Glorious
American Food

Glorious American Food

CHRISTOPHER IDONE

PHOTOGRAPHS BY TOM ECKERLE
FOOD ASSISTANT: RENA COYLE
WINE CONSULTANT: PENELOPE WISNER

A WELCOME BOOK
STEWART, TABORI & CHANG

GRAPHIC DESIGN BY R. D. SCUDELLARI

Text copyright © 1985 by Christopher Idone
Photographs copyright © 1985 by Welcome Enterprises, Inc.

Paperback edition published in 1994 and distributed in the U.S. by
Stewart, Tabori & Chang, 575 Broadway, New York, NY 10012.

Distributed in the English language elsewhere in the world (except
Canada and Central and South America) by Melia Publishing Services,
P.O. Box 1639, Maidenhead, Berkshire SL6 6YZ England. Canadian and
Central and South American accounts should contact Sales Manager,
Stewart, Tabori & Chang.

The recipes in Glorious American Food were created by Christopher
Idone specifically for this book, which has no connection with Glorious
Food Inc. of New York.

Grateful acknowledgment is made to the following for permission to
reprint previously published material:
The New York Times: "James Beard's Sourdough Rye Bread," by James
Beard, The New York Times, April 26, 1968. Copyright © 1968 by The
New York Times Company. Reprinted by permission.

Library of Congress Cataloging in Publication Data
Idone, Christopher.
      [Christopher Idone's glorious American food]
   Glorious American food / Christopher Idone ; photographs by Tom
   Eckerle ; food assistant, Rena Coyle ; wine consultant, Penelope
   Wisner.
         p. cm.
      "A Welcome Book."
      Originally published: Christopher Idone's glorious American food.
   1st. New York : Random House, c1985.
      Includes bibliographical references (p.) and index.
      ISBN 1-55670-361-9
      1. Cookery, American. 2. Menus. 3. Dinners and dining.
   I. Title.
   TX715.I227 1994
   641.5973–dc20   93-49625
                                                  CIP

10 9 8 7 6 5 4 3 2 1
Printed in Singapore

DEDICATION

FOR THE FARMERS, THE FISHERMEN,
THE RANCHERS AND THE VINTNERS
WHO LOVE THIS LAND.

TABLE OF CONTENTS

New England

Mid-Atlantic

South

Deep South

Southwest

Midwest

West Coast

Northern Regions

Northwest

INTRODUCTION

Every other Sunday, when I was young, my siblings and I were packed into the car and driven off to my maternal grandmother's house. It smelled of yeast and butter and roasting meats. My grandmother would drink a bit of port before dinner, and we children would drink milk warm from the cow when we sat down to mashed potatoes swimming in gravy and butter. On alternate Sundays, we visited my paternal grandfather. His house smelled richly of olive oil, garlic, and tomatoes bubbling on a wood-burning cast-iron cookstove, and a line stretched across the kitchen was hung with noodles like ribbons drying in the air until they were ready to be tossed into a cauldron of boiling water. While I sat on my grandfather's knee, I would chew a golden slice of bread with a crust so hard it hurt my teeth, and he would nibble slices of sausage spiced with fennel seeds or flecked with red hot pepper. My grandfather would take a glass of his own dark homemade red wine now and then, and he always encouraged me to take a few good

sips—because it was good for me. Later, my father would tell me I did not have to drink the wine if I really didn't like it, and he added that it was good only when it turned to vinegar—a fact I did not understand at that time.

At home we drank milk from our pet goats (long before I knew what a chèvre was). The goats lived among the menagerie of rabbits, chickens, and dogs that always were around. Sometimes we ate cream cheese with jelly and sometimes we had fresh mozzarella melted on fragrant oily bread. We bought our vegetables from a local farm stand and every Friday a truck pulled up with fish, clams, and mussels from the harbor fishing boats. The fisherman—for that's what we called him—would draw back the canvas to reveal all kinds of terrors pulled from the local waters, all spread out on heaps of snow-white crystals of ice. He weighed my mother's choice, collected her money, and wrapped our dinner in newspaper. We pulled up rhubarb stalks out behind the shed, and my mother served them stewed, with puddles of thick cream—I was somehow always amazed that the rhubarb came back each spring.

Rhubarb was followed by a season of asparagus and strawberries picked from a local patch. We cranked out ice cream tinted with the luscious berries and peaches of a hot summer. I remember dinner at a friend's house: We always started with chicken soup and matzo balls, and my favorite was their potato pancakes—fried golden and sweet, the color of buckwheat inside. There was always meat boiled tender and brown, whose only taste came from salt and a horseradish so hot it burned your nose and made you cry. Sour cream and cherries seemed an odd way to end it all.

In winter, our table was set with jars of jams, each topped with its layer of paraffin, and larger jars, brought up from the cellar near dinnertime, revealed tomatoes, corn, lima beans, and string beans. Sometime in 1944, there was a series of explosions in our cellar—violent and fierce, one after another, shattering glass, followed by thuds and splats. From that day on, no jar of pickles or put-up fruits would come out of that larder. My mother quit canning and frozen foods replaced the winter larder. Life changed and our food changed quickly.

Such childhood memories as these are, I suppose, the roots of my love for honest food, and formed the beginning of my curiosity. It was a long while before I realized that food served in one house differed from that served in another—that food tastes different in different places, that what flourishes in one area withers somewhere else. But now, I know. Surely food will always vary from home to home, and dishes will vary from cook to cook. American cooking developed with a sense of thrift— simple, basic, rooted to the land—it didn't lack inspiration. When I set out to "do" this book, I had an idea of what I might find in America. Certainly I thought I knew a great deal about this country's food. I'd read and traveled and tasted dozens and dozens of dishes. What I had suspected, but was not

sure of, was the truth about the source of our food: that it springs from great pride, and tremendous bounty.

I divided the United States into regions, not so much geographically as historically, following the food. The experience was a history lesson for me, one I wanted to record. I wanted to follow our entry into the magnificent ports and harbors of the continent and to trace the paths of pioneers who crossed what was then an unimaginable expanse of land. I wanted to see first-hand how people cook at home, in what ways their cookery depends on local produce, if local cookery is still based on regional dishes of the past or if it has become homogenized. My plan was to steer clear of restaurants catering to the "visiting firemen"—places meant to show off a city's sophistication. After all, we can enjoy a meal in Miami and have that same meal again in Philadelphia or Tulsa. But you need more than a local guidebook to get you to the blue highways 100 miles outside New Orleans where you'll find the best crawfish étouffé (served on Formica under fluorescent lights), or to taste trout, pulled

from a rocky pool by the Snake River and pan-fried, eaten by the light of kerosene lamps, miles from anywhere in Idaho. So I went to find the farmers and fishermen and ranchers, people of the country. I went to the source and found cooks, wonderful cooks, young and old cooks who shared their company, their charm and generosity, their experience and their own memories.

There were so many things I thought I knew. I've always known, of course, that hunting is popular across the country, but I never imagined that game still is such a basic food in so many areas. I found that the "western cowboy" works from Texas to Montana, from Bakersfield, California to the Santa Lucia Range on the Pacific. I tasted the beef the ranchers keep for themselves—from cattle that aren't sent off to the corn feedlots for a final fattening—much gamier to my city palate, but delicious and pleasing. Whole communities eat this way, eating beef as they prefer it; who outside of these communities would ever know of it?

I followed the water everywhere I went. Many of the fishermen I met are doing the

work their families have done for 13 generations—300 years! The haulseiners of Long Island depend on a depleting population of bass and are further hampered by state laws and by the sportsfisherman who claims this fish as his trophy. The old-time baymen of the East coast who hand-shuck scallops are the best in the land, slowly losing their livelihood as the scallop beds are overfished or polluted. Shrimp boats rot in the channels along the intercoastal water route from Charleston to the Bayou, because the independent shrimper has lost his mortgage to the banks and his catch to the trawlers that sift our waters and send back to us "fresh frozen" seafood. I've seen the versatile rice grower of the South turn his off-season fields into flooded crawfish farms or catfish ponds. I've watched the delicate shad travel up a cleaned-up Hudson River to the point where sweet water meets the salty current—so docile in their abundance that they are netted like pets, deposited in aerated water tanks, and trucked to the Susquehanna to replenish the stock there. And I have stood in the wood shavings of the first skipjack to be built on the Chesapeake in more than 70 years. I spoke with the children who had been to college and pursued a career, and had then experienced a change of heart, returning to the farm that was their birthright. I talked with the professor who gave up his tenure to cultivate his very own small parcel of land, growing tender lettuces, herbs, and vegetables. I was invited out in a Maine lobster boat to share in a lesson a lobsterman gave to his 12-year-old son: guiding his boat to the lobster pots, emptying them, banding the lobsters, and fetching a fair price at the local cooperative.

I was looking for the flavor of America, and I found that no single flavor exists. The menus and recipes I've devised rely on regionally available foods, the ingredients and techniques adjusted to reflect local influences. I followed tradition and custom to the point where it made sense to me. In essence, I took the liberty of adapting these dishes to please contemporary palates. I realized, too, that if indeed there exists a homogenized "American flavor," it belongs on only one level: fast food. But, around the corner there is always a reminder: overstuffed sandwiches of pastrami and corned beef, pickled, cured, peppered and smoked on the premises; a toasted roll filled with half a lobster, boiled up on a one-burner stove and moistened with mayonnaise and a hint of celery; a burrito chock with beans and sauce lovingly simmered for hours; a trio of steamed dumplings selected on the street, served up from a bamboo steamer. Eclectic, yes; foreign, no—all these foods have become part of the lexicon of American food, part of our culture, adding pleasure to our lives.

I chatted with the farmer who left his farm at 4 A.M. to drive 140 miles to the Decatur Street Market in New Orleans, his pickup filled with the most beautiful ivory turnips I have ever seen—he just beamed when they were photographed. I bought an overripe melon for a dime from a dejected farmer who sat on the tailgate sipping coffee from a tin cup, knowing his day was over before it had started. At times, I wondered whether what I was seeing and recording would ever be seen by a future generation. But ways of life are ever-changing; the side of American life that fascinates me so has been in the process of fading since long before I was around, or my grandmother and grandfather, for that matter. Every generation talks of hope and despair as though experiencing it for the first time.

If I discovered nothing else about America, I learned about pride. The best is all about us. The farmer who trucks his vegetables to the nearest highway to sell by the roadside has it. The farmer who has thousands of acres of peach trees has it. The cheesemaker and the winemaker have it. The cattlemen with their sturdy-shouldered stock have it. The fishermen have it. They seem humble and sometimes reticent about the good of what they do, but their commitment is inspiring and their devotion to the land and sea, almost religious. These were the people I spoke with, and I took pleasure in recording what they shared with me. And I take pleasure in passing on the result of our odyssey to you.

New
England

"I have had reason to think, in recent years, that as cooking in America has become more elegant, it has arrived at the point known to veteran State-of-Mainers as 'a pretty pass.'" –Kenneth Roberts, in his introduction to Marjorie Mosser's book GOOD MAINE FOOD *published by Doubleday & Co., New York 1947*

In the beginning, the crow flew from the great fields of the Southwest, whence came all the corn and the beans in the world. The crow carried a kernel of corn in one ear and an Indian bean in the other. So goes the myth of how farming was brought to the Indians of the New England coast.

Where are the sources of American cookery more invitingly encountered than in New England's familiar and fertile tradition? It was, after all, the settlers' first chapter. Any American schoolchild knows that those early colonists surely would have perished without the single greatest gift from the Indians: corn, a precious kernel, not to be squandered. In 1605 the explorer Champlain records that planting should begin no sooner than "when a white-oak leaf approximated a red squirrel's foot-print, or—as a double check on dimensions—when it was the size of a mouse's ear." Captain John Smith (whose expedition of 1614 landed the first Englishmen on these shores) records that squaws roasted corn at the side of the very fields they were tending. For the 102 Pilgrim settlers who followed in Smith's wake, Indian corn became the mainstay. They ate it roasted, grilled, or pounded to a paste and formed into little hot cakes called "bannocks." When the hogs the settlers brought from the homeland multiplied, these early New Englanders would pull back the corn husks to remove the silk, wrap the ear with thin slices of bacon, pull up the husks, and roast the corn to succulence. They popped corn in hot kettles as the

Indians taught them adding a little of their treasured lard. They ate succotash fresh in the summer, and in the winter they would make the same dish from dried beans and a dry-roasted corn, called samp. They planted corn in rows and grew beans between the corn rows that then served as nature's beanpoles.

To this day, descendants of some of those first families celebrate Forefathers' Day (December 21st), dining on succotash at the Old Colony Club in Plymouth. Corn was a part of early New England clambakes, which remain the quintessential New England summer feast; settlers learned from the Indians of Cape Cod and Nantucket how to build a fire in a rock-lined pit on the beach, how to add more rocks and cover the heated rocks with a layer of seaweed. Lobsters, clams, and corn were placed on top—all packed with seaweed kept steaming with water from the sea. In time the settlers learned to grind and sift corn by mill and left their mortars and pestles behind. As the coast became more diversely and widely settled, different regions came to be known for their own corn specialties (pones, hush puppies, corn sticks, corn bread, johnnycakes, Indian mush, and so on). Far into the 19th century corn was indispensable to the diet not only of New Englanders but of colonists of the South, the Deep South, and the Midwest as well.

In early spring the New Englanders caught herring with their bare hands, selecting the swollen roe-filled females as the prize and discarding their partners on the rocks. They feasted on the bass, shad, salmon, trout, and sturgeon that spawned upriver from the ocean. They ate sweet scallops harvested from shallow bays, oysters and clams the size of hazelnuts, mussels picked from rocks and periwinkles plucked from stony beaches. They fished for lamprey, flounder, whiting, cod, and its smaller cousin haddock. Erecting wooden frames for drying the cod, they found a market for this dried fish, sending shiploads to England and to Catholic Spain, and thus built a thriving commerce. Smith called this land Massachusetts.

Surely there was much to marvel at in unfamiliar foods. John Smith describes dining on stewed squashes and varieties of pumpkins, watermelons, and what we know today as Jerusalem artichokes. They snacked on pemmican, a paste made of dried venison strips pounded together with berries and bear or deer grease. They gorged on wild berries and smoked tobacco. Game there was in plenty: swans, geese, ducks, woodcocks, pheasants, partridges, deer, rabbits, squirrels, turkeys. Still, the Pilgrim newcomers, familiar as they were with the country of rolling green meadows which reminded them of their own southern England, were probably as unaccustomed to handling a gun as they were to plowing or clearing a field. In their homeland, hunting remained the privilege of the landed gentry, and few of the virtuous Pilgrims were accomplished hunters, let alone crack shots. An old muzzle-loading gun could in no way promise a brace of birds or a five-point buck, at least not until the development of a shotgun and an accurate rifle with a sight.

Farming was a communal effort for the Indians and it became so for the colonists. Planting and cultivation were commonly the work of the native women, children, and older men of the villages. They worked with crude hoes, sometimes fashioned of long poles with a large clamshell fixed to the end. Most English farms of that time were villages adjoining the great estates, with houses, stables, and gardens clustered near the village church and to the one or two highways that led to the fields. The early settlers adhered to this feudal arrangement in the colonies, the close-knit community providing mutual protection and governing authority. Barns and sheds were often connected to their dwellings, and the family garden and fruit trees flourished close by. Crops were planted on individual plots apportioned according to the size of the family, in one common field, and the town provided an ox or two to cultivate them. A town herdsman collected the one or two cows, sheep, or goats each farmer owned and took them to pasture as a common herd.

Everyday life encompassed a hundred small economies, but was softened by some few luxuries the colonists had brought from their homeland such as onions, leeks, cabbages, and turnips. Craving more luscious fruits than the tart beach plums, cranberries, and other wild berries they found here, they soon imported apple, pear, plum, and even apricot trees and seeds from Europe. Longing to recreate dishes from home and of course missing beer fiercely, they rushed to import wheat, rye, barley, and hops. As early as 1640 the first licensed brewery was established! Sadly enough, wheat and barley grew poorly in the rocky Eastern soil, and if ever it chanced to mature it was beset by hawks, blackbirds, and (ironically) the imported rat.

And so the beer they loved was replaced by hard cider from the flourishing apple trees, and when the cider turned they used it for vinegar. (Wine vinegars were the province of 19th century immigrants. Wine and sherry vinegars were used in Catholic California long before, but the American diner didn't really encounter these until just before the "food explosion" of the 1960s.) In those colonial cellars another alcoholic drink called "perry" was made from pears, and there were many wines made with cherries, mulberries, and of course dandelion blossoms. By the late 17th century, rum had won tremendous popularity among the colonists, a new rival to hard cider. A profitable exchange of cows, beef, hogs, sheep, dry biscuits, butter, salt cod, and tobacco were being shipped to New York ports and the West Indies in return for molasses (that thick, black, syrupy by-product of the sugar plantations). To some extent molasses was used for sweetening, though maple syrup and maple sugar were used regionally in northern Massachusetts, Vermont, and New Hampshire by the close of the 18th century. For the most part molasses was used to make rum, and many of the existing cider mills of the day were converted to that purpose. This rum was shipped to Africa in exchange for slaves, who then were sent to the cane fields of the West Indies and later to Virginia plantations and the prosperous estate farms of Massachusetts, Rhode Island, Connecticut, and Long Island.

The hearth was the heart of early American homes and farmhouses, the one unfailingly warm corner. A large iron pot invariably hung over glowing coals all day, stewing and bubbling with boiled chickens, corned beef, codfish, hams, and the vegetable greens that would become known as "pot liquor." The result was a plain style of cooking, but a style just the same. The cooking pot was brought directly to the table, where each family member ladled out a portion into shallow wooden bowls or trenchers; poorer families carved hollows in the tabletop itself and ate their portions with a wooden spoon. Preparation for winter was a year's occupation—the growing and putting up of fruits and vegetables, and the fattening of the hog, looked forward to the long winter ahead.

The network of one-farmer households spread as towns grew and generations settled further into the woodlands. The old New England villages remain, a reminder of those first dependent, frightened folds. At the outset of the 19th century, most of New England looked as Iowa does today. Hills and valleys were denuded of their timber to be used for building homes, barns, ships, and for desperately needed warmth. In turn those soft, fertile, but rocky rolling hills were cultivated and the rocks themselves were used to fence open fields and separate neighbor from neighbor. Today one finds those walls on walks through groves of birch, pine, and maple. Those farmers, like the native Americans before them, moved on to more fertile fields when the land was exhausted. And eventually they would move west.

Breakfast

OATMEAL

CODFISH BALLS*

BACON

CURRIED STEWED
TOMATOES*

RYE AND CHEDDAR
BISCUITS*

TEA

GAVILAN VINEYARDS VIN GRIS
or EDNA VALLEY VINEYARDS
VIN GRIS

Our customs have changed, and this hearty break-fast would make an ideal weekend lunch or dinner. In days past, codfish balls were a standard Sunday breakfast—especially from Boston up through Maine—quite often served up with Saturday night's baked bean dish. The pork barrel supplied the salt pork to flavor and season vegetables, meats, poultry, and fish and was a foundation for main dishes when nothing else was available. The lard was used for frying, as well as in the making of sweets and pastries—it was their butter. Coupling fish and pork renderings may seem odd, but it satisfied the New Englander's craving for the flavor of meat, and "Cape Cod turkey" wasn't

turkey at all, but rather cod larded with salt pork or bacon. The China trade and whaling expeditions brought in a profusion of spices and tropical fruits which swiftly found their way into the kitchens of the colonies. Rye flourished in the rocky New England soil, and provided a pleasant change from corn breads.

CODFISH BALLS

INGREDIENTS

1 cup salt cod, shredded (about ⅓ pound)
1 cup hand-mashed boiled potatoes
3 eggs, lightly beaten
Freshly milled black pepper
¼ cup milk plus additional milk for soaking the
    salt cod
Dried unseasoned bread crumbs
Lard or vegetable oil

METHOD

Soak the cod in cold water to cover for 12 hours,
    changing the water two or three times.
Soak the fish in milk to cover for
    another 6 hours.
In a bowl, shred the fish and mash together with the
    potatoes.
Combine with 1 of the eggs and pepper to taste. Shape
    the mixture into walnut-sized balls.
In a shallow bowl, combine the remaining 2 eggs with
    the ¼ cup milk. Place the bread crumbs in another
    shallow bowl.
Dip each ball in the egg and milk mixture and roll in
    the bread crumbs. Refrigerate for 20 minutes.
Fill a large skillet with 1½ inches of melted lard or oil.
    Set over moderately high heat.
When the oil just begins to simmer, add as many balls
    as will fit without touching.
Fry quickly, turning, until golden brown.
Drain on paper towels and cover to keep warm.
Fry the remaining balls and serve hot.

Makes 12 codfish balls or 4 or 6 codfish cakes.

RYE AND CHEDDAR BISCUITS

INGREDIENTS

1 cup rye flour
1 cup all-purpose flour
1 tablespoon baking powder
1 teaspoon baking soda
½ teaspoon salt
6 tablespoons unsalted butter, slightly chilled and cut into bits
¾ cup buttermilk
4 ounces cheddar cheese, grated (about 1 cup packed)

TOOLS

3-inch cookie cutter

METHOD

Preheat the oven to 450°.
In a mixing bowl, combine all of the dry ingredients.
Using your fingers or an electric mixer, blend the butter into the dry ingredients.
Add the buttermilk and cheese and mix thoroughly.
Place the dough on a lightly floured surface and knead for 2 minutes.
Roll out the dough ¾-inch thick. Cut the dough with a 3-inch round cutter and place the biscuits on an ungreased baking sheet.
Bake for 12 to 15 minutes, or until golden brown. Serve warm.

Makes 8 to 10

CURRIED STEWED TOMATOES

INGREDIENTS

4 large ripe tomatoes, peeled and seeded, with the juice reserved (about 5 cups)
Salt and freshly milled black pepper
1 teaspoon curry powder
1 tablespoon chopped fresh chives

METHOD

Coarsely chop the tomatoes and place them in a heavy saucepan. Add the reserved juice and set over moderate heat.
Bring the tomatoes to a slight boil and reduce the heat to low.
Add salt and pepper to taste and the curry powder and simmer 15 to 20 minutes, or until the tomato pulp is soft.
Place in a serving bowl and sprinkle with the chives.

Makes 5 cups

Succotash Dinner

GREEN TOMATO TART *

SUCCOTASH WITH THREE
STEAMED FISH *

STEWED TOMATOES
WITH ROSEMARY *

GRITS WITH BUTTER AND GRATED
CHEDDAR CHEESE *(see page 112)*

JASON'S BLUEBERRY PIE WITH
ROSE HIP PETAL ICE CREAM *

BRANDER VINEYARD

SAUVIGNON BLANC

At harvest's end, green tomatoes were put up as pickles, fried, or seasoned with sugar and spices and baked into pies. This tart fruit on a flaky crust coated with sweet honey mustard is a savory introduction to an end-of-summer menu. It was not uncommon to add bits of meat, fowl, or fish to succotash, which frequently was a meal in itself. Today's conception of succotash as corn with lima beans leaves most of us flat; however, the addition of fish, rendered pork, and string beans restores this dish to its former glory. The wild beach rose, Rosa rugosa, *grows in the crests and valleys of the*

dunes on the Atlantic coast. This Arabian strain flourished here purely by accident when English wrecks washed up on our Eastern shore. The fragrant petals found their way into potpourris and recipes, and the rose hips made delicious jelly. Those who live far from the sea can substitute a few drops of rose water to make this romantic whimsy.

GREEN TOMATO TART

INGREDIENTS

½ recipe Pie Dough, made with lard (see Basics,
    page 346)
2 teaspoons vegetable oil
1 large onion, thinly sliced
⅓ cup honey mustard
2 medium-size green tomatoes, cut in ¼-inch slices
Salt and freshly milled pepper
2 tablespoons unsalted butter, melted
2 tablespoons lightly chopped fresh Italian parsley

METHOD

Preheat the oven to 350°.
Prepare the pie dough according to the directions
    in Basics.
While the pastry is chilling, heat the oil in a skillet
    and add the onions. Slowly cook the onions, stirring
    from time to time over low heat, until wilted and
    brown, about 20 minutes. Reserve and let cool.
On a floured surface, roll out the dough into a
    10-inch circle.
Carefully lift the pie dough and place on a baking
    sheet.
Evenly spread the mustard over the surface of the pie
    dough, leaving a 1-inch band around the circum-
    ference of the dough.
Evenly spread the onions over the mustard.
Arrange the tomatoes in a spiral, covering the
    caramelized onions.
Lightly season the tomatoes with salt and pepper.
    Bake the tart for 25 minutes, or until the edges of
    the crust are crisp.
Remove the tart from the oven, brush with the melted
    butter, and sprinkle with the parsley. Serve warm.

Serves 4 to 6

SUCCOTASH WITH THREE STEAMED FISH

INGREDIENTS

10 ears fresh sweet corn
2 cups small, shelled fresh lima beans
2 cups fresh string beans, cut into 1-inch pieces
¼ pound unsalted butter
⅓ pound salt pork, cut into ¼-inch cubes
1 quart Court Bouillon (see Basics, page 343)
3 pounds (1 pound each) firm white fish fillets,
    such as scrod, halibut, bass, or weakfish
1 bunch small scallions, include some of
    the green, trimmed
2 to 3 tablespoons heavy cream

METHOD

Cut the kernels of corn from the cobs into a bowl.
With a large spoon, scrape the milk from the cob into
    the bowl with the corn. Reserve.
Blanch the lima beans in boiling water until
    almost tender.
Cool under cold water. Reserve.
Blanch the string beans and reserve.
In a large heavy saucepan, melt the butter and add the
    corn and its juices. Cook over moderate heat for 10
    minutes, stirring from time to time.

Meanwhile, in a skillet, render the salt pork until
    golden brown. Set aside on paper towels to drain.
In a large makeshift steamer, bring the court bouillon
    to a simmer over moderate heat. Add the fish and
    steam for 10 minutes per inch of thickness. If
    necessary, cook thicker pieces such as cod first, and
    add thinner fillets such as bass or weakfish after a
    few minutes, so that all will be cooked at the
    same time.
When all of the fish is in the steamer, place the
    scallions over the fillets.
While the fish is cooking, add the lima and string beans
    to the corn, stirring from time to time. Stir in the
    cream to loosen the mixture.
Pour the succotash on a heated platter, then arrange
    the fish and rendered salt pork over the succotash.
Set the scallions over the fish and serve.

Serves 6

STEWED TOMATOES WITH ROSEMARY

INGREDIENTS

4 to 5 large, very ripe tomatoes (about 3 pounds)
1 sprig fresh rosemary
Salt and freshly milled pepper

METHOD

Blanch, peel, and seed the tomatoes, reserving
    the juice.
Chop the tomatoes.
Place the tomatoes and their juice in a heavy non-
    aluminum saucepan.
Crush the rosemary by bruising it between your hands.
    Add the rosemary and salt and pepper to taste.
Simmer over moderate heat, stirring from time to
    time, until the liquid reduces and the tomatoes are
    cooked through.
Serve hot.

Note: Fresh ripe tomatoes are one of summer's joys.
    They need little seasoning and the fresh taste is
    incomparable. After stewing, the tomatoes may be
    cooled and frozen in plastic containers or put up in
    jars for a wintertime treat.

Makes 1½ to 2 quarts

Fill the pan with the blueberry mixture.

On a floured surface, roll out the pie dough ¼-inch thick.

Cover the berries with the dough. Trim and crimp the edges.

Bake in the center of the oven for 35 minutes, or until golden.

Serve warm with vanilla ice cream or the rose hip variation.

Serves 6

ROSE HIP PETAL ICE CREAM

INGREDIENTS

1 quart English Cream (see Basics, page 348), made without the vanilla

2 cups rose petals from *Rosa rugosa* (see Note)

TOOLS

Ice cream maker

METHOD

Prepare the English Cream, omitting the vanilla.

Freeze the cream in an ice cream maker, following the manufacturer's directions. When the cream begins to thicken, fold in the rose petals.

Spoon the ice cream into a container and freeze for 1 hour before serving.

The ice cream will take on the perfume flavor of the petals.

Note: *Rosa rugosa* flourish in the dunes along the Eastern shoreline. The fruit is rich in vitamin C and is considered medicinal as well as wonderful for making jellies. It is one of nature's most fragrant and natural roses indigenous to this area. The petals are five to a blossom, ranging in color from white to pale pink to rich pink to a deep pink.

You may substitute a few drops of rosewater in place of the petals.

Makes 1 quart

JASON'S BLUEBERRY PIE

INGREDIENTS

½ recipe Pie Dough, made with lard (see Basics, page 346)

2 pints blueberries, washed and drained

¼ cup sugar

1½ tablespoons quick cooking tapioca

1 lemon, seeded and thinly sliced

METHOD

Preheat the oven to 400°.

Prepare the pie dough and chill it.

In a mixing bowl, mix the blueberries with the sugar and tapioca.

Line a 9-inch pan with enough lemon slices to cover the bottom.

Baked Bean Dinner

BAKED BEANS WITH
BLACK DUCK BREASTS
AND LINGUIÇA SAUSAGES*

BROWN BREAD*

SUSAN WILBUR'S CORN RELISH*
AND PICKLES

APPLE CHARLOTTE*

BEER or RED & GREEN
VINEYARD ZINFANDEL

Though they take hours of slow cooking, baked beans require little tending. To a New Englander the dish is not just a pot of beans, but a casserole that might be cooked with a partridge, accompanied by a fresh goose breast, or finished with the addition of Portuguese linguiça sausage. Rich, dark molasses flavored the dish but was used sparingly so as not to oversweeten. With these embellishments the simple pot of beans becomes a New England cassoulet. Steamed brown bread, with or without raisins, always accompanied the dish, likewise pickles and relishes to satisfy the Yankee passion for sweet and sour. The apple was the one fruit that thrived, and the colonial housewife's countless variations on the apple dessert are a credit to her imagination.

BAKED BEANS WITH BLACK DUCK BREASTS AND LINGUIÇA SAUSAGES

INGREDIENTS

BEANS:

2 pounds dried navy, cranberry, or Yellow Eye (favored in Maine) beans
1 pound salt pork with skin attached (see Note)
2 tablespoons dry mustard
1 teaspoon cider vinegar
¼ cup dark rum
½ cup molasses
1 teaspoon salt (optional)
1 medium-large onion, studded with 12 cloves

MEAT:

3 linguiça sausages
¾ pound lean pork fat, cut into ¼-inch cubes
6 boneless, skinless Black Duck breasts (also called Canadian Redleg), or substitute Mallard or Muscovy duck breasts
Salt and freshly milled pepper
½ pound unsalted butter, clarified (see Basics, page 344)
Small bunch fresh sage

TOOLS

Bean pot or deep casserole
Kettle or stockpot
Cast-iron skillet or ovenproof large heavy sauté pan

METHOD

The beans:

Thoroughly wash and pick over the beans. Place in a pot with plenty of water and set aside to soak overnight.

Drain the beans, place them in a large kettle and add cold water to cover.

Bring to a boil over high heat. Reduce the heat to low and simmer for 30 minutes.

Drain the beans and reserve the cooking liquid.

Preheat the oven to 200°.

Cut away the salt pork skin in one sheet.

Line the bean pot with the skin, skin side up.

In a small bowl, combine the dry mustard, vinegar, rum, molasses, and salt. Mix into the beans and fill the bean pot one-third full with the bean mixture.

Add the clove-studded onion and top with more beans and the salt pork. Cover with the remaining beans.

Cover the bean pot and bake for 10 to 11 hours, checking the liquid from time to time. If the beans begin to dry out, add some of the reserved bean liquid to moisten them. Uncover the beans for the last hour of cooking and bury the linguiça sausages in the beans. About 30 minutes before serving, render the cubed pork fat over moderately low heat until golden, draining off the fat as it cooks.

Drain the cubes on paper towels and set aside in a warm place.

The duck breasts:

Lightly season the duck breasts with salt and pepper.

Warm the butter in a large ovenproof skillet set over moderately high heat.

Add some of the sage leaves and sauté the breasts for 2 minutes on each side, until rare.

Place the skillet in the oven for 3 to 4 minutes while you assemble the dish.

To assemble:

Remove the onion from the beans and discard it.

Remove the sausage from the beans. Peel off the skin and slice ¼-inch thick.

Arrange the sliced sausages in the center of a warm platter.

Surround the sausages with the duck breasts and place one or two whole sage leaves over each breast.

Sprinkle with the reserved rendered pork fat.

Serve with the beans.

Note: If the salt pork is very salty, boil it first. Otherwise it will burn and brown before the fat is rendered.

Serves 6 to 8

BROWN BREAD

INGREDIENTS

2 tablespoons butter, for the mold
1 cup whole wheat flour
1 cup all-purpose flour
1 cup yellow cornmeal
2 teaspoons baking soda
1 teaspoon salt
2 cups buttermilk or sour milk
⅔ cup molasses
1 cup seedless raisins

TOOLS

Two 1-quart steamed pudding molds or one 2-quart
    steamed pudding mold
Large pot with cover, to hold the mold

METHOD

Butter the steamed pudding mold, including the cover.
In a large bowl, combine the flours, cornmeal, baking
    soda, and salt.
Add the buttermilk and molasses and stir thoroughly.
Fold in the raisins.
Pour the mixture into the mold and cover tightly.

Place the mold in a large pot and fill with hot water to
    reach halfway up the sides of the mold.
Cover the pot and steam over moderate heat for 3
    hours, replenishing the water as necessary every 30
    to 45 minutes.
When the bread is cooked, unmold and serve warm,
    slicing the loaf with a strong string.
Makes 1 loaf

SUSAN WILBUR'S CORN RELISH

INGREDIENTS

2 dozen large ears sweet corn, husked
1 large green cabbage (about 3 pounds)—outer leaves
    removed, cut in half, and cored
4 green bell peppers—halved, cored, seeded, and
    deveined
1 sweet red bell pepper—halved, cored, seeded,
    and deveined
4 large onions
2 quarts cider vinegar
1 cup all-purpose flour
4½ cups sugar
¼ cup salt
3½ tablespoons dry mustard
1 teaspoon turmeric

METHOD

Using a sharp knife, cut the corn kernels from the cobs
    and reserve in a large bowl.
Using a spoon, scrape the milky liquid from the cob
    into the bowl of kernels.
Thinly slice the cabbage and chop medium fine.
Cut the green and red peppers into thin strips
    and dice.
Chop the onions.
In the kettle, bring 1 quart of the vinegar to a simmer
    over moderate heat.
Whisk in the flour, sugar, salt, dry mustard,
    and turmeric.
Add the remaining 1 quart vinegar and simmer
    for 30 minutes.
Stir in the vegetables and simmer for 10 minutes.
Ladle the relish into sterilized jars and seal.
Makes 5½ quarts

APPLE CHARLOTTE

INGREDIENTS

8 to 10 thin slices white bread, crusts removed and cut
   in half (see Note)
½ pound unsalted butter, melted
6 pounds semi-tart apples, such as Rome, Idared, or
   Cortland—peeled, cored, and thinly sliced
2 cups dark brown sugar
¾ teaspoon ground cinnamon
½ teaspoon ground mace
½ teaspoon ground allspice
Heavy cream or whipped cream, for serving

TOOLS

1½—quart soufflé dish

METHOD

Preheat the oven to 350°.

Working in batches, dip the bread in ¼ pound of the
   melted butter and brown lightly in a heavy skillet set
   over moderate heat.

Line the bottom and sides of the soufflé dish with
   bread, cutting as necessary to fit the dish. Reserve
   the remaining slices of bread.

Add the remaining ¼ pound butter to the skillet and
   return it to moderate heat.

In a bowl, toss the apples with the sugar and spices
   and turn the mixture into the skillet.

Cook, stirring, until the apples wilt and the sugar
   melts. The filling will resemble a chunky sauce.

Pour the filling into the lined dish and top with the
   reserved slices of bread.

Place the mold in a hot water bath and bake for 40 to
   50 minutes, until crisp and golden.

Remove from the oven and cool on a rack for
   15 minutes.

Place a serving dish over the mold and invert
   to unmold.

Serve warm with heavy cream or whipped cream.

Note: Slice some of the bread crosswise to line the
   sides of the dish. Diagonal slices are easier to fit on
   the top and bottom.

Serves 6 to 8

Lobster Lunch

WHITE FISH CHOWDER*

BOILED LOBSTERS*

BLACKBERRY COBBLER* WITH
CREAM OR VANILLA ICE CREAM

TREFETHEN VINEYARDS
CHARDONNAY

At one time, Nantucket's chowder was a simple combination of fish or clams with water, pork, and onions, thickened with flour. The Portuguese prepared a more Mediterranean version using olive oil, tomatoes, peppers, and garlic. By the middle of the 19th century, a true New England chowder was a milky stew, served with water biscuits or hardtack of a rocklike texture and meant to be crumbled and soaked in the chowder as filler. Salt cod substituted when fresh fish was lacking; both are used here for a salty richness.

Lobster, not an everyday treat, is served here at its simplest: boiled. A true down-easter prefers his lobster boiled or steamed, flavored with nothing more than the sea water in which it cooks.

WHITE FISH CHOWDER

INGREDIENTS

1 pound salt cod (as prepared on page 19)
1 pound fresh cod fillet, skin removed
1 pound halibut fillet, skin removed
4 tablespoons unsalted butter
1 medium yellow onion, chopped
4 cups heavy cream
2 cups milk
1 teaspoon fresh thyme leaves
¼ pound fresh pork fat back
2 cups peeled, diced potatoes
Freshly milled black pepper
3 tablespoons chopped fresh parsley

METHOD

Cut all of the fish into 1½-inch cubes. Cover and refrigerate.

In a soup kettle, melt the butter over moderate heat. Add the onions and sauté until translucent, 3 to 5 minutes.

Add the heavy cream, milk, and thyme and reduce the heat to low. Simmer for 20 minutes.

Meanwhile, dice the fat back and cook over moderate heat until rendered golden brown. Drain on paper towels and set aside on a warm part of the stove.

Add the potatoes to the chowder and simmer until the potatoes are almost fork-tender.

Add the fish and simmer for about 10 minutes, until just cooked through. Season to taste with pepper. Serve the chowder in warmed soup bowls and sprinkle with the parsley. Serve the rendered pork on the side and let each guest sprinkle some over the chowder.

Serves 6

COOKING LOBSTER

The sweetest and tenderest lobsters are under 1½ pounds, and the easiest way to cook live lobsters is by boiling or steaming them.

To boil lobsters, fill a lobster kettle with water to cover the lobsters and add 1 teaspoon of salt for every quart of water if you are not using sea water. Cover the kettle and bring to a rolling boil.

Plunge the lobsters head first into the pot and cover. When the water begins to boil, cook the 1-pound lobsters for 10 minutes, 1¼-pound lobsters for 12 minutes, and 1½-pound lobsters for 14 minutes. Cold live lobster will cool down the water and it will take from 3 to 5 minutes for the water to return to a boil.

When steaming lobsters, if possible, layer the bottom of the kettle with about ½ pound of seaweed. Add several quarts of water, and bring to a boil, covered. Add the lobsters, cover, and cook according to the individual size. Most lobster kettles will hold 4 to 5 lobsters at a time, but it is best to cook them a few at a time rather than overcrowding the pot. If steaming, the lobsters on the bottom will cook fastest. Lobsters should cool slightly before handling.

For easy serving, use a sharp sturdy knife to cut the lobsters from the point where the tail and body meet down to the tail. Turn the lobster around and cut through the head. Remove and discard the sand sac from the head of the halved lobster. Crack each claw at its widest point and serve with lobster crackers.

Boiled or steamed lobster may be served plain or with warm drawn butter.

BLACKBERRY COBBLER

INGREDIENTS

2 quarts blackberries
About ½ cup sugar, depending on the sweetness of the berries

BISCUIT DOUGH:

4 cups all-purpose flour
2 teaspoons salt
2 tablespoons baking powder
2 teaspoons sugar
2 cups heavy cream

Heavy cream, for serving

TOOLS

2-quart ovenproof casserole

METHOD

Preheat the oven to 400°.

Toss together the berries and sugar in the casserole.

Place in the oven for 20 minutes, until the sugar melts and the berries soften.

Meanwhile, prepare the biscuit dough:

In a large bowl, combine the dry ingredients.

Gradually pour in the cream and mix into a sticky dough.

Remove the casserole from the oven and spoon the biscuit dough over the berries.

Reduce the heat to 350° and bake from 20 to 25 minutes, or until the cobbler is golden brown.

Serve warm with heavy cream.

Serves 6

time, hashed. The cornmeal johnnycake, sweetened with molasses, was one of the first faintly elaborate breads. The name "johnny" came from journey and the cakes, tucked into saddlebags, traveled to the four corners of the country. Long before pie à la mode became the mode, cheddar was the common accompaniment to homemade apple pies. Americans had not yet developed their legendary "sweet tooth" and preferred to end the meal with a savory. The cheese is served at the end of the meal, exactly where it should be, to be enjoyed with the last of the wine.

RHODE ISLAND STEAMED MUSSELS

INGREDIENTS

¼ cup olive oil

2 cups dry white wine

1 small fennel bulb—halved, cored, and cut into 2-inch julienne

4 quarts mussels, scrubbed and debearded

1 bunch scallions, including some of the green, thinly sliced lengthwise.

1 teaspoon finely chopped cilantro

½ cup chopped fresh dill

Freshly milled black pepper

METHOD

In a large kettle, combine the oil and wine over high heat.

Bring to a boil, add the fennel julienne and reduce the heat to low. Simmer until tender, about 8 minutes.

Increase the heat to moderately high and add the mussels and remaining ingredients. Cover tightly and steam until the mussels open. Discard any that do not open. Serve the mussels in heated bowls with some of the liquid ladled over.

Note: Place the mussels in the freezer for 10 minutes before cooking so they will open faster.

Serves 6 to 8

Boiled Dinner

RHODE ISLAND STEAMED MUSSELS*

GLAZED CORNED BEEF
WITH ROOT VEGETABLES*

PIQUANT RELISH (see Basics, page 343)

JOHNNYCAKE*

APPLE PIE WITH CHEDDAR CHEESE*

BEER or FROG'S LEAP
SAUVIGNON BLANC

In addition to the pork and apple barrels, most homes had a pickling barrel. The process of salting and brining beef resulted in corned beef, so called because the pellets of salt resembled grains in size, and at that time all grains were called "corn." Until the invention of the icebox, homemakers depended on snow and pickling to preserve their meat. The corned beef is dressed up with a sweet glaze and an assortment of winter vegetables. It was often something of an "extender" meal that made a weekly appearance. The leftover beef was served up cold, which was the preference, with hot vegetables and then a third

GLAZED CORNED BEEF WITH ROOT VEGETABLES

INGREDIENTS

BRISKET:

1 corned brisket of beef (4 to 5 pounds)
2 bay leaves
8 peppercorns
2 allspice berries
1 small cinnamon stick
1 teaspoon mustard seed

GLAZE:

1 cup dark brown sugar
1 tablespoon dry mustard
¼ cup molasses
⅓ cup bourbon

VEGETABLES:

8 small golden beets
12 small new potatoes, with a strip of peel removed around the center
12 large scallions, trimmed
12 baby carrots, including ½ inch of the green tops, peeled
12 white radishes, including ½ inch of the green tops, peeled
2 parsnips—peeled, cut lengthwise in half, and quartered lengthwise

1 pint Brussels sprouts, cleaned and trimmed
1 small head Savoy cabbage or white cabbage, cored and cut into 1-inch-thick slices

METHOD

Wash the brisket thoroughly to remove any brine. Place the brisket in a large kettle with the spices and add enough water to cover.

Bring to a boil and simmer over moderately low heat for about 1 hour per pound, or until the center of the meat can be pierced easily with a 2-prong kitchen fork.

Meanwhile, make the glaze:

In a bowl, mix the sugar with the dry mustard. Add the molasses and fold in the bourbon. Set aside for at least 45 minutes to thicken.

Wash the beets thoroughly, leaving the roots and 2 or more inches of stem attached to prevent bleeding while cooking.

Cook the beets in a pot of lightly salted boiling water until tender, about 12 minutes.

Place in cold running water and slip off the skins.

Return the beets to the pot and keep warm.

When the corned beef is cooked, preheat the oven to 375°.

Remove the beef brisket and 2 cups of the cooking
liquid to a large baking pan. Set aside.
Bring the remaining cooking liquid to a rolling simmer
and cook the vegetables, starting with the potatoes
for 10 minutes. Add the radishes and scallions and
simmer for 10 minutes. Add the remaining vegetables and cook for 10 minutes.
While the vegetables cook, spoon over enough
thickened glaze to coat the corned beef and bake in
the oven, basting with additional glaze, for 10 to
15 minutes.
Serve the corned beef on a large platter, surrounded
by the vegetables.

Serves 6 to 8

JOHNNYCAKE

INGREDIENTS

Butter, for the baking pan
1 cup yellow cornmeal
¼ cup sugar
½ teaspoon baking soda
1 teaspoon cream of tartar
¼ teaspoon salt
1 cup buttermilk
1 egg, well beaten
1 tablespoon molasses
1 tablespoon unsalted butter, melted

TOOLS

8-inch square baking pan

METHOD

Preheat the oven to 425°.
Lightly butter an 8-inch square baking pan.
Sift together the dry ingredients in a large mixing
bowl. Add the buttermilk, beaten egg, molasses, and
melted butter and mix until smooth.
Pour the mixture into the prepared baking pan and
bake for 30 minutes.
Unmold the johnnycake and let cool slightly before
cutting into diamonds.
Serve warm.

Serves 6 to 8

APPLE PIE WITH CHEDDAR CHEESE

INGREDIENTS

2 recipes Pie Dough, made with lard (see Basics,
page 346)
9 cups sliced apples, such as Greening, Cortland,
Winesap, or other hard cooking apples (8 to
10 apples)
Juice of 1 lemon
⅓ cup sugar
½ teaspoon cinnamon
1½ teaspoons quick cooking tapioca (if apples
are very juicy)
3 tablespoons unsalted butter, cut into bits
1 egg yolk beaten with 2 tablespoons cold water,
for egg wash
Cheddar cheese, sliced

TOOLS

10-inch deep dish pie pan (about 2 inches deep)

METHOD

Preheat the oven to 425°.
Prepare the pie dough and line a 10-inch deep dish
pie pan with half the dough.
Peel and core the apples and slice into eighths.
In a bowl, toss the apples with the lemon juice, sugar,
and cinnamon. Stir in the tapioca.
Turn the filling into the pie pan and dot with the butter.
Roll out the remaining dough into a circle. Moisten the
edges of the pie crust with water and set the top
crust in place. Seal and crimp.
Brush the crust evenly with the egg wash.
Cut vents in the top crust by inserting a paring knife
¼ inch through the dough.
Bake in the center of the oven for 20 minutes. Reduce
the heat to 350° and continue baking for 45
minutes more.
Cool for 1 hour before serving.
Serve with the cheddar cheese.

Serves 8 to 10

Red Flannel Hash

RED FLANNEL HASH * WITH
POACHED EGGS, RED PEPPER
RELISH, AND KETCHUP *

INDIAN PUDDING SOUFFLÉ
AND WHIPPED CREAM *

BLOODY MARYS,
BEER or ROBERT PECOTA WINERY
GAMAY BEAUJOLAIS

The name "red flannel" originated when red beets were chopped into the corned beef hash, along with whatever leftover vegetables were handy. Though frugal and fast, this leftover meal is an all-time favorite, brightened up with a hot poached egg. Homemade ketchup, neither sweet nor tart, and the ever-present jar of relish or pickles were served alongside. "Come at pudding time" was an invitation to dinner because the pudding opened the meal. Puddings were based on old English recipes. There's nothing Indian about this pudding at all, the name being derived from the commonly-used term "Indian cornmeal."

RED FLANNEL HASH

INGREDIENTS

2 cups diced corned beef
2 cups diced boiled potatoes
1 cup diced large scallions
1 cup diced carrots
½ cup chopped Brussels sprouts
½ cup diced parsnips
1 cup diced red beets
Salt and freshly milled black pepper
¼ pound unsalted butter
2 to 3 tablespoons heavy cream
Ketchup (see Basics, page 346)

METHOD

Use the leftover meat and boiled vegetables to prepare the hash.

In a large bowl, mix together the meat and all of the vegetables, except the beets.

Lightly salt and pepper the mixture to taste. If the corned beef is very salty, do not add any salt.

Over moderate heat, melt the butter in a large cast-iron or other heavy skillet.

Fold the beets into the hash mixture and turn the mixture into the skillet.

Pack firmly, cover, and cook for 10 minutes.

Uncover and drizzle the cream over the hash.

Cover and continue cooking for an additional 10 to 15 minutes, until crusty and well browned.

Turn hash over with a spatula and pack firmly again.

Continue to cook for another 15 minutes.

Serve the hash with a poached egg for each guest, and red pepper relish and ketchup as condiments.

Makes 5 hearty portions

INDIAN PUDDING SOUFFLÉ

INGREDIENTS

Butter and sugar for the mold
½ cup yellow cornmeal
4 cups milk, scalded
2 tablespoons melted butter
½ cup molasses
1 teaspoon cinnamon
½ teaspoon ground ginger
1 teaspoon salt
2 eggs, separated
Whipped unsweetened heavy cream, for serving

TOOLS

1½-quart soufflé dish or baking dish
Double boiler

METHOD

Preheat the oven to 350°.
Butter and sugar the soufflé dish.
Place the cornmeal in the top of the double boiler, over boiling water, and gradually add the scalded milk, stirring constantly for 20 minutes.

Remove from the heat and stir in the butter, molasses, spices, salt, and egg yolks. Set aside to cool slightly.
In a clean bowl, beat the egg whites until stiff but not dry. Fold into the pudding mixture.
Turn the batter into the prepared mold and bake for 40 to 45 minutes, until puffed and brown.
Serve with the whipped cream.

Serves 4 to 5

Steak on the Rocks

An old Maine islander told me how generations of people had been cooking meat out of doors. They pulled a flat rock from the sea, and heated it in a roaring fire. The rock was then pulled out with a board or shovel and dusted off, and a steak set on top to quickly sizzle, the fat from the meat acting as a good, natural grease. The rock actually imparts a sea salt flavor to the meat. He said he knew about this from his grandfather, and his grandfather before that, and so on, putting it back a dozen or so generations—in all probability this method came from the Indians. After the steak is cooked, after you've had your meal, the rock is thrown back into the sea.

Yankee Fourth of July

BEET SOUP*

POACHED SALMON* WITH
HOLLANDAISE SAUCE*

SWEET SNAP PEAS AND
RED POTATOES WITH DILL,
KOSHER SALT, AND BUTTER

STRAWBERRY ICE CREAM*

BRIDGEHAMPTON CHARDONNAY

The Fourth of July heralds summer throughout New England. Around July 4th was just about when New England salmon, in their heyday, began to spawn. Before pollution, some of the great salmon catches were from rivers in the East. It was the custom to serve salmon on the Fourth of July, with new peas and new potatoes. Eastern salmon is best poached. It is a rather delicate fish, unlike the King Salmon of the Pacific Northwest which is bigger and gamier. Oddly enough, Easterners, unlike Indians of the Northwest, never planked their salmon as they did their shad. I chose the sugar snap pea, a recent popular strain

that is eaten pod and all. They should be treated like any good variety pea: thrown in salted water, cooked until tender, and not tinkered with beyond that. Hollandaise was a later accompaniment— thanks to Fannie Farmer—and became one of the preferred sauces with many a fish dish. Hollandaise like mayonnaise is one of the few untranslatable words that have entered the culinary vocabulary. New Englanders suffer from berry fever—from strawberries to blueberries to huckleberries to gooseberries—they do everything with berries, ending with cranberries, and it's just one perpetual berry season.

BEET SOUP

INGREDIENTS

3 pounds small new beets, with their leaves
1 bunch scallions, including some of the green, halved lengthwise
2 lemons, cut into eight wedges
5 stems fresh dill
2 quarts Chicken Stock (see Basics, page 343)
Salt and freshly milled black pepper
Sour cream, chopped fresh dill, and grated lemon zest, for garnishes

METHOD

Trim the beets, leaving 2 inches of the stems and the root ends attached to prevent bleeding. Reserve the leaves.

Wash the beets and leaves thoroughly.

Place the beets and leaves in a soup kettle and add the remaining soup ingredients. Pour in 1 quart of water.

Bring to a boil over high heat and reduce the heat to low. Simmer until the beets are tender.

Remove the beets and turn off the heat.

Under cold running water, slip off the skins and stems.

Cut the beets into fine julienne.

Strain the broth, discarding the solids, and add the beet julienne to the soup. Refrigerate until thoroughly chilled.

Serve with a spoonful of sour cream with a little chopped dill and grated lemon zest.

Note: This soup can be made one day ahead of time.

Serves 8

POACHED SALMON WITH HOLLANDAISE SAUCE

INGREDIENTS

1 whole salmon (5 to 6 pounds), gutted, gills removed with head and tail intact

2 sprigs fresh tarragon

Court bouillon (see Basics, page 343, double the recipe but do not use the double quantity of wine)

Vegetables (see Note)

TOOLS

Fish poacher large enough to hold the fish comfortably

METHOD

Wash the fish thoroughly and place the tarragon in the cavity.

Wrap the fish tightly in lengths of plastic wrap.

Place the fish in a poacher, add the court bouillon and enough water to cover.

Place the poacher on two burners over moderately high heat and cover.

When the liquid begins to bubble, reduce the heat to low and simmer slowly for 20 to 25 minutes.

Remove from the heat and allow the fish to cool.

Remove the fish to a platter and carefully remove the plastic wrap.

Peel away the skin and dark flesh to reveal the salmon flesh. Blot away excess juices.

Arrange the vegetables on either side of the fish and serve with the Hollandaise Sauce.

Note: Wrapping the fish in plastic wrap will produce a firm, flavorful fish.

Fresh garden peas with butter and a sprinkling of mint are a traditional accompaniment to this festive dish.

Sweet snap peas are a simpler vegetable to serve. Remove the stems, cook until tender and toss with melted butter, salt, and freshly milled pepper.

Culls are the tiny potatoes left behind in the fields after harvesting. Some farmers grow tiny potatoes the size of shooting marbles such as these. They should be cooked in their skins until tender, a matter of 5 minutes after the water comes to a boil. Serve with melted sweet butter, kosher salt, a little chopped dill, and grated lemon zest.

Serves 6 to 8

HOLLANDAISE SAUCE

INGREDIENTS

3 egg yolks, at room temperature
1 tablespoon fresh lemon juice
Salt and freshly milled white pepper
Pinch of cayenne
1 tablespoon cold unsalted butter
¼ pound plus 4 tablespoons unsalted butter, clarified
(see Basics, page 344)

METHOD

Off the heat, whisk the egg yolks in a nonaluminum
saucepan until they become thick and lemony
in color.
Add the lemon juice and seasonings.
Add the cold butter and place the saucepan over very
low heat, whisking constantly until the mixture
thickens and becomes creamy.
Remove from the heat.
Beat the mixture with the whisk, adding the melted
butter in droplets. When the sauce begins to take on
the thickness of heavy cream, start adding the
butter in a steady stream.
Taste for seasoning and hold, off the heat, on a warm
corner of the stove.

Note: Hollandaise is easily made in a blender or food
processor. Egg yolks, lemon juice, and seasonings
are blended and the clarified butter is incorporated
in a slow steady stream. This is a fail-safe method;
however, the flavor of the lightly cooked yolks and
the whisking in of the butter result in a fluffier and
richer tasting sauce.

Makes about 1 cup

STRAWBERRY ICE CREAM

INGREDIENTS

1 quart cold English Cream (see Basics, page 348)
1 quart cold ripe strawberries, hulled and crushed

TOOLS

Ice cream maker

METHOD

Combine the English Cream and the strawberries.
Place the mixture in the ice cream maker and freeze
according to the manufacturer's directions.

Makes 1¾ to 2 quarts

Fish Fry

CORN COB CHOWDER*

FRIED WHITEBAIT*

PAN-SAUTÉED OYSTERS*

FRIED CLAMS*

TARTAR SAUCE (see Basics, page 345)

COLE SLAW (see page 120)

RASPBERRIES AND CREAM

MATANZAS CREEK WINERY
CHARDONNAY

Corn chowder is as native to New England as clam chowder. Most chowders were made with pork fat. I've chosen to leave it out, especially because this corn is freshly picked off the stalks, the kernels tender and creamy, requiring only the infusion of good corn flavor from the cobs themselves. A hint of scallion is sufficient. The fish fry that follows the chowder begins with tiny whitebait, which is baby herring, dusted with flour and thrown into hot fat while still kicking—a lilliputian fish fry. Whitebait should be consumed on the spot, and eaten with your fingers like potato chips, with

perhaps a sprinkle of fresh lemon. They also make perfect little appetizers with a prefatory cocktail. Generally speaking, New England shellfish is dusted with flour and cooked in butter, while Southern shellfish is tossed with cornmeal and fried in fat. Here I've done one of each. The standard seashore accompaniments are tartar sauce and creamy cole slaw.

CORN COB CHOWDER

INGREDIENTS

6 ears fresh white sweet corn, kernels not too closely removed and each cob cut into three pieces

4 cups milk

1 quart Chicken Stock (see Basics, page 343)

2 teaspoons salt

1 teaspoon sugar

6 scallions

5 tablespoons unsalted butter

1 tablespoon all-purpose flour

Freshly milled black pepper

⅛ teaspoon cayenne pepper

METHOD

Place the corn cobs in a soup kettle.

Add the milk and chicken stock. Bring to a boil and simmer for 1 hour.

Remove the cobs and add the corn kernels, salt and sugar. Continue to simmer as the corn cooks.

With a small spoon, scrape away the pulp from the cobs and add it to the chowder.

Chop the scallions, including most of the green tops, and briefly sauté them in 4 tablespoons of the butter. Set aside.

In a small bowl, blend the remaining 1 tablespoon butter with the flour.

Whisk the flour mixture into the chowder. Season with pepper to taste and the cayenne and cook for another 15 minutes.

Fold in the scallion mixture. Taste for seasoning and serve in heated soup plates.

Serves 5 to 6

FISH FRY

INGREDIENTS

1 quart whitebait
Vegetable oil
All-purpose flour
Salt
24 oysters, shucked
½ cup clarified butter (see Basics, page 344)
24 cherrystone clams, shucked
Cornmeal

METHOD

Whitebait:

Carefully wash the whitebait in 2 to 3 changes of cold
water. Drain and pat dry.

In a deep heavy pot or skillet, heat 3 cups vegetable oil
until hot.

Working in 1-cup batches, lightly dredge the whitebait
in flour and cook until crisp and golden.

Remove with a flat slotted skimmer and drain on paper
towels.

Salt lightly and serve immediately.

Oysters:

Drain the liquor from the oysters. Discard it or save for
another use.

Dredge the oysters lightly with flour, shaking to remove
any excess.

Sauté the oysters in clarified butter until they begin to
brown.

Remove with a slotted spoon.

Serve immediately.

Clams:

Drain the juice from clams. Discard it or reserve for
another use.

Dredge the clams lightly with cornmeal, shaking to
remove any excess.

Fry the clams in 1 inch of hot vegetable oil until crisp.

Serve immediately.

Note: Oysters and clams can be dipped in beaten egg
and then flour or bread crumbs. They may be
sautéed in clarified butter or vegetable oil.

Serve with Rémoulade (see page 167), or Tartar Sauce
(see Basics, page 345).

Serves 6 to 8

Capon Dinner

COLD JELLIED VEGETABLE SOUP*

STUFFED CAPON*
WITH OYSTER SAUCE*

RASPBERRY TART*

PEACH PIE*

WAGNER VINEYARDS
CHARDONNAY

All varieties of vegetable soups open meals, or are meals in themselves. Rather than give a plain hot soup, I've turned this one into a cold, rich broth, so it's very jellied. Combinations of meat and fish were very common in early cookery. We know that the skins and flesh of bass and haddock were scored and filled with chunks of bacon (the early Americans loved that pork flavor). Likewise, they would stuff their chickens and turkeys with oysters. I don't like oysters in stuffing, and have reversed the tradition, filling the bird with bread and sausage, and incorporating the oysters in the sauce. A capon is larger and meatier than a chicken; it will feed a lot of people, and if you're going to stuff something, you might as well stuff something big. Serving more than one dessert was a habit that ran across New England into the heartland. Women just liked to bake; it was an expression of bounty and hospitality.

COLD JELLIED VEGETABLE SOUP

INGREDIENTS

3 quarts Chicken Stock (see Basics, page 343)
1 veal knuckle, cut in half

FOR CLARIFICATION:

6 celery ribs with leaves, finely chopped
1 medium onion, chopped
1 pound lean top round of beef, ground
3 egg whites, including the shells (do not use brown
    eggs)
⅛ teaspoon saffron threads

VEGETABLES:

1 small bunch golden beets (about 5—red beets may
    not be substituted)
2 medium zucchini
4 very ripe tomatoes—peeled, seeded, and juiced
8 baby carrots, peeled and cut diagonally into ¼-inch
    slices
½ pound green beans, trimmed and cut into 1½-inch
    lengths
1 bunch small scallions, including some of the green—
    cleaned, trimmed, and quartered lengthwise
Salt

TOOLS

Large nonaluminum kettle
Fine wire mesh sieve

METHOD

Prepare the chicken stock according to the method in
    Basics, with the addition of the veal knuckle.
To clarify the stock:
Bring the finished stock to a boil in a large soup kettle.
Reduce the heat to a simmer.
In a mixing bowl, combine the celery, onions, ground
    beef, egg whites, and egg shells.
Stir the mixture into the stock and let simmer gently
    for 30 to 45 minutes, or until a crusty "raft" forms
    on top.
Using a ladle, gently press the "raft" down, filling the
    ladle with the stock. Pour the liquid through a fine

wire mesh lined with a damp soft cotton kitchen
    towel or a triple thickness of dampened cheesecloth.
Pour the clarified stock into a clean large saucepan.
    Add the saffron and place over low heat.
The vegetables:
Trim the beet stems, leaving 2 or more inches attached
    to prevent excess bleeding. Wash thoroughly.
Place the beets in a pot of lightly salted water. Bring
    the water to a boil and cook until tender.
Drain the beets and cool under cold running water.
    Slip off the outer skins and stems. Cut the beets into
    ¼-inch slices. Reserve.
Trim the top and bottom ends off of the zucchini. Cut
    crosswise into thirds.
Cut each third lengthwise in half and then cut each
    half lengthwise into three pieces.
Slice the tomatoes and reserve.
Increase the heat and bring the stock to a
    moderate boil.
Add the carrots and green beans and cook for 4
    minutes.
Add the scallions and zucchini and cook for 3 minutes.
Add the tomatoes and cook for 2 minutes.
Check the seasonings.
Remove from the heat and pour the consommé into a
    bowl.
Let cool for 20 minutes and refrigerate, uncovered.
When the soup begins to gel, swirl the vegetables 2 or
    3 times every 30 minutes, until they begin to float.
Stir in the sliced beets.
Refrigerate again and chill until the consommé sets.
Ladle the soup into a glass bowl and serve.

Note: This soup can be prepared a day in advance.

Serves 8 to 10

STUFFED CAPON WITH OYSTER SAUCE

INGREDIENTS

CAPON:

1 capon, with neck and wings reserved (9 to 10 pounds)
4 cups day-old French or Italian bread, cubed
3 cups milk
⅓ pound pork sausage
1 medium-size yellow onion, finely chopped
1 celery rib, finely chopped
1 clove garlic, minced
1 to 2 tablespoons butter (optional)
1 teaspoon chopped fresh tarragon
1 teaspoon thyme leaves
1 egg
2 to 3 tablespoons heavy cream
Salt and freshly milled black pepper

STOCK:

1 celery rib, chopped
1 small yellow onion, quartered
3 fresh parsley sprigs
1 small carrot, coarsely chopped
4 black peppercorns

SAUCE:

2 dozen oysters, shucked, with their liquor reserved
2 cups heavy cream

METHOD

Preheat the oven to 450°.
Wash and pat the capon dry with paper towels. Reserve.
In a large mixing bowl, soak the cubed bread in the milk. Set aside.
In a heavy medium skillet, render and brown the sausage over moderately low heat.
With a slotted spoon, remove the sausage meat to a large mixing bowl.
Sauté the onion in the rendered sausage fat.
When the onions are wilted, add the celery and garlic, and cook for about 10 minutes, until the celery is tender. (If the mixture becomes dry and sticks to the pan, add 1 to 2 tablespoons of butter.)
Remove from the heat and add to the mixing bowl with the sausage.
Squeeze the milk from the bread cubes and add the bread to the sausage-stuffing mixture. Discard the milk.
Add the herbs, egg, cream, and salt and pepper to taste. Check the seasonings.
Stuff the capon and truss the bird.
Place the capon on a rack in a roasting pan. Roast for 20 minutes, reduce the oven temperature to 325°, and roast, basting frequently, for 2 hours more.
While the capon is roasting, prepare the stock.
In a medium saucepan, combine the reserved capon pieces with the remaining stock ingredients. Pour in enough cold water to cover.
Bring the stock to a boil, reduce the heat to low, and simmer, skimming the surface.
Simmer for 1½ hours, adding more water, if necessary. Reserve.
Meanwhile, drain off the oyster liquor and place the liquid in a small saucepan. Reduce the liquor over low heat to ½ cup.
Pour the heavy cream in a small saucepan, and reduce over low heat to 1 cup.
Pierce the leg joint with a sharp paring knife; when the juices run clear, remove the bird from the oven. Place on a warm platter and keep warm.
Make the sauce:
Pour off most of the fat on the roasting pan. Place the pan over high heat.
Strain the reserved stock into the pan and deglaze, scraping up the brown bits that cling to the bottom of the pan.
Strain the stock into the reduced cream and bring to a boil.
Add the oysters and simmer until the oysters plump and their edges curl slightly. Add the reduced oyster liquid.
To serve, ladle a few spoonfuls of sauce and oysters over the capon and pour the remaining sauce into a heated bowl.
Serve with steamed baby squash and zucchini with their flowers, and parslied potatoes.

Serves 6

RASPBERRY TART

INGREDIENTS

ALMOND PASTRY:

1½ cups ground almonds, with their skins
½ cup sugar
½ pound unsalted butter
1½ cups all-purpose flour, sifted

2 quarts fresh raspberries
1 tablespoon sugar

TOOLS

Electric mixer
9-inch fluted, loose-bottomed tart pan

METHOD

In a small mixing bowl, combine the almonds with ¼ cup of the sugar. Set aside.

With an electric mixer, cream together the butter and the remaining ¼ cup sugar. Gradually add the flour and blend. Add the almonds and mix well. Cover and chill for 20 minutes.

Preheat the oven to 350°.

On a lightly floured board, roll out two-thirds of the dough ¼-inch thick.

Place the dough in the pan, fitting it evenly over the bottom and sides. Roll over the pan with the rolling pin to trim off the excess dough. Combine the pastry scraps with the remaining dough and roll out ¼-inch thick.

Place the berries in the tart shell and lightly sprinkle with the sugar.

Cut the pastry into ribbons and cover the pie, interweaving the strips in a lattice fashion. Trim the excess dough, and crimp the edges.

Bake for 30 minutes.

Cool the tart on a rack for 20 minutes. Chill for 30 minutes. Remove the sides of the tart pan before serving.

Serves 6 to 8

PEACH PIE

INGREDIENTS

½ recipe Pie Dough made with butter (see Basics, page 346)
8 firm, ripe peaches—blanched, skinned, stoned, and cut into 1-inch slices
Juice of ½ lemon
⅓ cup sugar
2 teaspoons quick cooking tapioca
1 tablespoon sugar, for crust

METHOD

Preheat the oven to 450°.

On a lightly-floured surface, roll out half of the pie dough ¼-inch thick.

Place the dough in the pan, fitting it evenly over the bottom and sides.

Place the peach slices in a bowl and toss with the lemon juice, sugar, and tapioca.

Turn the peach slices into the shell.

Roll out the remaining dough ¼-inch thick.

Cut a 1-inch round vent in the center of the dough.

Place the pie crust dough over the peaches. Trim and crimp the edges.

Bake for 15 minutes. Reduce the heat to 350° and continue baking for 20 to 25 minutes, until pale gold in color. Remove and place on a rack and sprinkle with 1 tablespoon of sugar.

Cool before serving.

Serves 6

Swordfish Dinner

STEAMED LITTLENECK CLAMS*

THE BENCHLEY'S GRILLED
SWORDFISH WITH SALT CRUST*
AND GIN-LIME BUTTER
(see Basics, page 345)

DILLED KIRBY CUCUMBERS*

BRAN POPOVERS* WITH
ROSE HIP BLOSSOM BUTTER*

BLACK PLUMS, CURRANTS,
AND GOOSEBERRIES

CHAPPELLET VINEYARDS
CHARDONNAY

Swordfish adapts itself to the grill perhaps better than any other fish. It is too often underrated and overcooked. Usually swordfish is cut one-half to one inch thick; this recipe works only if it is cut 2-inches thick and thinly sliced at the table as one would a steak. The salt crust doesn't penetrate the flesh but rather seals in the juices before it burns off during cooking. Cucumbers are a wonderful foil for fish. Don't overlook the Kirby cucumber (usually associated with pickles), with seeds so tiny that they don't have to be removed. The common popover is best served with meat and gravy, but wouldn't make sense with this meal. The bran makes it grainier and gritty, a nice complement in texture and taste.

STEAMED LITTLENECK CLAMS

INGREDIENTS

4 dozen small littleneck clams, scrubbed
3 cloves garlic, minced
½ cup finely chopped fresh parsley
2 tablespoons chopped fresh chives
1 tablespoon chopped fresh tarragon leaves
2 sprigs thyme or lemon thyme, leaves only (or any combination of fresh herbs you have on hand)

TOOLS

Large steamer

METHOD

Place the clams in the freezer for 10 minutes before cooking. (This will cause the clams to open quickly.)
Place 1 cup cold water or a combination of dry white wine and water in a large steamer.
Cover, and bring to a rolling boil over high heat.
Add the garlic.
Place the clams in the steamer basket, cover, and cook the clams just until they open. (To ensure a tender clam, remove the clams with tongs or a slotted spoon as soon as they open. Reserve in a covered bowl. Keep the cover on the steamer as they cook, checking from time to time to remove the opened clams. Discard any clams that do not open.)
When all the clams have been removed, remove the steamer container and toss in the herbs.
Pour the cooking liquid over the clams and serve immediately.

Note: This makes a great lunch course with crusty bread. A combination of ½ cup good olive oil and ½ cup white wine used in the steaming process is a nice Mediterranean variation on this dish, and makes a wonderful sauce to sop up with the bread.

Serves 6 to 8

THE BENCHLEY'S GRILLED SWORDFISH WITH SALT CRUST

INGREDIENTS

1 thick cold swordfish steak, cut 2 inches thick (about 4 pounds)
¼ pound unsalted butter, melted
Kosher salt

TOOLS

Grill and charcoal

METHOD

Brush one side of the cold fish with some of the melted butter.
Dredge liberally in the kosher salt.

Refrigerate for 20 minutes, or until the butter has congealed.
Turn the fish over and butter and salt that side. Refrigerate for 20 minutes, or until ready to cook.
Place the fish on a hot grill and cook for 10 minutes on each side, turning only once. The fish will be moist and tender.
Serve with Dilled Kirby Cucumbers.

Serves 6 to 7

DILLED KIRBY CUCUMBERS

INGREDIENTS

18 Kirby cucumbers, peeled and quartered lengthwise
Salt
4 tablespoons unsalted butter
2 tablespoons chopped fresh dill

METHOD

Preheat the oven to 350°.
Lightly salt the cucumbers and let stand in a colander for 20 minutes.
Place the cucumbers in a small ovenproof casserole and dot with the butter.
Cover tightly and bake, tossing once or twice while they cook, for 25 to 30 minutes, or until the Kirbys are limp but not soft.
Toss the cucumbers with the dill and serve.

Serves 6

BRAN POPOVERS

INGREDIENTS

Bacon fat, butter, or margarine, for the muffin tins
Unprocessed bran, to dust the tins
1 cup all-purpose flour less 1 tablespoon
¼ teaspoon salt
2 tablespoons unprocessed bran
1 cup milk
2 eggs, lightly beaten
1 tablespoon melted unsalted butter

TOOLS

12-cup muffin tin

METHOD

Preheat the oven to 450°.
Grease the muffin tins and dust with bran.
Sift the flour into a mixing bowl. Add the salt
   and the bran.
Whisk in the milk, eggs, and melted butter.
Fill the muffin cups three-quarters full and dust the
   top of the batter with additional bran.
Bake at once for 15 minutes. Reduce the heat to 350°
   and continue to bake for 20 minutes.
Serve immediately.

Makes 8 to 10 popovers

ROSE HIP BLOSSOM BUTTER

INGREDIENTS

1 pound unsalted butter, at room temperature
6 rose hip blossoms

METHOD

In a bowl, cream the butter with a wooden spoon or
   electric mixer.
Select a glass container that will comfortably hold the
   butter and place a rose hip blossom, face up, on the
   bottom of the container.
Using a bit of butter to hold them in place, arrange 4 of
   the blossoms, facing out, on the sides of the
   container. Fill the container with the butter, pressing carefully against the flowers. When filled, place
   one blossom on top. Cover and refrigerate for 24
   hours. The butter will take on the perfume of the
   flowers and taste even richer.
Remove from the refrigerator to soften for 20 minutes
   before serving.

Makes 1 pound flavored butter

Long Island Fish Dinner

SCALLOP STEW*

STEAMED BASS WITH
CIDER AND GINGER*

STEWED RUM PLUMS*

MAPLE WAFER COOKIES*

CARMENET VINEYARD
SAUVIGNON BLANC

Mid-autumn opens the scallop season. The sweetest of all scallops are those harvested by the fishermen from the eastern shore of Long Island north to Maine. They are harvested from the sea like oysters from flat-bottomed dredging boats. This beautiful shell, familiar to most of us through gas station logos, is too fragile to be shipped live and is shucked immediately before being sent to market. This luscious, pearly shellfish should be eaten as fresh as possible, cooked as briefly as possible. The fish is steamed in cider. Cider got into everything, just as pork did, and was probably used in the place of wine, which was not generally available in early days. We tend to lose sight of the fact that the trade routes had opened beyond anyone's expectations, and with the discovery of this country, new things were coming into this world left and right. I don't think the colonists quite knew what was hitting them. Bass with cider and ginger may sound like a modern interpretation, but the novelty of vanilla, rums, ginger, and other spices belonged to the 17th century, when these luxuries were carried into American harbors.

Both wild American and established European plums have been cultivated here since the early 17th century. P. americanus is a golden plum, varying in hue from burnished yellow to almost red. In early years, colonial women didn't poach twelve plums for guests, they poached a barrelful. When the plums were ripe, they had to be preserved, put up, put down, dried, or whatever. They had to help get a family through the winter.

SCALLOP STEW

INGREDIENTS

3 cups heavy cream, reduced over moderate
  heat to 2 cups
2 cups Fish Stock, reduced over moderate heat
  to 1½ cups (see Basics, page 344)
1 quart bay scallops
Worcestershire sauce
Cayenne pepper
Salt

¼ cup chopped fresh chives

METHOD

In a large nonaluminum saucepan, combine the reduced cream with the reduced fish stock over moderately low heat. Add the scallops and seasonings to taste and simmer for about 8 minutes, until the scallops are just opaque. Do not overcook or the scallops will toughen.

Season with cayenne and salt to taste and pour into heated soup plates. Sprinkle with the chives.

Makes 4 large or 6 medium servings.

STEAMED BASS WITH CIDER AND GINGER

INGREDIENTS

Vegetable oil

1 whole bass (about 5 pounds), spine removed with head and tail intact

1-inch piece fresh ginger, peeled and cut into fine julienne (about ¼ cup)

1 small hot red chile pepper, seeded and cut into fine julienne

2 ripe tomatoes—peeled, seeded, and thinly sliced

3 small carrots, cut into 2-inch julienne and blanched for 1 minute (about 1 cup)

2 medium leeks—halved lengthwise, washed, cut into 2-inch julienne, and blanched

Salt

¼ cup lightly chopped Italian parsley

½ cup apple cider

METHOD

Preheat the oven to 400°.

Place a sheet of foil, large enough to envelope the fish, on a large baking sheet or baking pan. Line it with parchment paper.

Brush the parchment lightly with oil so the fish will not adhere after cooking.

Set the fish on the parchment, lightly salt the cavity, and scatter some of the vegetables and ginger inside the fish.

Scatter the remaining ingredients over the fish and pour the cider over the fish.

Tightly close the foil and bake the fish for 20 to 25 minutes, or for 10 minutes per inch of thickness.

Serves 4 to 5

STEWED RUM PLUMS

INGREDIENTS

2 dozen golden plums
2 cups dark rum
2 cups sugar
1 vanilla bean, split
3 small cinnamon sticks
2 tablespoons peppercorns

METHOD

Place the plums in a single layer in a large shallow
    nonaluminum pan.
Add the rum, sugar, spices, and enough water to cover.
Bring the liquid to a boil, reduce to a simmer, and
    poach until the fruit can be pierced easily
    with a knife.
Remove from the heat and let the fruit cool in
    the liquid.
Serve 2 plums per person with Maple Wafer Cookies.

Note: These Stewed Rum Plums can be put up in
    sterilized jars or refrigerated for up to 5 days.

Serves 8 to 12

MAPLE WAFER COOKIES

INGREDIENTS

1 cup all-purpose flour
½ teaspoon baking powder
¼ teaspoon baking soda
½ cup maple syrup
½ cup sugar
¼ pound unsalted butter
½ cup chopped walnuts

TOOLS

2 to 3 baking sheets

METHOD

Preheat the oven to 350°
Fill a large saucepan with about 2 inches of water,
    place over high heat, and bring to a simmer.
Sift the flour, baking powder, and baking soda into a
    mixing bowl and reserve.
In a heavy medium-large saucepan, bring the maple
    syrup, sugar, and butter to a boil and continue
    boiling for 30 seconds, or until the sugar is
    dissolved.
Stir the dry ingredients into the sugar mixture and
    fold in the nuts.
Place the smaller saucepan over the saucepan filled
    with simmering water.
Remove from the heat (keeping the mixture warm will
    prevent it from hardening or seizing up).
With a large dessert or soup spoon, spoon out the
    mixture onto ungreased or foil-lined baking sheets,
    spacing the spoonfuls 3 inches apart.
Bake for exactly 7 minutes.
Allow the wafers to cool before removing from the
    sheets. Store in an airtight container.

Makes 2 dozen wafers

Chowder Picnic

Tomato-based clam chowder was being served up at the beginning of this century, from Coney Island to Delmonico's. How it came to be called "Manhattan" no one really knows, but it was a distinct departure from the creamy chowders of New England. Manhattan, or Long Island, clam chowder is done with a strong addition of herbs, specifically thyme, and the addition of tomatoes and potatoes. All of the ingredients should be as fresh as possible. The herbs are fresh, the fish are fresh, and one shouldn't take short-cuts, such as using clam broth. The addition of several types of fish makes this chowder more of a meal.

By the 18th century, there were over 400 varieties of gooseberries, as well as numerous cultivated and wild currants. The berries never appealed to the American eating public much beyond New England. Affected by a blight that attacked the American white pine, both gooseberries and currants were outlawed and fell almost entirely from popular use. The berries are once again beginning to capture the fancy of home gardeners. Gooseberries give off an enormous amount of pectin and the fruit is jelly-like—ideal for a fool, that most English of desserts. Lorna Doones seem to be the closest we Americans get to shortbread.

MANHATTAN FISH CHOWDER

INGREDIENTS

1 quart shucked quahog or cherrystone clams, with
    their liquor
¼ pound salt pork or slab bacon, diced

1 large onion, minced (about 1 cup)

4 ripe tomatoes—peeled, seeded, and chopped with juices reserved (about 3 cups)

1 teaspoon fresh thyme leaves

1 teaspoon chopped fresh rosemary leaves

1 teaspoon fresh tarragon leaves

Freshly milled black pepper

1½ cups small, peeled and quartered new potatoes

3 small carrots, diced (about 1 cup)

2 dozen small littleneck clams—washed, drained, and chilled

1 pound firm white fish fillets, such as weakfish or bass, cubed

¼ cup chopped fresh parsley

Oyster crackers, for serving

TOOLS

Meat grinder or food mill

METHOD

Strain the clam liquor into a small bowl.

Chop the shucked clams with a sharp knife, or put through the medium disk of a meat grinder or food mill. Cover and set aside.

In a large soup kettle, render the salt pork over moderate heat until the cracklings are golden.

Remove the cracklings with a slotted spoon and reserve.

Add the onions and sauté in the fat until translucent.

Add the tomatoes and their juices.

Add 2 cups cold water, the herbs, and seasonings.

Add the reserved clam liquor, the potatoes, and carrots.

Cover and simmer for about 8 minutes.

When the potatoes are cooked, add the reserved chopped clam meat and cook for 5 minutes.

Remove from the heat, cool, and refrigerate, covered, overnight.

To assemble:

Place the littlenecks in the freezer for 10 minutes to facilitate quick opening.

Meanwhile, skim off any fat that is congealed on the surface of the stew.

Bring the stew to a simmer over moderately low heat.

When the chowder bubbles lightly and is hot, add the littlenecks. Cover and continue to simmer.

When the clams begin to open, add the cubed fish and simmer just long enough for the fish to become tender, about 5 minutes.

Add the reserved cracklings and parsley and serve with oyster crackers.

Note: This chowder is best when allowed to ripen in refrigerator for one day before serving. The chowder freezes well before the addition of the littlenecks and fish.

Serves 6

GOOSEBERRY FOOL

INGREDIENTS

1 quart fresh gooseberries

1 pint fresh currants, if available

About ½ cup sugar

1 cup heavy cream, lightly whipped

METHOD

Separately wash and drain the fruits.

In a nonaluminum saucepan, toss the gooseberries with ½ cup sugar or a little more, depending on the tartness of the fruit.

Warm the gooseberries over moderate heat just until they begin to collapse and give off their juices.

Turn the gooseberries and juices into a bowl and refrigerate for at least 2 hours.

Repeat this method with the currants, adding 1 to 2 tablespoons sugar and warming the berries just until the sugar dissolves. Refrigerate.

When ready to serve, place layers of gooseberries, currants, and cream in a glass beaker or bowl, repeating the layering until all of the fruits and cream are used.

Swirl the mixture slightly before serving with Lorna Doones.

Serves 6

STREET FOOD

The Lobster Roll

All good cooks tend to treat the lobster with reverence. Even when served cold in salad it takes on proportions that go beyond a treat. That treat really started in the lobster shacks and fish houses that follow the coast from Maine to Montauk. It is their hot dog, and they serve it on a toasted and buttered frankfurter roll. They have made it one of life's simple pleasures.

INGREDIENTS

2 cooked lobsters, each about 1¼ pounds, shelled (see
    page 32)
2 celery ribs, peeled and finely diced
½ cup homemade Mayonnaise (see Basics, page 345)
4 hot dog rolls
4 tablespoons unsalted butter, melted

METHOD

Remove the lobster meat from the tails and claws and
    cut it into ½-inch pieces.
Combine the meat with the celery and mayonnaise,
    cover, and chill for 30 minutes.
Preheat the broiler.
Open the hot dog rolls and brush with the melted
    butter.
Place the rolls, buttered side up, in a hot broiler and
    toast lightly, until golden.
Fill each roll with the lobster salad and serve
    immediately.

Serves 4

Rum Punch

In the early 1800s, there was a wonderful drink called "yard of flannel," made with steaming ale, lemons, eggs, sugar, spices, and rum. Our taste in drinks has become simpler. We drink eggnog once a year, our syllabub has become a dessert, and wine has become a cocktail. Hot drinks are still a satisfying pick-me-up that in the cold of winter warm the spirit, the head, and the belly.

HOT BUTTERED RUM

INGREDIENTS

¼ pound unsalted butter, at room temperature
3 tablespoons brown sugar
Pinch of ground cloves
4 navel oranges
8 small cinnamon sticks
2 cups dark rum
Boiling water, hot tea, or hot cider

TOOLS

6- to 8-ounce glasses or mugs
8 metal spoons

METHOD

In a small bowl, cream the butter with the
    brown sugar and ground cloves; reserve.
Remove the zest from each orange in one
    spiral strip. Cut each strip
    in half.
In each glass or mug, place one spoon, a strip
    of zest, 1 cinnamon stick, and 2 ounces
    of rum.
Pour 4 to 5 ounces of boiling water, tea, or
    cider into each glass and float 1 tablespoon
    of the softened butter mixture on top. Serve.

Makes 8 drinks

Mid-Atlantic

"Fain would I pause to dwell upon the world of charms that burst upon the enraptured gaze of my hero, as he entered the state parlour of Van Tassel's mansion. Not those of the bevy of buxom lasses, with their luxurious display of red and white; but the ample charms of a genuine Dutch country tea-table in the sumptuous time of autumn. Such heaped-up platters of cakes of various and almost indescribable kinds, known only to experienced Dutch housewives! There was the doughty dough-nut, the tenderer oly koek, and the crisp and crumbling kruller; sweet-cakes and shortcakes, gingercakes and honey-cakes, and the whole family of cakes. And then there were apple-pies and peach-pies and pumpkin-pies; besides slices of ham and smoked beef; and, moreover, delectable dishes of preserved plums, and peaches, and pears, and quinces; not to mention broiled shad and roasted chickens; together with bowls of milk and cream, all mingled higgledy-piggledy, pretty much as I have ennumerated them, with the motherly teapot sending up its clouds of vapour from the midst—Heaven bless the mark!"
—THE LEGEND OF SLEEPY HOLLOW *by Washington Irving*

Ⅰn a land of valleys jeweled with orchards from the Hudson west to Pennsylvania, carefully tended hot-houses and sheltered gardens glowed with delicate cuttings and seeds brought by settlers from plants as various as the apple, peach, plum, cherry, apricot, fig, and wild persimmon. And the myth of Johnny Appleseed grew from tales of a vagrant horticulturist named John Chapman, who wandered from the Alleghenies to Ohio, planting and tending nurseries. Apples were important food, and all the more so for their long storage life, for an apple barrel could be kept year-round. Apples were sliced in rings and dried for winter use. A child's thirst was quenched with cider, and a man's, slaked with hard cider, rather decent brandy, and potent applejack. Expatriate Europeans missed their clarets, but these apple beverages kept many an Englishman and Dutchman happy. Settlers were remarkably self-sufficient, and a newcomer was quick to clear a field and sow an acre or two with

corn, potatoes, and garden vegetables. (If his family was too young or sickly, he might hire a wandering laborer or, if he were fortunate, depend on a slave or indentured servant for help.) The hills were cleared to provide pasture for dairy cows which yielded milk, rich cream, butter, and even a cheddar to rival that of Vermont and England. Streams and lakes were aboil with trout and bass, and the Hudson gave much of the East Coast sturgeon and shad, and delicate shad roe in the springtime. Traditionally, buck shad has been smoked to juicy perfection, and the roe-heavy females still sell briskly throughout the Eastern seaboard. Eel was packed in great quantities and shipped to Holland for smoking, early Dutch farmers considering this a more valuable cash crop for export than for local market.

Frugality was the watchword of the prosperous small farm. The larder was stocked with basics—pork and apple barrels, dried corn, a root cellar—to stave off hunger over winter's long course. The home cook put up preserves, jams, vegetables, and pickles, and a smokehouse filled with wild game, fish, hams, and bacon would give peace of mind. These little farms survived because they wasted nothing; even corn cobs and apple tree prunings were used, investing smoked pork, chickens, and wild game with their sweet flavors.

An early sophistication graced the southern end of Pennsylvania. While the Philadelphia Germans ate pickled pig's feet, jellied pig's knuckles, hard-boiled eggs pickled in beet juice, and crunchy Reading pretzels, the Quaker Philadelphians preferred more lux-

urious tables. Lordly landowners, powdered and puffed to suit the mode of their century, indulged themselves, and Quaker William Penn himself enjoyed living well, rarely inclined to forgo a social evening (typically dining on turtle from the West Indies, oysters from the Chesapeake, local game, syllabubs, flummeries, trifles, and fools, all washed down with Madeiras, ports and another imported wines). Philadelphia, hub of the colonies, hosted glittering evenings of mock Regency and was this country's capital until 1800 (excepting a brief year of glory for New York City).

Fried scrapple and eggs were everyman's breakfast. (The menu for a turn-of-the-century dinner given by the Pennsylvania Society in "Commemoration of the 200th Anniversary of the Birth of Benjamin Franklin" lists as a fifth course, scrapple, served with Moët et Chandon.) Hot pepper pot—a filling bowl of tripe, veal, vegetables, herbs, and whole spoonfuls of pepper, reportedly tossed together by a Pennsylvania Dutchman for Washington's troops at Valley Forge—appeared on the menus in Philadelphia and around the countryside. By the 19th century it was hawked from steaming cauldrons in the city streets. The formal dinners attended by our Founding Fathers were staggering two course affairs: soups and fishes, served with game, poultry, roasts of beef and mutton, chops, and vegetables and sweets were the second course. Fifty dishes might ornament such a function, attended by gallons of wines, beer, cider, and rum. (When Mr. Washington ran for the legislature in 1758, his agents doled out three Imperials, or three-and-a-half gallons, of one of the same to each voter, and worried that the quantity might be stingy!) Penn, whose Philadelphia was as German as it was English Quaker, established that city's first brewery, which succeeded where the New England ones had failed. Yeasty brews made from pure local water met with approval, and dark Bock or "Easter beer" was the companion drink to the Lenten weisswurst flecked with spring chives. Bock was left behind in favor of a lighter and more sparkling beer (the preference of today's taste), brewed here in the 18th century by German refugees of the European potato famine who immigrated to Ohio, Minnesota, and Wisconsin.

The rising cities of Boston, New York, and Philadelphia could boast restaurants with service of silver, fine china, and crystal, in proud imitation of European custom and of the luxury enjoyed by owners of local estates. Dining clubs became havens of the select. The oldest of these, the Schuylkill Fishing Company (known simply as the Colony in Schuylkill) was established in 1732 and is further renowned as the birthplace of the infamous Fish House Punch, a fairly lethal combination of rum, Cognac, peach brandy, citrus juices, and sugar. (Indoctrination into the club required a new member to fry carefully a half dozen perch in a long-handled skillet—as long as a man is tall—and to flip the fish perfectly in the air when they were ready to be turned.)

From early days, land in New York was expensive. The Pennsylvania government, on the other hand, offered some of the richest farmland in the east for 10 cents an acre. This was particularly fortunate for Germans seeking relief from religious persecution. Penn's royal grant was open to persecuted societies from other countries, and soon sects such as the Moravians, Amish, Shakers, and Schwenkfelders arrived. These folk joined the company of 13 Mennonite and Crefelder families already here, who had left their native Rhine Valley still in ruins some 35 years after the Thirty Years' War.

The character of these people set standards for this country. The Shakers spread across the Mid-Atlantic as far as Ohio, Indiana, Illinois, and Iowa, their celibate communities always tiny and on the verge of extinction. For all the Shakers' austerity, their cooking is brilliant, coupling asparagus with mint, spinach with rosemary, omelettes with blue chive blossoms, and apple pie with rose water. Their most influential innovation, pearl-ash, became a staple colonial leavening for dough: modern baking powder. It might almost be said that the Shakers, with their elementary formula for muffins, cakes, biscuits, and pancakes (consisting of flour, salt, sugar, and baking powder)

were virtually the originators of packaged baking mixes.

Unlike some other sects, the Mennonites did not travel far west, and together with the Amish greatly influenced American cookery throughout the middle and northern regions of this country. Like the Shakers they maintained an austere way of life refusing to this day the use of electricity and automobiles. (Some communities circumvent denial by sharing a communal tractor, because their huge land holdings defy the handheld plowshare.) They became known as the "Pennsylvania Dutch" (a corruption of "Deutsche" meaning German). Their lives are ruled by simplicity: their children run barefoot in fine weather. Mothers and daughters wear hand-sewn buttonless dresses, and their hair in neat white caps; fathers and sons go about their farm chores in white shirts and black trousers with suspenders, usually sporting flat-topped straw hats. They grind their flours and meals, buckwheat and rye-barley, in the 18th-century way. But in truth their larders are full and their tables abundant

with wonderful food—sweet, sustaining breakfasts of hot cakes and waffles, fruit and nut-stuffed coffeecakes with sugar icing, small swirled buns redolent of cinnamon and sticky with honey, bacon, and hams. Jersey and Guernsey cows are free to graze on the grasses of rolling soft hills, but the pig, who can quite happily eat anything and still turn into pork, is fussed over and fattened with apples to perfume his tender flesh. A Pennsylvania Dutch table is not properly set without an assortment of "seven sweets and seven sours"—chowchow, corn relish, spiced cantaloupe, bread-and-butter pickles, cole slaw, crab apple jelly, creamy cottage cheese, and apple butter.

Pennsylvania Dutch cookery is famous for scrapple, and of course for its dumplings and noodles. Chicken pot pies and stews were laced with threads of aromatic saffron that enhanced game sauces in this region as early as 1683. Saffron-scented chicken broth comes forth with chunks of chicken, fresh corn, and popcorn floating on top. Hickory smoke flavored their meats, sweet hams, and sausages; sometimes they served their bologna sliced with apple pie, as the New Englanders did with cheese, and their ring bologna would develop later into the hot dog. Typically their pot roasts and sauerbraten were spiked with cloves, cinnamon, and ginger, and set to bake in Dutch ovens in a bath of beer or red wine. And surely most representative of their farmhouse sweets is the shoofly pie, a sticky concoction of molasses, brown sugar, spices, and sweet crunchy crumbs. Americans have always been fond of sweets, and marble cake and sweet chocolate sauces were riches of the Mennonite table, satisfying their passion for this devilish sweet. As early as 1765, the first chocolate mill, in Lansdale, Pennsylvania, combined cocoa and milk in Swiss fashion. By 1780 New England's Walter Baker Cocoa and Chocolate Company was supplying chocolate to all of the original colonies. It was the only packaged and advertised item in the store operated by Abraham Lincoln and his partner in Illinois in 1833! (The Baker Company went so far as to ship their products around the Horn to early California outposts.) And of course the town of Hershey, Pennsylvania, has long been renowned for chocolate. It would be almost 100 years before the first book of confections would be published in America, but the tradition of sweets continued across the plains with the pioneer woman's memories of her grandmother's favorite recipes.

Farmhouses still sell preserves, pickles, pies, and scrapple along many country roads, and many homemade jams are sold at the Lancaster Farmers' Market. This market, set up in perpetuity by Royal Charter during the reign of George II in 1742, is a reminder of how little the cooking of that region has changed. The bottled, freshly grated horseradish, prepared by local Mennonite and Amish womenfolk and strong enough to blow your head off, is not to be missed.

It was still in recent memory that these "market" or "truck" farms supplied the large city wholesale markets, which in turn sold to the small grocery stores. This was a time when the baker sold his own bread, and one visited the butcher for his meats and poultry, the fishmonger for his fish, and the cheese shop for eggs, cream, and cheese. But the small groceries and markets have fallen away as the small farms have succumbed to new technology. The great urban sprawl,

begun in the 1950s, inexorably has encroached on our farmland, and at this writing some three million acres of farmland are lost every year. Our produce, once brought to town by pick-up, is now shipped in bulk from national and even international producers, much of it packed even before it has ripened. Now we usually buy only half-ripe bananas, and we optimistically leave tomatoes to sit in brown paper bags, hoping they'll turn from pale woolly things into the juice-filled fruits we remember. One can even buy a plastic "ripening bowl" for pears! More than three-quarters of the produce eaten in the Northeast comes to our supermarkets from thousands of miles away.

And so many a small farmer, who husbanded his animals and tended his few acres, was unable to eke out a living. Some of the old family farmers managed to hold on, surviving long enough to be joined by younger generations who find relief in bucolic settings. It is this "new blood," coupled with the sophisticated urbanite's rarefied demand for good quality, all-but-forgotten, that has been a boon to the local farmer. The Greenmarket at Union Square in New York City is one of the larger town markets on the East Coast. Harking back to the traditional markets of days gone by, the fringe of the square is given over to the farmers who truck in their greens and herbs, rhubarb and strawberries, their peas in spring, corn and tomatoes in summer, and pumpkins, apples, cider, fresh eggs, homemade cheese, and chickens. By mid-December the market is quite over, but it has sustained the farmer for another year.

Breakfast

ASPARAGUS*

SHAD ROE*

RHUBARB PIE*

CLINTON CORNERS
SEYVAL BLANC,
HUDSON RIVER REGION

Shad roe is the caviar of the East. The Hudson River has been cleaned up, which is encouraging and should be commended, and shad once again thrive to such a degree that they are being used to stock other depleted rivers in the East. Shad roe is too often broiled or fried, overwhelmed with rashers of bacon, and served so tough that understandably few people are aficionados of the dish. Shad roe should be submerged in melted butter and gently poached, so that the grains of eggs are gossamer forkfuls of spring's first treat. To complete the celebration, I choose crisp young stalks of asparagus and sour sorrel. Rhubarb grew wild in the East, and was a favorite of the Holland Dutch and the English before they settled here. These foods are natural complements, and together create a regional meal.

ASPARAGUS

INGREDIENTS

4 pounds thin asparagus spears, ends trimmed
Melted butter
Freshly squeezed lemon juice

METHOD

Bring 3 inches of lightly salted water to a boil in a
   large shallow pan.
Add the asparagus and bring to a simmer. Simmer for
   6 to 8 minutes, just until tender.
Drain and serve hot with melted butter and
   lemon juice.

Serves 4

SHAD ROE

INGREDIENTS

ROE:

1 pound unsalted butter
2 pairs shad roe, washed in cold water

SAUCE:

3 tablespoons unsalted butter
3 tablespoons all-purpose flour
1½ cups half-and-half
Salt and freshly milled pepper
1 cup sorrel leaves, washed and cut into ribbons

METHOD

In a large deep saucepan, melt the butter and bring it
   to a mild simmer over moderate heat. Set the shad
   roe in the butter, cover, and poach gently for 10 to 12
   minutes, turning once.
Meanwhile, prepare the sauce:
Melt the butter in a saucepan set over moderate heat.
   When the foam subsides, remove the pan from the
   heat and whisk in the flour.
Return the sauce to the heat, gradually pour in the
   half-and-half, and whisk vigorously.

Cook, whisking, until the sauce thickens, about
10 minutes.

Season to taste with salt and pepper and fold in
the sorrel.

When the shad roe are cooked, slide a slotted spoon
under them, and remove to a heated serving plate.
Set aside and keep warm.

Continue cooking the sauce for 2 to 3 minutes, stirring
with a wooden spoon, until the sorrel wilts.

Spoon the sauce over the shad roe.

Serve with steamed or boiled new potatoes, sprinkled
with a combination of finely chopped lemon zest
and cilantro.

Note: This amount of roe will serve two handsomely
but, due to its richness, is adequate for four.

Serves 2 to 4

RHUBARB PIE

INGREDIENTS

½ recipe Pie Dough, made with butter (see Basics,
page 346)

1½ pounds young, pink rhubarb stalks, cut into 1-inch
pieces (about 5 cups)

¾ cup sugar

2 tablespoons quick cooking tapioca

MERINGUE:

2 egg whites, at room temperature

¼ cup sugar

TOOLS

9-inch pie pan
Electric mixer
Pastry bag fitted with a star tube

METHOD

Preheat the oven to 425°.

Prebake the pie crust until golden, following the
directions in Basics.

Remove to a cooling rack. Reduce the oven temperature
to 350°.

Wash the rhubarb pieces and drain.

In a nonaluminum saucepan, combine the rhubarb
with the sugar and tapioca.

Cover and simmer over moderately low heat until the
rhubarb is tender, about 12 minutes.

Turn the mixture into a bowl to cool to room
temperature.

When cooled, spread the rhubarb filling evenly in the
pie shell.

Prepare the meringue:

With an electric mixer, beat the egg whites until foamy.

Gradually add the sugar, and beat until the whites are
stiff and glossy.

Place the meringue in a pastry bag fitted with a star
tube and pipe the meringue in lattice fashion over
the rhubarb mixture.

Bake the pie for 10 minutes, or until the meringue
is golden.

Serve at room temperature.

Serves 6

Pig Roast

ROAST SUCKLING PIG*
WILTED GREENS AND CORN BREAD
TURNIP AND RHUBARB KRAUT*
SPICED PEACHES*
CHERRY PIE*

BEER or SONOMA-CUTRER
VINEYARDS CHARDONNAY

The Pennsylvania Dutch feast on roast suckling pig for any occasion. It is usually stuffed, spitted and roasted, served with sauerkraut, apples, and the perpetual accompaniment of seven sweets and seven sours. Shreds of turnip can be brined just like cabbage, and with the addition of rhubarb the result is a seasonal kraut. Likewise the customary onslaught of relishes is replaced by spiced peaches. Wild greens and grasses are picked from nearby fields, and when wilted with hot pan juices from the pig, this field green salad becomes a pot liquor. Most of the early settlers depended on wild vegetation, and today, handfuls of these wild greens make a delightful addition to a meal. The greens with their hot dressing should be served on fresh baked corn bread following the recipe on page 250, omitting the vegetables.

ROAST SUCKLING PIG

INGREDIENTS

1 suckling pig (14 to 16 pounds)
Salt and freshly milled pepper
6 tart apples, quartered
2 sprigs fresh thyme
2 sprigs fresh rosemary
2 lemons, halved
Vegetable oil
Wild flowers or fresh herbs, for serving

METHOD

Preheat the oven to 450°.
Remove the liver, kidneys, heart, and other organs
    from the cavity of the pig and thoroughly
    scrub the pig.

Towel dry thoroughly, inside and out.
Salt and pepper the cavity, and stuff it with the apples,
    herbs, and lemon halves. Sew the cavity shut with a
    larding needle or close it with skewers and string.
Place the pig in a large roasting pan in a sitting
    position with its back legs folded under its rump and
    its front legs forward.
Brace the mouth open with a 2-inch ball of foil.
Cover the ears with foil to protect them from burning.
If the pig is too large for the roasting pan, surround
    the pan with a double thickness of heavy-duty foil.
Roast the pig for 30 minutes.
Brush on vegetable oil to coat the skin, and reduce the
    temperature to 350°.
Roast for 30 minutes and baste again.
Continue roasting for 2½ hours more, basting every
    30 minutes with the pan juices.
Insert a meat thermometer into the fleshiest part of
    the thigh. When the internal temperature reaches
    185°, the pig is roasted.
Remove the pig from the oven and let rest for
    30 minutes.
Transfer the pig to a serving board or platter and
    remove the foil.
Fill the mouth with wild flowers or fresh herbs, and
    surround the roast with more flowers or herbs.
Meanwhile, skim off as much fat as possible from
    the pan juices and pour the liquid into a small
    saucepan.
Cook the juice until heated through and reserve ¾ cup
    to wilt the salad greens.
Serve the remaining juices with the roast.

Serves 8 to 10

TURNIP AND RHUBARB KRAUT

INGREDIENTS

3 pounds small white turnips
3 tablespoons salt
1 cup cider vinegar
2 pounds fresh rhubarb spears
½ to ¾ cup sugar, depending on the redness
    of the rhubarb

METHOD

Peel the turnips and coarsely grate them into a bowl.
Toss with the salt and vinegar.
Cover and set aside at room temperature for 1 hour.
Cut the rhubarb into 2-inch pieces. Cut each piece
lengthwise into 3 strips. Wash in cold water
and drain.
Place the rhubarb in a large saucepan and toss with
the sugar.
Cook the rhubarb over moderate heat for 5 minutes,
or until the rhubarb begins to wilt but still is
slightly crisp.
Drain the grated turnips in a colander or strainer,
pressing out as much liquid as possible. Fold the
turnips into the rhubarb and cook until heated
through.
Serve immediately.

Serves 8 to 10

SPICED PEACHES

INGREDIENTS

12 firm, ripe peaches, blanched and peeled
1 bottle (25.4 ounces) dry white wine
1 cup white wine vinegar
3 small cinnamon sticks
6 whole cloves
8 peppercorns
1 lemon, halved and squeezed
About 2 cups sugar, depending on the
sweetness of the fruit

METHOD

In a large nonaluminum kettle, combine the peaches
with all of the other ingredients.
Bring to a simmer over moderate heat and poach until
the peaches can be pierced easily with a sharp
knife, 10 to 15 minutes. Discard the lemons.
Let the peaches cool in their liquid, and serve at room
temperature.

Note: The peaches can be put up in sterilized jars.

Serves 8 to 12

CHERRY PIE

INGREDIENTS

1 recipe Pie Dough (see Basics, page 346)
2½ cups pitted tart cherries
About ⅓ cup sugar, depending on the sweetness of
the fruit
2½ tablespoons quick-cooking tapioca
Zest of ½ lemon
1 egg, beaten with 2 tablespoons water, for egg wash

TOOLS

9-inch pie pan

METHOD

Preheat the oven to 350°.
On a floured board, roll out half of the dough about
¼-inch thick. Fit it evenly into a 9-inch pie pan,
pressing gently against the bottom and sides.
In a bowl, toss the cherries with the sugar, tapioca,
and lemon zest.
Pour the mixture into the pie crust.
Roll out the remaining dough and set the top crust
in place.
Trim the dough and crimp and seal the edges.
Cut 3 small steam vents in the center of the pie crust.
Brush the egg wash over the top.
Bake the pie in the center of the oven for about 1 hour,
until the crust is lightly browned.
Let cool before cutting.
Serve slightly warm.

Serves 8 to 10

Dumpling Dinner

CHICKEN WITH DILL DUMPLINGS*

MINTED PEAS*

GLAZED CARROTS*

STEAMED GINGER PUDDING*
SERVED WITH POACHED PEARS

ROBERT MONDAVI WINERY
FUMÉ BLANC

The sects that settled in Eastern Pennsylvania brought with them an epicurean style that was fascinating, intelligent, and wholly their own. The abandon with which they would spike their dishes with fresh herbs, and their cakes and desserts with spices is brilliant. Light, fluffy dumplings are refreshing with dill and elevate the simple farm chicken beyond the usual fricassee. Gingerbread and its variations were all-time favorites. Gingerbread cake came warm to the table in New England with whipped cream, here with sour cream and applesauce, in the West with chocolate sauce. This variation is served steaming, spiked with crystallized ginger and accompanied with poached pears.

CHICKEN WITH DILL DUMPLINGS

INGREDIENTS

CHICKEN:

2 whole chickens (each about 3½ pounds), cut into small serving pieces with breast and thigh boned and bones reserved

Salt and freshly milled black pepper

3 tablespoons unsalted butter

2 celery ribs, chopped

1 medium onion, chopped

3 tablespoons all-purpose flour

2½ cups Chicken Stock (see Basics, page 343)

2 cups heavy cream

½ cup chopped fresh dill

DUMPLINGS:

2 cups all-purpose flour, sifted

1 teaspoon baking powder

¼ teaspoon baking soda

1 teaspoon salt

3 tablespoons unsalted butter, melted

¾ cup buttermilk

½ cup chopped fresh dill

1½ quarts Chicken Stock (see Basics, page 343)

METHOD

Preheat the oven to 300°.

Prepare the chicken:

Wash and dry the chicken pieces with paper towels.

Lightly salt and pepper the chicken.

In a large heavy skillet, melt the butter and brown the chicken pieces over moderate heat until golden brown.

Remove to a heatproof platter and reserve in the preheated oven.

Add the bones to the skillet and cook, stirring, until browned.

Add the chopped celery and onions, and cook until they wilt.

Add the flour and cook, stirring, for 5 minutes.

Add the chicken stock and cream, and reduce the heat to low. Simmer for 30 minutes.

Strain the sauce into a serving tureen, discarding
the solids.

Fold the dill into the sauce.

Add the chicken pieces to the sauce and place
in the warm oven.

Prepare the dumplings:

Sift the dry ingredients into a large mixing bowl.

Add the melted butter and buttermilk and blend
until smooth.

Fold in the chopped dill.

In a large pot, bring the stock to a simmer.

Drop the dumpling mixture by soup spoonfuls into the
simmering stock.

Cover and cook for 5 minutes.

With a slotted spoon, turn the dumplings over. Cover
and cook 5 more minutes.

Continue poaching the dumplings until puffed and
cooked in the center.

Place the dumplings on top of the chicken and sauce
and serve with Glazed Carrots and Minted Peas.

Serves 6 to 8

MINTED PEAS

INGREDIENTS

3 pounds fresh green peas, shelled (3½ to 4 cups)
¼ teaspoon sugar
3 tablespoons unsalted butter
Salt and freshly milled black pepper
8 fresh mint leaves, cut into thin ribbons

METHOD

In a saucepan, bring 2 cups of lightly salted
water to a boil.

Add the peas and the sugar.

Simmer for 8 to 10 minutes, or until tender.

Drain.

Fold in the butter, salt and pepper to taste, and the
mint. Serve at once.

Serves 6 to 8

GLAZED CARROTS

INGREDIENTS

8 to 10 medium carrots
3 tablespoons unsalted butter
1 tablespoon sugar
Salt and freshly milled black pepper

METHOD

Peel and trim the carrots.
Cut the carrots into thirds. Cut each third lengthwise
    into ½-inch sticks.
In a pot of salted boiling water, cook the carrots
    until tender.
Drain and reserve.
Melt the butter in a skillet over moderate heat.
Add the sugar, and stir until dissolved.
Add the carrots and toss in the butter and sugar until
    thoroughly coated. Season with salt and pepper and
    cook until heated through.

Serves 6 to 8

STEAMED GINGER PUDDING

INGREDIENTS

2 tablespoons softened unsalted butter, for the mold
3 cups all-purpose flour
1 teaspoon baking soda
1 tablespoon ground ginger
1 tablespoon ground cinnamon
½ pound unsalted butter, at room temperature
1 cup packed dark brown sugar
4 eggs
1 cup molasses
1 cup heavy cream, lightly whipped
4 pieces crystallized ginger, cut into
    fine julienne

TOOLS

2-quart steamed pudding mold with cover or 2-quart
    pudding basin
Electric mixer

METHOD

Use the 2 tablespoons butter to coat the pudding mold
    and its cover. Set aside.
Put a kettle of water on to boil.
Meanwhile, sift together the dry ingredients. Reserve.
In a mixing bowl, cream the butter with the sugar.
Add 2 of the eggs and blend thoroughly.
Add half of the sifted dry ingredients and blend.
Add the remaining 2 eggs and mix well.
Add the remaining dry ingredients and blend.
Stir in the molasses and mix thoroughly.
Turn the batter into the prepared mold, and tap on a
    hard surface to settle the batter.
Cover the mold tightly with the buttered cover.
Place the mold in a large pot.
Fill the pot with boiling water to reach two-thirds of
    the way up the sides of the mold.
Cover the pot and steam over moderate heat for 1¾
    hours, adding additional boiling water after 30 to 45
    minutes, if necessary.
Unmold and let cool.
Coat the top of the pudding with some of the whipped
    cream. Sprinkle with the crystallized ginger.
Serve with the remaining whipped cream and
    poached pears.

Serves 8

Dutch Brisket Dinner

DUTCH BRISKET WITH
BRAISED ONIONS*

HORSERADISH BEETSAUCE*

SPAETZLE*

SAUTÉED RED
AND WHITE CABBAGE*

SPICED CANTALOUPE*

DILL PICKLES*

APPLE CAKE*

BEER, STOUT or
HERMANN J. WEIMER
VINEYARD RIESLING

Throughout history spices have been used to disguise meat that was beginning to turn, but without refrigeration, even pickled meat could turn. Sauerbratens and marinated meats were a German custom and an extender meal that was served both hot and cold. The marinade is pungent, but the spices give an illusion of sweetness, and the dish becomes a sweet and sour. The cabbage is a fresh hot slaw served up with caraway, a seed favored in the breads, dumplings, and cheeses of the area. The cantaloupe, briefly sautéed and spiced, plays the part of a glorified

pickle. Pickling is one of the easiest forms of cooking, requiring no great skill. Limp store-bought pickles can never touch the homemade variety. The deep dish apple cake is just one of countless filling desserts quickly thrown together by the competent hand of a farm wife.

DUTCH BRISKET WITH BRAISED ONIONS

INGREDIENTS

1 beef brisket (6 to 7 pounds)

MARINADE:

1 bottle (25.4 ounces) dry red wine
1 cup tarragon wine vinegar
4 celery ribs, coarsely chopped
1 large onion, coarsely chopped
6 peppercorns, crushed
1 bay leaf
2 sprigs fresh thyme

ONIONS:

Salt and freshly milled black pepper
All-purpose flour
¼ teaspoon ground cinnamon
½ teaspoon ground cloves
4 pounds yellow onions, thinly sliced
4 tablespoons butter

METHOD

In a nonaluminum bowl or pan, combine the brisket with the marinade ingredients. Refrigerate for 24 hours, turning once.

Preheat the oven to 400°.

Remove the brisket from the marinade and dry with paper towels. Reserve the marinade.

Rub in the salt and pepper and spices. Lightly dredge with flour.

In a large heavy skillet, brown the brisket, fat side down, over moderate heat. Turn and brown all over.

Remove the meat to a large nonaluminum ovenproof casserole or Dutch oven.

Strain the marinade, discarding the solids. Pour the liquid into the skillet and deglaze over moderately high heat, scraping up the brown bits that cling to the bottom of the skillet. Simmer for 5 minutes.

Pour the liquid over the meat and cover with the onions.

Cover the casserole and bake for 30 minutes.

Remove the cover and continue cooking for 1 hour.

Cover again and cook for 1 to 1½ hours more, until the meat is fork-tender.

Let the brisket rest for 10 to 15 minutes.

Serve with the onions and pan juices.

Serves 12

HORSERADISH BEET SAUCE

INGREDIENTS

3 small beets, peeled and finely grated
1 cup freshly grated horseradish
¼ cup sour cream
¼ cup heavy cream, whipped

METHOD

In a small serving bowl, fold together all of the ingredients.

Chill and serve.

Makes 2 cups

SPAETZLE

INGREDIENTS

4 cups all-purpose flour
6 eggs
1½ teaspoons salt
3 to 4 gratings fresh nutmeg
¼ pound unsalted butter
Salt and freshly milled black pepper

METHOD

Combine the flour, eggs, salt, nutmeg, and 1¼ cups cold water in a large bowl. Mix with a wooden spoon and reserve.

Bring a large pot of salted water to a boil.

Pick up small amounts of dough with a teaspoon and push the dough into the water with another, or push the dough through a colander. Dip the spoons in the boiling water to avoid their becoming sticky and unmanageable.

Using a wooden spoon, stir the spaetzle off the bottom of the pot and cook for 2 minutes.

With a slotted spoon, remove the spaetzle to a bowl of ice water.

Repeat the process until all of the dough has been used. Rinse and drain well. Refrigerate until ready to serve.

In a large skillet, melt the butter over moderate heat. Add the spaetzle and lightly sauté until warmed through.

Season with salt and pepper and serve warm.

Serves 12

SAUTÉED RED
AND WHITE CABBAGE

INGREDIENTS

1 small head red cabbage, outer leaves removed
1 small head white cabbage, outer leaves removed
½ pound lean slab bacon, cut into ¼-inch slices and cubed
1 teaspoon caraway seeds
½ cup sour cream
Salt and freshly milled black pepper

METHOD

Halve the cabbages and core them.

Slice into thin strips.

In two separate pots of boiling water, blanch each type of cabbage for 5 seconds and drain immediately.

In a large skillet, render the bacon until golden brown.

Drain the bacon on paper towels, and reserve.

Add the cabbage to the skillet and cook, tossing over moderate heat, to coat it with the rendered fat.

Add the caraway seeds.

Fold in the sour cream and season to taste.

Toss and cook until the cabbage is tender.

Fold in the bacon pieces and serve.

Serves 12

SPICED CANTALOUPE

INGREDIENTS

2 small ripe cantaloupes
2 small cinnamon sticks
2 tablespoons sugar
Juice of ½ lemon
1 teaspoon curry powder

METHOD

Halve the melons and seed them.
Cut each half into ½-inch-wide strips and remove the rinds with a paring knife.
Place the melon in a nonaluminum saucepan and add the cinnamon sticks, sugar, and lemon juice.
Cook over moderate heat, stirring gently until all of the sugar melts, about 5 minutes.
Add the curry powder and cook for another 5 minutes.
Serve warm.

Serves 12

DILL PICKLES

INGREDIENTS

½ cup pickling salt or kosher salt, for brining
4 pounds Kirby cucumbers, freshly picked and washed thoroughly
3 cups good quality distilled white vinegar
1 tablespoon sugar
6 large cloves garlic, blanched in their skins for 3 minutes and peeled
3 whole allspice berries
6 peppercorns
1 bunch fresh dillweed with flowers

TOOLS

Large stoneware or glass crock, stainless steel kettle, or other large nonaluminum pot
2 large kettles, one with a rack, or a lobster pot and rack
Canning tongs
3 quart-size or 6 pint-size sterilized canning jars

METHOD

In the stoneware crock, combine the pickling salt with 2 quarts cold water. Add the cucumbers and soak for 24 hours.
When ready to put up:
Bring a large kettle of water to a boil.
In a large nonaluminum saucepan, combine the vinegar, sugar, and 3 cups water. Bring to a boil over high heat.
Remove the Kirbys from the brine with a slotted spoon and drain. Plunge the cucumbers into the pot of boiling water.
Drain immediately and pack the Kirbys into sterilized jars. Divide the garlic, spices, and dillweed equally among the jars, filling up to within 1 inch from the top.
Pour in the hot vinegar liquid to reach ½ inch from the top of each jar.
Tightly seal the jars.
Place the jars on a rack in the kettle, making sure they do not touch.
Add enough hot water to cover the lids by 2 inches.
Cover and bring to a boil. Continue to boil for 15 minutes if using pint-size jars, or 20 minutes, if packed into quarts.
Remove the jars from the water bath with the canning tongs and set on a rack to cool.
Store in a cool place.
Note: Kirby cucumbers are small, firm 3½- to 4-inch cucumbers. Vegetables and fruits used for canning should be fresh-picked and put up within 24 hours.

Makes 3 quarts

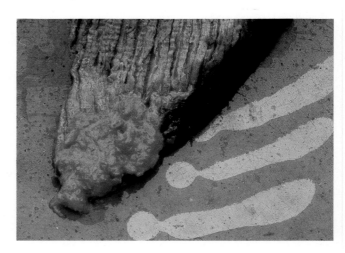

APPLE CAKE

INGREDIENTS

2 to 3 tablespoons unsalted butter, for the pan
10 large apples (preferably McIntosh), peeled
    and cored
½ pound unsalted butter, at room temperature
2 cups sugar
2 eggs
3 cups all-purpose flour
2 teaspoons baking soda
½ teaspoon ground cinnamon
1 teaspoon freshly grated nutmeg
1 teaspoon ground allspice
1 cup heavy cream, whipped, for serving

TOOLS

14-inch ovenproof oval baking dish, 2½-inches deep
Electric mixer

METHOD

Preheat the oven to 350°.
Butter the baking dish.

Roughly chop the apples.
Reserving 1 cup, place the apples in a large pot with
    ½ cup water. Simmer over moderately low heat until
    the apples begin to soften but do not turn to sauce.
    The mixture should be *very* chunky.
Remove from heat and set aside.
In a mixing bowl, cream together the butter and sugar.
One at a time, add the eggs.
Sift together the dry ingredients and incorporate.
Fold in the apple mixture with a rubber spatula.
Turn the batter into the prepared baking dish.
Sprinkle the reserved 1 cup apples over the dough and
    pat down with a spatula.
Bake for 1 hour, or until golden brown.
Serve warm with unsweetened whipped cream.

Serves 12

Beer and Pretzel

*The New England settlers brought beer, but the
Germans perfected it. The flavors and varieties are
almost numberless, and it is the one beverage we
understand at an early age, developing a fondness
for a particular brand and sticking with it for life.*

Deli Food

New York City may be the last bastion of ethnic food. Best representing the hunger for "what was" is the proliferation of Jewish delis throughout this town. From a style of cooking based on "don'ts," they have provided us with the best pastrami, the best rye bread, rich chicken soup, and, if you are a careful cook, your matzo balls can be as light as air. Blintzes burst with farmer's cheese, and tubs of sour cream and preserves can fill you up.

MATZO BALL SOUP

INGREDIENTS

STOCK:

2 quarts Chicken Stock (see Basics, page 343)
1 chicken (about 3 pounds)
2 celery ribs, cut into 2-inch pieces
1 medium carrot, cut into 1-inch pieces
3 parsley sprigs
Salt

MATZO BALLS:

3 eggs
¼ cup plus 2 tablespoons seltzer or soda water
3 tablespoons chicken fat (skimmed from the chilled chicken stock or store-bought, called *schmaltz*)
⅔ to ¾ cup matzo meal
1 tablespoon finely chopped fresh parsley
Salt and freshly milled white pepper
¼ cup minced fresh parsley, for serving

METHOD

The stock:

Place the stock ingredients in a soup kettle and bring to a simmer over moderate heat.

Partially cover the kettle and poach the chicken for 30 to 40 minutes, or until the thigh juices run clear when pierced with a kitchen fork.

Remove and discard the vegetables from the soup and let the chicken cool in the stock.

When the stock is cool, remove the poached chicken and refrigerate the stock and the chicken separately.

Reserve the chicken for sandwiches and chicken salads.

The matzo balls:

In a bowl, lightly beat the eggs and combine with the seltzer.

Add the chicken fat and blend.

Gradually add the matzo meal, stirring until the mixture is spongy and lightly thickened.

Add the parsley and seasonings and blend.

Cover and refrigerate for at least 30 minutes.

Remove the mixture and the stock from the refrigerator 30 minutes before preparing the soup.

Skim the stock of all fat and bring to a simmer over low heat.

Shape the matzo mixture into 1-inch balls, wetting your hands in cold water from time to time to prevent sticking.

Increase the heat to produce a gentle boil and add the matzo balls to the soup. Partially cover the kettle and poach the matzo balls for 20 to 25 minutes, until cooked through. Test one to be sure it is cooked in the center.

Ladle 2 matzo balls and broth into each heated bowl and sprinkle with the additional parsley.

Serves 5 to 6

The best hot dogs are made in lamb casings. It's very difficult to find a good hot dog these days, but they definitely are around. There is nothing like a "dirty," in-the-street, New York City, out-of-the-steam-wagon hot dog. We eat them everywhere—in arenas, in parks, at concerts, and at ball games.

Martini

A good cocktail must be made with the finest liquor. It should be made with care; the over-zealous can just as easily ruin the drink as the careless. The martini is a drink I associate with Manhattan, but the finest bartender for the job lives in Venice. As the good cocktails and the good barmen become more and more scarce, my advice is to end your day and begin your evening with the perfect martini you make yourself.

GIN MARTINI

INGREDIENTS

Ice cubes
Splash of imported dry vermouth
2½ ounces dry gin, chilled
Small strip of lemon zest or 1 large green olive

TOOLS

Cocktail pitcher and stirrer
4-ounce glass, chilled
Cocktail strainer

METHOD

Fill the pitcher with 6 to 8 ice cubes.
Add the vermouth and gin and stir briskly.
Strain the martini into the chilled glass and twist the
   lemon zest over the top of the liquor or add the olive.
Serve and sip.

Serves 1

THE STEVENS BROTHERS' VODKA MARTINI

INGREDIENTS

Ice cubes
Splash of Dry Punt é Mes
3 ounces vodka, chilled
Small strip of lemon zest or 1 green Niçoise olive

TOOLS

Cocktail pitcher and stirrer
3- to 4-ounce glass, chilled
Cocktail strainer

METHOD

Fill the pitcher with 6 to 8 ice cubes.
Add the Punt é Mes and vodka and stir briskly.
Strain the martini into the chilled glass and twist the
   lemon zest over the top or add the olive.

Serves 1

South

"Our countryside's cooking came to its full flower for the bran-dances—which came into being, I think, because the pioneers like to shake limber heels, but had not floors big enough for the shaking. So in green shade, at some springside they built an arbor of green boughs, leveled the earth underneath, pounded it hard and smooth, then covered it an inch deep with clean wheat bran, put up seats roundabout it, also a fiddlers' stand, got the fiddlers, printed invitations which went far and wide to women young and old, saw to a sufficiency of barbecue, depended on the Lord and the ladies for other things—and prepared to dance, dance from nine in the morning until two next morning. Men were not specifically invited—anybody in good standing with a clean shirt, dancing shoes, a good horse and a pedigree, was heartily welcome." —Martha McCulloch-Williams, DISHES AND BEVERAGES OF THE OLD SOUTH, *1913, New York*

Thomas Jefferson, who returned to Monticello to resume life as a gentleman farmer after his eight-year presidency, called himself the most "ardent farmer in the state." William Byrd, founder of Richmond, called Virginia the "Garden of Eden," and recorded in his 1737 *Natural History of Virginia* that the colony was growing all manner of European produce—artichokes, cauliflower, peaches, pears, quince, figs, cherries, pomegranates, and the coffee and tea that grew on the great estates. It was really Jefferson who cultivated this garden. Jefferson, America's first man of style, took advantage of his duties at the court of Louis XVI to travel Europe widely. So delighted was he with the olive oil he found there that he sent cuttings from Provence to North Carolina, where he hoped they might thrive. He rhapsodized about this oil, for him a necessary luxury, and attributed his long life to a diet largely of vegetables and salads bathed in it. (Perhaps his love of vegetables inspired the southern vegetable dinner: a summer harvest in bowls of creamed corn, okra and tomatoes, butterbeans and black-eyed peas, cucumbers in cream, and on and on, all sopped up with hot

corn bread.) When the olive tree did not take to the southern climate, Jefferson experimented with an oil from benne seeds (known also as sesame). Long a staple of the southern kitchen, benne is not native. According to legend, the seeds were snatched by desperate blacks even as they were seized from their African fields into slavery; the seeds, plugged into their ears and thus hidden, crossed the ocean to southern soil where they flourished, a melancholy reminder of their homeland. How different from the forward-looking New England settlers, enthusiastically tucking apple pips into their baggage and sacks.

Jefferson was the model of a southern host, hospitable and ebullient. Frugal New Englander John Adams, once president himself, was driven to remark, "I dined a large company once or twice a week. Jefferson dined a dozen every day. I held levees (receptions) once a week. Jefferson's whole eight years was a levee!" Jefferson held wine to be one of the table's great merits, and once intoned, "No nation is drunken where wine is cheap; and none sober, when the dearness of wine substitutes harder spirits as a common beverage." Relentlessly inquisitive, he studied the wine country of France, Germany, Italy, and Spain, and sent vine cuttings to Virginia in attempts at viniculture. He took frequent notes and kept meticulous accounts, calculating that a bottle of Champagne served 3½ guests. His own consumption of Champagne numbered more than 500 bottles annually, and his notorious Washington cellar at one time held 400 bottles of claret, 540 of Sauternes, and casks of Madeira and port. (During his first year as president, he frightfully exceeded the wine budget, spending nearly $3,000.) His unfailing good taste was well known, and he was not reticent to share it. He advised wine purchase for the table of President George Washington (ordering 65 dozen bottles in 1790). Even his congratulatory letter to President James Monroe offered only a few correct formalities, and rushed on to a discourse recommending which wines are best served at which occasions. In the White House he brilliantly entertained visiting foreign ministers, congressmen, and assorted dignitaries and citizens, undoubtedly to the enjoyment and great admiration of some and to the rankling envy of others.

The nuances of Jefferson's kitchen were Virginian and French: velvet brown sauces, clear soups, custards, meringues, macaroons, blancmange, wine jellies, trifles, bread puddings, even floating island in a pool of syllabub. He treasured the receipts of his best cooks, as did his daughter Mrs. Randolph, who added greatly to the repertoire of local dishes; she is said to be the author of macaroni and cheese, a dish she created for her father using Parmesan. Jefferson had particular fondness for local foods: sweet potatoes, black-eyed peas, turnip greens, ham, and crab. Much credit is due him for the endive, cress, cucumbers, asparagus, tomatoes, and almond trees that flourish here. In his own gardens, he enthusiastically forced over 30 varieties of peas! At this time, the potato was newly vindicated in Europe as an acceptable, if plebian, food, and its blossom was sported at the elegant French court by the king himself. And although Jefferson is said to have personally preferred the potato to corn, he nevertheless took pains to introduce maize to his French hosts, growing it in his Paris garden and serving it up to his dazzled guests. Always Jefferson's interest and loyalty lay with an agrarian nation, moving him to pronounce that "the introduction of anything which will divert our attention from agriculture must be extremely prejudicial if not ruinous to us."

A southern plantation was society in miniature. Self-sufficient, its success depended wholly on slaves and servants. Plantations raised cash crops for trade, most notably tobacco and cotton destined for England. Their own blacksmiths made the ploughs, wagons, gates, and fancy ironwork. Their cattle filled the larder and supplied skins for the plantation tanner's shoes and saddles. Their sheep furnished wool, the fields, cotton; their carpenters repaired the homes, barns, and stables; no one was idle.

From the very early days in the southern colonies, hospitality was a custom of both the wealthy and the poor. Friend or stranger was invited to dine, to stay for a night, a few days, a few weeks—some abused the privilege and stayed a month here and a month there! Balls and parties brought the gentlefolk from far and near. Lavish picnics were held in cool woods, and barbecues and fish feasts on the river bank by the

plantation house. Prosperous plantations dotted the banks of rivers for miles into the interior from Charleston to Virginia.

Pig raising was to become a major industry. (So sweet and tender were these porkers, fattened on African peanuts and corn, that Queen Victoria had them sent to her along with her favorite Belons, oysters from Maine.) The South was a congenial home for the pig, the southern larders so bursting with pork and hams that William Byrd wrote in 1720 that he found "the people extremely hoggish in temper and prone to grunt rather than speak." Hog killing was an event that brought out the full platoon of servants, slaves, and family. "Kill your hogs when the wind is from the northwest," was heard from Kentucky through North Carolina, and all at once the hogs were killed, hung, scalded, and scraped. Butchered to use every morsel right down to the tail, the pig yielded heavy roasts, hams, and bacon (to be salted, hickory-smoked, or sugar-cured), mounds of snow-white lard, chitterlings, sausage-skins, masses of rendered fat, and the tripe, backbones, and livers sent straight into the kitchen for the traditional "hog-killing day" dinner, complete with crackling bread.

The blacks, treated as a separate society, ate differently from their masters. In the evenings when the manor slaves and the field slaves got together, they would make do with the chitterlings, jowls, ears, tails, maws, snouts, hocks, or whatever else from the pig might be given to them. They gathered wild greens, beet tops, and turnip and mustard greens to be cooked slowly with a hock or jowl until nearly soup. This "mess o' greens" or "pot likker" was served up with hot pones and black-eyed peas. It was the beginning of "soul." The "mammy cooks" (and every big house had one) took this soul with them into the manor and combined it with the French and English preferences of their masters, creating a unique style that warms the heart. Wheat was the status grain for breads and cakes in the great houses, but the black cook had her own particular status, ruling her kitchen with an iron hand and often dishing out her own earthy pones of Indian meal and hominy (dried Indian corn soaked, broken in a mortar, hulled, and then boiled).

Settlers of the South found the native American living off wild oats, sunflower seeds, pumpkins, strawberries, melons, and corn. They gathered chestnuts, hickory nuts, and black walnuts. By southern tradition, mush, grits, and hominy were set at almost every table, with some sort of corn bread (pones, hoe cakes, corn cakes), biscuits, crackling bread, and "oyster cakes," a paste of grated green corn mixed with egg, wheat flour, and butter, fried to simulate an oyster. (In the antebellum South, it was customary for plantation owners to eat white corn and foist the yellow off on their slaves. This practice diminished when it became known that, in that respect, the slaves were actually better off, yellow corn being more nutritious.)

Throughout the South, the hog was considered to be the only meat. The favored method of preparation in the North Carolina back country was to dry-roast the hog in hickory coals for 8 to 12 hours. (Nowadays, it's still to be found cooked just so, then hacked with a cleaver, seasoned with salt, pepper, and vinegar, and served on good, reliable packaged white bread.) This type of cooking, long known as the "barbecue," came to the South through the Caribbean, and, at its simplest, is a method of cooking meat on a grid of sticks raised on forks above coals. This typically southern barbecue is at odds with the spicy tomato and sweet-sour sauces found from Texas to Kansas. (Just off the highway on the Maryland-D.C. border is a shack with a painted sign advertising "RIBS," half a dozen of them slapped between slices of Wonder bread; getting this down is one of the miracles of the human mouth.)

At the end of the 18th century, the region west of the Appalachian Mountains was referred to as the "western country." The inhabitants, many of them Irishmen and Scotsmen, were by reputation skilled hunters. Fall was the season there to trap bears for their invaluable warm pelts and nourishing fat flesh; the hind legs when smoked made delicious hams. Squirrel hunts too were a popular pastime, and sporting parties would roast hundreds of these exceedingly tender, white-fleshed rodents. Dishes of this "western country" were somewhat influenced by the South, but here rabbits, brains, sweetbreads, possum, wild turkey, and quail were especially choice. Squirrel was baked, fried, fricasseed, coupled with dumplings or rice, or served in a rich stew-like soup they called burgoo. These folk too, cultivated corn, but most of it was destined for the city ports of Charleston and Savannah. Their rustic bread was ground Indian meal, shaped into heavy loaves and baked in ovens, or baked as small cakes on a board before a fire. Peaches were cultivated (especially around Lexington) and often made into a popular brandy.

It was these same Scot and Irish settlers who introduced whiskey. The prevailing spirit of the day was rum, but transporting it across the United States was too expensive, and so they distilled corn and rye. Moonshine, though, was most widely enjoyed and is by no means forgotten today.

The frontier folk were a poor lot who managed to get by with little. Here the countryside was speckled with tree stumps and peppered with rude wood cabins and their stone chimneys. A young visiting Frenchman, François Michaux, recorded that there was not "a single family without milk, butter, salted or dried meats, and Indian corn generally in the house." Still, it would be many years before the luscious ham, grained with moist fat running through the rosy meat, so unlike the hams of Virginia and the Carolinas, would appear on the Kentucky table. Today on Derby Day, luncheon is silver dollar-size biscuits with paper-thin slices of ham served with corn pudding and frequently-freshened mint juleps. For dessert? The juleps will do just fine.

So much southern cooking has depended on the sea's harvest. The Chesapeake Bay (fed by the York, Susquehanna, Potomac, Rappahannock and James Rivers) and its backwash seep into the swamps of North Carolina and reach the barrier islands at the Atlantic. It is the largest estuary on the American continent, its shoreline a welcoming cradle for the settlers led by John Smith who discovered it in the early 17th century. This watershed supplies most of the Eastern seaboard with oysters, crabs, clams, herring, shad, bass (what locals call "blackfish"), perch, and an impressive amount of eel (most of which is shipped to Scandinavia and the low countries, where it is smoked). The shoreline teems with birds, filling the air with an incessant cacophony of chirping, honking, and trumpeting: herons and ospreys, swans, ducks of all varieties, woodcocks, larks, partridges, pheasants, over a half million Canadian geese, and enough migratory blackbirds to darken winter's bright blue sky. From Tilghman Island to Cape Charles, this area known as the "Eastern Shore" is a poignant reminder of the beauty that met the new arrivals at Charlestown harbor 300 years ago. The South begins here!

The families who have fished these waters trace their beginnings to the stalwart Elizabethans who clawed their way up the Bay. Their language, spicy as a blue crab boil, smacks still of old English. These isolated watermen patiently crab from spring to fall and dredge and tong for oysters when winter turns the bay's blue foamy peaks to murky black swells. A waterman does daily battle with the sea, a heritage passed from father to son, rewarded with a decent, hard-earned wage.

When the crabs leave their burrows in the basins along the Atlantic and migrate to the bay, when the blue crab reddens and the sook's (female crab's) claws turn bright nail-polish red, it is spring. The crabs journey up the grassy sea shoals at the sides of the bay to molt and spawn. Two or three days before the female molts, the hard-shelled jimmie (male) grabs her from above and then, gently cradling her face up, carries her off to the lush protection of the eelgrass. When she begins to shed, the jimmie will copulate from six to as long as 12 hours. He will continue to cradle her for another two or three days, while her new shell hardens. The jimmie will go on to mate again, but the sook, with her million eggs, is fertile for the rest of her life.

This is the time watermen set out their nets and baited crab pots. The catch is sorted on deck or in long, narrow tubs in the crab shacks along the shore: the greens will molt in a couple of weeks or less, the pinks within a week, and the busters will shed in mere hours. Once they have shed, they are boxed in eelgrass and ice. Huge numbers of these softshell crabs are sent live to the Fulton Fish Market in New York City, making their first appearance just as shad and shad roe are on the wane. They must be crawling and kicking to be worth the price, for a dead crab just isn't worth cooking.

Down on the Eastern Shore softshells can be had lightly floured (perhaps with a shake of cornmeal) and fried in rendered fatback, or sautéed, or deep-fried in batter (the custom as far south as New Orleans and the Gulf). Further east they are tossed lightly in a hot pan with sweet butter and a scattering of herbs and

garlic, and the pan then is deglazed with wine or vermouth. When the she-crab grows into her new shell, the city of Charleston makes exquisite soup of her tender meat and golden egg sacs, combining them with butter, cream, sherry, and spices. Come late August the watermen pull in their catch, fat from a rich summer diet, by crab pot or net, or hooked on eel-baited cotton trotline that stretches three-quarters of a mile.

Virginia's tidewater shores are lined with picking houses. Throughout the autumn, the crab picking houses, staffed mostly by women, are busy cooking, pasteurising, and packing the various grades of prized lump, special, regular, and claw meat. Picking is a difficult job, a skill paid by the pound. A consumer cussing his way through a pound of the cheaper crab when making a crab cake hasn't a hint of how difficult it is to pick this meat. Shore residents and vacationers crowd into crab houses to dine on the hard, hot-spiced red crabs piled on newspapers and served with wooden mallets to aid in the cracking and sharp knives to catch every flake, and with pitchers of beer to reward the thirsty task. The voluptuous hot spices used in boiling the crabs permeate the flesh, and the residue, left on claws and fingers alike, smarts the tongue. This is truly the flavor of the South, from the elegant large pincers packed with delicate meat and served with spicy rémoulades to the baskets of hundreds of whole crabs unceremoniously steamed in huge caldrons.

Just when the crabs start to burrow, big white sails appear on the horizon, blowing across the bay. The mast rises above the sea, a single tree carefully chosen from nearby forests, all hooped with leg o' mutton rig, cotton jib, and her gold and painted prow rising and falling, reflected on the water's surface. It is a flat-bottomed boat, the "skipjack," a dredger, the last surviving working sail in America. First built by local watermen in the latter half of the 19th century, some of the 33 remaining boats have survived nearly 100 seasons of oystering on the bay. The skipjacks are a far cry from the almost 7,000 "sailing canoes" that worked these waters in the 1880s; the 19th century was oyster-crazy, and new railways sent the still-living oysters far west. The Wellfleet captains of Cape Cod

indiscriminately ravaged the natural stock, starting in Buzzard's and Narragansett Bays, working their way to Long Island Sound, Staten Island, down the Jersey shore to Delaware and the Chesapeake. Once the bay gave up millions of bushels every year—more than twice the amount of oysters eaten from coast to coast today.

Plundering nature was long thought to be this country's birthright, and in the 18th century nature's delicate balance was rarely considered. This was a dark period in the bay's history as well. Crews were "picked up" on the waterfront with billy clubs, and those who resisted were sometimes "paid off with the boom." Many skipjacks, owned by shucking houses, were rented to any captain who claimed a good haul. To this day, sleek patrol boats navigate among the skipjacks, checking the legal size of the dredged oysters and recording hauls. Because "tongers" (flat-bottomed motorboats from which some oystermen "tong" up oysters by hand) can't compete with the skipjacks and their catch, the tonger season is two months longer than the skipjack's.

To open the oyster season, the skipjacks race their annual meet. These beautiful hulls, gleaming afresh, tack on a dime with their sails pressed to the wind. And all their seemingly fragile brilliance is put to the test when their iron-spiked chain baskets drag along the bay floor, hauling in the oysters. Teams of two and three cull the live oysters from the dead shells and shovel the shells and debris back into the sea. Some of the oystermen who dredge from the sweet waters of the Choptank and Chinkatink Rivers haul their catch to the salty water at the mouth of the bay, were they leave the oysters for a couple of weeks to develop a more saline flavor. These oysters, and those dredged from deep waters, fetch higher prices at market than tonged ones pulled from close to shore or in the shallower waters of the bay.

It is a long day for the oystermen. From early morning until dusk, they cluster at the sides of the skipjacks, bent and spread-legged over the dredges. With a break for lunch hot from the galley (often cooked by the seafaring wife of the captain), after maybe 12 hours they head with their quota to the small towns and island ports.

Breakfast

COUNTRY-FRIED HAM
WITH REDEYE GRAVY*

FRIED EGGS

SPOON BREAD*

NELL DILLOW THOMAS'
PICKLED PEARS*

BLACK COFFEE

TUALATIN VINEYARDS
PINOT NOIR BLANC

To the uninitiated, the salty cured hamsteak of the South is a rude awakening. Making a "sauce" with coffee or water was just an afterthought to juice up the sometimes dry cured meat. The term "redeye" refers to the red flecks of fat that surface in the gravy. The spoon bread is the morning's grits. Southerners will pickle anything from peanuts to watermelon rind, and the pickled winter pears just make the ham go down easier.

COUNTRY-FRIED HAM WITH REDEYE GRAVY

INGREDIENTS

4 slices country ham, each 1/4–inch thick (preferably
    with the bone)
Milk
½ to ⅔ cup black coffee

TOOLS

Bacon press (optional)

METHOD

Trim the skin off the ham, leaving as much of the fat as
    possible.
Soak the ham in enough milk to cover for about 20
    minutes.
Drain and pat dry with paper towels.
In a large heavy skillet over moderate heat, brown the
    ham on each side, using a bacon press to keep the

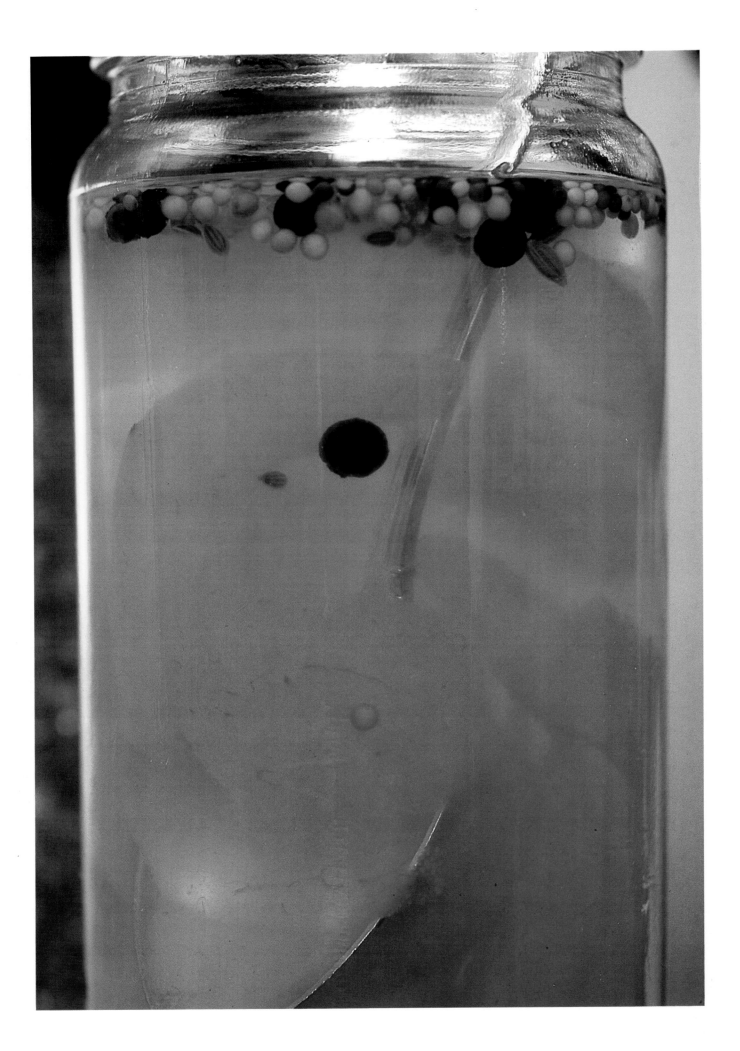

ham from curling and to help it to cook evenly.

Remove the ham to a warm plate.

To deglaze the skillet, add the black coffee and cook, scraping up the brown bits that cling to the bottom of the pan.

Reduce the mixture over high heat for about 1 minute.

Pour the redeye gravy over the ham and serve hot with fried eggs.

Serves 4

SPOON BREAD

INGREDIENTS

Butter, for the mold
2 cups milk
⅔ cup yellow cornmeal
1 teaspoon salt
1 tablespoon sugar
2 tablespoons butter
3 eggs, separated
2 teaspoons baking powder

TOOLS

2-quart soufflé dish or ovenproof baking dish

METHOD

Generously butter the soufflé dish.

Preheat the oven to 350°.

In a heavy medium saucepan, scald the milk. Do not let it boil.

Combine the cornmeal, salt, and sugar, and slowly stir into the milk.

Add the butter and stir constantly over moderate heat for 10 minutes.

Off the heat, stir in the egg yolks and baking powder. Let cool.

In a bowl, beat the egg whites with a dash of salt until they form soft peaks.

Thoroughly blend about ½ cup of the egg whites into the cornmeal mixture to lighten it.

Gently fold in the remaining egg whites; do not overblend.

Pour the mixture into the buttered mold and bake for 30 to 35 minutes, until golden.

Serves 4 to 5

NELL DILLOW THOMAS' PICKLED PEARS

INGREDIENTS

About 16 Kiefer or other hard winter pears—peeled, cored, and cut into medium-thin slices (4 cups)
Juice of 1 lemon
4 cups cider vinegar
4 cups sugar
2 teaspoons pickling spices

TOOLS

3 quart-size or 6 pint-size sterilized canning jars

METHOD

In a bowl, toss the sliced pears with the lemon juice so they do not discolor.

In a heavy nonaluminum kettle, combine the pears with the remaining ingredients and 1 cup of cold water.

Bring to a boil over high heat. Reduce the heat to low and simmer the pears for about 45 minutes, or until almost tender.

Place the pears in sterilized jars, dividing the spices among the jars.

Add syrup to reach ½-inch from the top.

Seal the jars at once.

Makes 2½ to 3 quarts

Oyster and Buckwheat Dinner

TOMATO SOUP*

BEATEN BISCUITS

CREAMED OYSTERS AND HAM*

BUCKWHEAT CAKES AND
MELTED BUTTER*

LADY BALTIMORE CAKE*

CATOCTIN
VINEYARDS SEYVAL BLANC
OR CHARDONNAY (MARYLAND)

Oyster and ham pie is very common along the Atlantic coast, but it tends to be overly doughy. What makes the following recipe legitimate, I suppose, is the fact that they eat a lot of buckwheat down there; I've taken this traditional filling and just poured it on top of a stack. The infamous beaten biscuit is about as close as you can get to softtack. The most famous are prepared down along Maryland's Eastern Shore, where a local cook beats them with an axe. I have refrained from including the recipe. The Lady Baltimore Cake was a specialty of a Charleston tearoom, but the recipe became popular up the Chesapeake and throughout that region. The leftover yolks inspired a Lord Baltimore cake, and the two together were often the bride and groom's cake at many a southern wedding. The sweet, gooey meringue, for good or bad, foreshadowed the marshmallow.

TOMATO SOUP

INGREDIENTS

4 pounds very ripe tomatoes—peeled, seeded, and
    coarsely chopped, with the juice reserved
3 fresh basil leaves
Salt and freshly milled white pepper
1 cup heavy cream, reduced over moderate heat by
    one-third

TOOLS

Food processor or food mill

METHOD

In a large nonaluminum saucepan, combine the
    tomatoes with the reserved juices, the basil, and
    salt and pepper to taste. Cook over moderate heat
    for about 20 minutes, or until the liquid begins to
    thicken.
Purée the tomatoes in a food processor or food mill.
Fold in the reduced cream.
Strain to remove any seeds. Check the seasonings and
    serve hot.
In summer, serve with a few ribbons of fresh basil.

Note: Peeled, seeded, and juiced tomatoes freeze
    very well.

Serves 4

CREAMED OYSTERS AND HAM

INGREDIENTS

16 to 20 large oysters, shucked with 1 cup of liquor
    reserved (4 to 5 oysters per person)
1 cup heavy cream, reduced over moderate heat by half
⅛ teaspoon cayenne pepper
¾ cup cured ham, cut into long, thin slivers

METHOD

In a small saucepan, reduce the 1 cup of oyster liquor
    by half over moderate heat.
In a medium saucepan, combine the reduced cream
    with the cayenne.
Strain the reduced liquor into the cream. Set aside and
    keep warm while you make the Buckwheat Cakes.
To serve, fold the oysters into the warm cream mixture
    and cook over moderate heat just until the edges
    begin to curl.
Stir in the ham. Keep warm.

Note: If the ham is very salty, let it steep in ½ cup milk
    for 15 to 20 minutes.

Serves 4

BUCKWHEAT CAKES WITH MELTED BUTTER

INGREDIENTS

1 cup buckwheat flour
1 cup sifted all-purpose flour
1 tablespoon sugar
2 teaspoons baking powder
1 teaspoon baking soda
½ teaspoon salt
2 eggs
2 cups buttermilk
¼ cup Clarified Butter (see Basics, page 344)

METHOD

In a mixing bowl, sift together all of the dry ingre-
    dients.
In another bowl, lightly beat the eggs and mix in the
    buttermilk and then ¼ cup of the butter.

Fold the egg mixture into the dry ingredients and blend
    well.
Cook the cakes on a well-buttered griddle.
Pour a little of the remaining clarified butter over each
    pancake and portion the creamed oysters and ham
    over the stacks.

Note: As the mixture sets, it thickens. You may want to
    add additional buttermilk to thin the batter out.

Makes about 24 small pancakes

LADY BALTIMORE CAKE

INGREDIENTS

CAKE LAYERS:

½ pound plus 4 tablespoons unsalted butter, at room
    temperature
2¼ cups sugar
5 cups cake flour
1 tablespoon plus 1 teaspoon baking powder
¼ teaspoon salt
1½ cups milk
1 tablespoon white rum
10 egg whites

FILLING:

⅔ cup chopped dates
½ cup raisins
¼ cup white rum
½ cup chopped walnuts

FROSTING:

4½ cups sugar
2 tablespoons light corn syrup
6 egg whites
Salt

ASSEMBLY:

Simple Syrup (see Basics, page 348)
⅓ cup white rum

TOOLS

Three 9-inch cake pans
Electric mixer
Candy thermometer

METHOD

The cake layers:

Preheat the oven to 350°. Butter three 9-inch round cake pans.

Using an electric mixer, cream together the butter and sugar in a large mixing bowl.

Sift together the dry ingredients and gradually incorporate them.

Slowly add the milk and rum.

In a mixing bowl, beat the egg whites with a dash of salt until stiff and glossy.

Fold the whites into the batter.

Divide the batter evenly among the cake pans.

Bake for 25 minutes, or until the cake pulls away from the sides of the pan.

Unmold the cake layers and let cool completely on a wire rack.

The filling:

In a small bowl, soak the dates and raisins in the ¼ cup rum for several hours; reserve.

The frosting:

In a heavy saucepan, bring the sugar, corn syrup, and 1½ cups water to a boil and cook until it reaches a temperature of 232°, or until the syrup threads 8 inches off the edge of the spoon without dripping.

In a bowl, beat the egg whites with a dash of salt until stiff and glossy. Gradually beat the hot syrup.

Drain the dates and raisins, reserving the rum.

Combine the fruits and chopped nuts with one-third of the frosting to make the filling.

To assemble:

Combine 1 cup of Simple Syrup with the ⅓ cup white rum and the reserved rum.

Trim the tops and bottoms of the cakes.

Brush the bottom layer with some of the rum syrup.

Spread half of the filling over the bottom layer.

Place the second layer on top of the first. Brush it with syrup and spread with the remaining filling.

Set the top layer in place and brush with a little of the syrup.

Frost the sides and top of the cake, using small circular motions to create swirling peaks.

Serves 8 to 10

Crab Lunch

SOFT-SHELL CRABS*

SALAD

STRAWBERRY SHORTCAKE*

ICED TEA

FISHER VINEYARDS
CHARDONNAY

Soft-shell crabs, a delicacy of the East, are at their peak in May and early June. It is a must that crabs be prepared alive—let the squeamish have their crabs cleaned by the fishmonger. They need no embellishment other than the juices they are cooked in, except perhaps thinly sliced bread fried in sweet butter. The hot, buttery shortcake will be your bread for this meal, covered with cream and fragrant sliced strawberries. Iced tea is the perennial beverage of the South, drunk throughout the meal. It is a drink every proper Southern lady has been making ever since there were porches to sit on.

SOFT-SHELL CRABS

INGREDIENTS

2 to 3 soft-shell crabs per person, depending on size
¼ pound unsalted butter
¼ cup chopped almonds
Juice of ½ lemon
¼ cup chopped fresh parsley

METHOD

Ask the fishmonger or use a sharp paring knife to fold back the soft carapace and trim off the head of the crabs. Remove the gills. Trim the apron from the underside of the crab.

Melt the butter in a large heavy skillet and sauté the crabs for 1 to 2 minutes on each side.

Remove to a heated platter, and keep warm.

Add the almonds and lemon juice to the butter, and toss until the almonds turn golden brown.

Stir in the parsley.

Pour the butter-almond mixture over the crabs and serve.

STRAWBERRY SHORTCAKE

INGREDIENTS

DOUGH:

2 cups all-purpose flour
1 teaspoon salt
1 tablespoon baking powder
1 tablespoon sugar
5 tablespoons unsalted butter
1 cup heavy cream

FILLING:

2 pints strawberries
¼ cup sugar
1 cup heavy cream, whipped, for serving

METHOD

The dough:

Preheat the oven to 350°.

In a large bowl, sift together the dry ingredients and
 mix in the butter.

Fold in the cream.

On a lightly-floured surface, divide the dough into 4
 pieces, and pat into 1-inch-thick rounds.

Bake on an ungreased baking sheet for 35 minutes,
 until golden.

The filling:

Hull and slice the strawberries.

Mix with the sugar.

Split the shortcakes and spoon the filling onto the
 bottom half.

Replace the tops and serve with the whipped cream.

Serves 4

Pan-Fried Dove Supper

PAN-FRIED DOVES*

BREAD SAUCE*

FRIED CRUMBS*

FRIED BAKED GRITS*

PARSLEY BUTTERED TURNIPS*

GLAZED TOMATOES*

SYLLABUB*

CRYSTALLIZED GRAPEFRUIT*

STAG'S LEAP
WINE CELLARS MERLOT or
SCHARFENBERGER CELLARS
SPARKLING WINE

More often than not, the eye-opener for a man was a brandy or a julep; sometimes a lady began her day with a glass of syllabub. It was the custom of guests at lordly manor houses along every river into Savannah to go dove hunting in the fall and spring. It's a rather comical sight to see these ladies and gentlemen going down oak-lined paths in their horse-drawn carts, with a couple of blacks walking in front, clapping their hands to startle the birds into flight. The gentlemen shoot a covey, the blacks run off to pick them up, and the cook later fries them up into a damn good breakfast.

PAN-FRIED DOVES

INGREDIENTS

8 doves, split
Salt and freshly milled black pepper
1 tablespoon juniper berries, bruised
¼ pound butter, clarified (see Basics, page 344)
2 tablespoons gin

METHOD

Lightly rub the doves with salt and pepper and the bruised juniper berries.

In a large heavy skillet, warm the butter over moderately high heat.

Add the birds, skin side down, and sauté for 4 to 5 minutes, until browned. Turn the birds and cook another 5 minutes, until pink and juicy.

Sprinkle with the gin and ignite, shaking the pan until the flames subside. Serve at once.

Serves 4

BREAD SAUCE

INGREDIENTS

2 tablespoons butter
2 tablespoons all-purpose flour
2 cups milk
⅛ teaspoon ground mace
Freshly milled white pepper
1 cup day-old white bread, crusts removed, and bread torn into small pieces (about 3 slices)
½ cup country cured ham, cut into julienne (about 3 ounces)

METHOD

In a small saucepan, melt the butter. Remove from the heat and whisk in the flour.

Return to the heat, add the milk, mace, and pepper to taste and whisk constantly until the sauce thickens and is velvety-smooth.

Fold in the bread and ham and pour into a heated sauceboat.

Serves 4

FRIED CRUMBS

INGREDIENTS

1 tablespoon butter
1 cup dried bread crumbs, made from stale bread
Salt and freshly milled pepper
Pinch of dried thyme

METHOD

In a medium skillet, melt the butter over moderate heat. Add the bread crumbs and the seasonings and sauté, tossing until golden brown.
Serve with the doves.

Serves 4

FRIED BAKED GRITS

INGREDIENTS

Butter, for the baking dish
4 cups milk
1½ cups quick cooking grits
¼ pound plus 4 tablespoons unsalted butter
1½ teaspoons salt
Dash of hot pepper sauce
1½ cups grated cheddar or rat cheese
3 eggs, well-beaten
Butter, for frying

TOOLS

Large rectangular ovenproof baking dish

METHOD

Butter the baking dish. Set aside.
Preheat the oven to 350°.
In a large saucepan, bring the milk and 2 cups water to a boil over high heat.
Pour in the grits, stirring constantly until moistened.
Remove from the heat and stir in the butter, seasonings, cheese, and eggs.
Pour into the prepared baking dish and bake for 1 hour.
Let cool to room temperature and cut into diamond shapes.

Pan fry in butter until golden on both sides.

Note: These grits can be served hot, direct from the oven, or made in advance and fried just before serving.

Serves 6 to 8

PARSLEY BUTTERED TURNIPS

INGREDIENTS

8 small turnips, trimmed and quartered, but not peeled
Salt
2 tablespoons butter
1 teaspoon sugar
1 tablespoon chopped fresh parsley

METHOD

In a large pot of salted boiling water, cook the turnips until tender. Drain.
Melt the butter in a large heavy skillet. Add the turnips and sugar and cook, tossing, until coated with the butter. Add the parsley, toss to coat, and serve.

Serves 4

GLAZED TOMATOES

INGREDIENTS

4 ripe tomatoes—cored, halved horizontally, and lightly squeezed of seeds
Salt and freshly milled pepper
1 teaspoon sugar
1 tablespoon chopped fresh parsley

METHOD

Preheat the oven to 350°.
Place the tomatoes on a lightly oiled baking sheet.
Sprinkle with salt and pepper, the sugar, and parsley.
Bake for 10 minutes, until softened.
Remove and place under the broiler for a few seconds, until glazed.

Serves 4

SYLLABUB

INGREDIENTS

8 to 10 dried macaroons
1 cup confectioners' sugar
1 cup heavy cream
½ cup dark rum
¼ cup fresh lemon juice
2 tablespoons powdered instant espresso coffee

TOOLS

Food processor

METHOD

In a food processor, lightly whirl the macaroons until finely crumbed. Do not overprocess. Measure out 1 cup of crumbs and set aside.

Place the sugar in the food processor and mix for about 1 minute.

Add the cream and process for 1 minute.

Blend in the rum and lemon juice. Turn into a bowl and refrigerate for 2 days.

When ready to serve, fold in the macaroon crumbs.

Serve in chilled cups, dusted with the instant espresso coffee.

Serves 4

CRYSTALLIZED GRAPEFRUIT

INGREDIENTS

3 grapefruits
2½ cups sugar

METHOD

Peel the grapefruits and cut the peel into long ¼-inch julienne.

Place the peels in a medium saucepan and add cold water to cover.

Boil for 10 minutes and drain. Repeat this process two more times with fresh water.

In the saucepan, mix 2 cups water with 1½ cups of the sugar.

Add the grapefruit peels and bring to a boil.

Boil until peels become translucent and the liquid becomes a thick syrup, about 45 minutes.

With a slotted spoon, remove the peels to a sheet of waxed paper.

Allow to set for 7 minutes. Transfer the peels to another sheet of waxed paper and sprinkle with the remaining 1 cup sugar.

Roll the peels in the sugar and let stand for 2 hours.

Serve 2 to 3 strips of peel per person and store the remainder airtight in a jar.

Makes about 1 quart

Crab Soup Lunch

SHE-CRAB SOUP*

SALT-CURED HAM BISCUITS*

SALAD

LIME CURD TARTLETS*

MEREDYTH VINEYARD
CHARDONNAY

She-crab soup is a delicacy of Charleston. The roe-filled sooks make the dish authentic, but a valid interpretation can be made with freshly pasteurised crab. A lighter version of the beaten biscuit, with flecks of salt cured ham, should come to the table so piping hot that the butter will be absorbed immediately. Lime curd, a twist on English lemon curd, is served in tart shells.

SHE-CRAB SOUP

INGREDIENTS

4 cups heavy cream
4 tablespoons butter
¼ cup finely chopped shallots
1 pound fresh lump crabmeat with roe
Freshly grated nutmeg
⅛ teaspoon cayenne pepper
Grated zest of ½ lemon
Salt
1 tablespoon finely chopped fresh parsley
Dry sherry (optional)

METHOD

In a small saucepan, reduce the cream over moderate heat by one-third.

In a large saucepan, melt the butter. Add the shallots and sauté until wilted.

Add the crabmeat and cook gently, tossing for 2 minutes.

Pour in the reduced heavy cream and simmer for 5 minutes.

Season with the nutmeg, cayenne, and lemon zest. Check the seasonings and add salt to taste.

Mound some crabmeat in each warm soup plate and pour the soup around it.

Sprinkle lightly with parsley.

Serve the sherry at the table, adding a spoonful to each portion, if desired.

Serves 4 to 6

SALT-CURED HAM BISCUITS

INGREDIENTS

2 cups all-purpose flour
2 tablespoons baking powder
⅛ teaspoon sugar
5 tablespoons shortening
1 cup milk
1 cup finely diced leftover salt-cured ham or sweet-cured ham

METHOD

Preheat the oven to 450°.

In a mixing bowl, sift together the dry ingredients.

Using your fingers, cut in the shortening until the mixture is coarse and crumbly. Add the milk and mix slightly.

Fold in the ham.

On a floured surface, roll or pat out the dough about ½-inch thick.

Cut out biscuits with a cookie cutter and bake on an ungreased baking sheet for about 12 minutes, or until the tops are brown.

Makes 2 dozen small or 1 dozen large biscuits

LIME CURD TARTLETS

INGREDIENTS

1 recipe Pie Dough, made with butter (see Basics, page 346)

½ cup fresh lime juice

½ cup sugar

1 tablespoon cornstarch

8 egg yolks, at room temperature

2 tablespoons unsalted butter

TOOLS

Six 3½-inch shallow tartlet molds

METHOD

Use the pie dough to make 6 pastry shells. Bake thoroughly and set aside to cool.

Place the lime juice, 1 cup of water, and the sugar in a saucepan and bring to a boil over high heat.

Meanwhile, in a mixing bowl, dissolve the cornstarch in ½ cup water. Whisk in the egg yolks.

Slowly pour 1 cup of the boiling lime syrup into the yolk mixture and blend thoroughly.

Pour the mixture back into the saucepan and bring to a boil, stirring constantly.

Remove from the heat, add the butter and mix.

Pour into the prebaked tart shells and let set for about 30 minutes before serving.

Serves 6

Southern Picnic

STRAWBERRY AND
CREAM CHEESE SANDWICHES*

DEVILED EGGS*

FRIED CHICKEN*

POTATO SALAD*
COLE SLAW* PICKLES

BISCUITS* COCONUT CAKE*
(see Page 121)

BERINGER VINEYARDS
CHENIN BLANC

Picnics were very much the custom in spring. Families and hoards of their friends went off into the woods and set out elegant picnics. Dainty strawberry sandwiches and stuffed eggs were served with white wine and Champagne, and the meal immediately took up its Southern roll. The key to good fried chicken is in the turn of the fork, and if you were not lucky enough to spend your youth at the elbow of an old mammy cook, the secret may elude you forever. There are as many ways to fry a chicken as to skin a cat. Chicken can be fried in vegetable oil or in shortening—but never, ever in butter.

STRAWBERRY AND CREAM CHEESE SANDWICHES

INGREDIENTS

1 large package (8 ounces) cream cheese, preferably without gum additives, at room temperature
1 tablespoon unsalted butter, at room temperature
¼ teaspoon ground cinnamon
16 slices very thinly sliced white bread
1 cup ripe strawberries
Granulated sugar

METHOD

In a bowl, cream together the cream cheese and butter with the cinnamon until soft and smooth.

Lightly spread the cream cheese on all of the bread slices.

Hull the strawberries and thinly slice. Arrange the slices on 8 slices of the bread, covering the entire surface.

Lightly sprinkle the berries with granulated sugar and top each sandwich with a remaining slice of bread.

Trim off the crusts and cut the sandwiches into 4 triangles.

Note: If making ahead of time, wrap in damp tea towels.

Makes 32 tea sandwiches

DEVILED EGGS

INGREDIENTS

1 dozen eggs
¼ cup homemade Mayonnaise
  (see Basics, page 345)
1 tablespoon Creole mustard
½ teaspoon finely minced fresh tarragon
1 tablespoon butter, softened
Salt and freshly milled pepper

TOOLS

Pastry bag fitted with star tube

METHOD

Place the eggs in a large pot of cold water.

Bring to a boil and cook for 12 minutes.

Set in the sink under cold running water.

Crack the shells while the water is still cooling the eggs.

When cool, remove the shells.

Cut the eggs lengthwise in half.

Remove the yolks to a separate bowl and discard 4 cooked whites.

Mix the yolks with the remaining ingredients.

When ready to serve, fill a pastry bag with the yolk mixture and pipe it into the egg whites.

Set on a platter and serve.

Makes 20 deviled eggs

FRIED CHICKEN

INGREDIENTS

3 chickens (each about 3½ pounds), cut into small serving pieces

2 cups all-purpose flour

1 tablespoon salt

½ teaspoon freshly milled white pepper

Vegetable oil, for frying

METHOD

Pat the chicken pieces dry with paper towels.

Mix the flour with the salt and white pepper and dredge the chicken pieces in it. Shake off any excess flour.

Pour ½ inch of vegetable oil into a heavy skillet and place over high heat.

When the oil is hot, reduce the heat to moderate.

Working in batches, fry the chicken slowly until cooked through and deep golden brown.

Keep the chicken warm in a 275° oven until all of the chicken has been cooked.

Serves 8

POTATO SALAD

INGREDIENTS

2 cups homemade Mayonnaise (see Basics, page 345)

3 tablespoons Dijon-style mustard

12 to 14 medium potatoes—cooked, peeled and sliced

2 bunches scallions, including some of the green, chopped

Salt and freshly milled pepper

METHOD

In a large bowl, mix the mayonnaise with the mustard.

Fold in the potatoes, scallions, and salt and pepper to taste.

Refrigerate and remove 20 minutes before serving. Check seasonings.

Serves 8 to 12

COLE SLAW

INGREDIENTS

1 medium head cabbage

Salt and freshly milled black pepper

1 cup homemade Mayonnaise (see Basics, page 345)

2 tablespoons tarragon vinegar

¼ teaspoon sugar

1 red or green bell pepper—cored, seeded, and cut into julienne

METHOD

Discard the outer cabbage leaves and cut in half. Core and, beginning at the core end, thinly slice.

Place the cabbage in a large mixing bowl.

Toss with 2 tablespoons salt and add cold water to cover. Let stand for 1 hour.

Drain and dry thoroughly.

In a large bowl, combine the mayonnaise with the vinegar and sugar.

Add the cabbage and red pepper and toss with the mayonnaise dressing. Season to taste with salt and pepper.

Refrigerate and remove 20 minutes before serving. Check the seasonings.

Serves 8

COCONUT CAKE

INGREDIENTS

CAKE:

Butter and flour for the pans
¼ pound unsalted butter
1 cup sugar
4 eggs, separated
2 cups all-purpose flour
1 tablespoon plus 1 teaspoon baking powder
½ teaspoon salt
⅓ cup fresh or canned coconut milk
Grated zest of 1 lemon

LEMON FILLING:

⅓ cup fresh lemon juice
½ cup sugar
1½ tablespoons cornstarch
8 egg yolks, at room temperature
2 tablespoons butter

SEVEN-MINUTE ICING:

1½ cups sugar
2 eggs whites, at room temperature
¼ teaspoon cream of tartar
¼ cup ice water

1 cup shredded unsweetened coconut, to dust the cake

TOOLS

Two 8-inch cake pans
Electric mixer

METHOD

The cake:
Butter and lightly flour the cake pans.
Preheat the oven to 350°.
Cream together the butter and sugar in the bowl of an electric mixer.
One at a time, add the egg yolks and mix until blended.
Sift together the flour, baking powder, and salt and add alternately with the coconut milk.
Stir in the lemon zest.
In another bowl, beat the egg whites until stiff and glossy. Fold the whites into the batter with a rubber spatula.
Divide the batter equally between the cake pans and bake for 40 minutes, or until the cake pulls away from the sides of the pan.
Remove from the cake pans and cool on wire racks.

The lemon filling:
In a medium nonaluminum saucepan, bring the lemon juice, sugar, and 1 cup water to a boil.
In a bowl, dissolve the cornstarch in ⅓ cup water and mix in the yolks.
When the lemon syrup boils, remove from the heat and gradually whisk it into the yolk mixture.
Return to a saucepan and bring to a boil.
Remove from the heat and whisk in the butter. Place a sheet of plastic wrap directly on the surface of the filling and set aside.

The seven-minute icing:
In a large heatproof mixing bowl, combine all of the ingredients.
Set the bowl over a pot of boiling water and beat with an electric mixer for about 7 minutes, until white peaks form.
Remove from the heat and beat until the icing stiffens and becomes spreadable.

Final assembly:
Trim the tops and bottoms of each cake with a serrated knife.
Cut the cakes horizontally in half.
One at a time, spread each layer with the lemon filling, stacking evenly.
Ice the cake with the seven-minute frosting.
Cover the tops and sides of the cake with the shredded coconut.

Serves 10

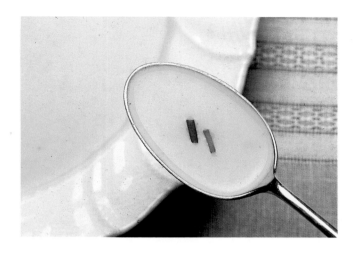

Beaufort Soused Corn and Shrimp Lunch

CURRIED BUTTERMILK
VICHYSSOISE*

BEAUFORT SOUSED CORN
AND SHRIMP*

FRIED GREEN TOMATOES*

CORN BREAD

PEACH COBBLER*

KENDALL-JACKSON VINEYARDS
SAUVIGNON BLANC

Vichyssoise is one of the most refreshing soups in warm weather, and it's certainly substantial. This soup, first served at the Ritz in New York, really is no different from potato soup, and seems elegant just because it's been puréed and doused with cream. Waters off the Carolina coast harvested some of the best shrimp available, and Beaufort is a small port that once was crowded with fishing boats. The shrimp industry has dwindled to a handful of boats, but, in that area, shrimp dishes and pies are still very popular. I took the shrimp and the corn out of the pie shell, and soused them

with a vinaigrette; it's lighter than a doughy pie. Cobbler is usually blanketed with biscuit dough; here a rich buttery crust is rolled out to fit the skillet, all baked into a lighter version of traditional cobbler.

CURRIED BUTTERMILK VICHYSSOISE

INGREDIENTS

4 medium leeks
4 medium potatoes
4 tablespoons butter
1 tablespoon curry powder
1 quart Chicken Stock (see Basics, page 343)
Salt and freshly milled pepper
1 quart buttermilk
2 tablespoons chopped fresh chives

METHOD

Discard the green tops of the leeks and split the leeks lengthwise.
Wash in cold running water to remove all sand. Drain and finely chop.
Peel and slice the potatoes.
Melt the butter in a large pot.
Add the leeks and sauté over moderate heat, until wilted.
Add the curry powder and cook for 1 minute.
Add the chicken stock and potatoes.
Bring to a boil, reduce the heat to low and simmer for 45 minutes to 1 hour, until the potatoes are tender.
Purée the mixture in a food processor. Cover and chill.
When ready to serve, whisk in the buttermilk.
Check the seasonings.
Serve in chilled bowls, with a sprinkling of the chopped chives and a grind of black pepper.

Serves 8 to 10

BEAUFORT SOUSED CORN AND SHRIMP

INGREDIENTS

5 pounds medium shrimp, peeled with tails intact
1 bay leaf
1 teaspoon crushed peppercorns
1 lemon, halved
12 ears sweet corn, cut from the cob
1 cup thinly sliced scallions
1 lemon, thinly sliced
Salt

VINAIGRETTE:

⅓ cup fresh lemon juice
½ cup olive oil
Salt and freshly milled black pepper
Salt

METHOD

In a large saucepan, place the shrimp in 2 quarts of
    cold water.
Add the bay leaf, peppercorns, and the halved and
    squeezed lemon.
Bring to a boil over moderately high heat.
Add the corn and remove from the heat. Drain and turn
    into a serving bowl.
Remove and discard the halved lemon and bay leaf.
Fold in the scallions and lemon slices.
Make the vinaigrette and pour over the corn and
    shrimp, tossing to coat.
Let stand for 15 minutes.

Season to taste with salt and serve warm.
Note: To serve with Corn Bread, follow the recipe on
    page 250, omitting the vegetables.
Serves 8

FRIED GREEN TOMATOES

INGREDIENTS

4 green tomatoes
1 cup all-purpose flour
¼ cup rendered ham fat

METHOD

Slice the tomatoes ¼-inch thick.
Lightly dredge with flour, shaking off any excess.
In a large heavy skillet, preferably cast-iron, melt the
    fat. Coat and fry the tomatoes until lightly golden
    on each side.

Serves 4

PEACH COBBLER

INGREDIENTS

COBBLER DOUGH:

2 cups all-purpose flour
1 tablespoon sugar
¼ teaspoon salt
½ pound unsalted butter,
cut into chips and chilled
3 tablespoons ice water

FILLING:

12 large ripe peaches
Juice of 1 lemon
¼ cup sugar

1 tablespoon sugar, for the top of the crust
Heavy cream or vanilla ice cream, for serving

TOOLS

10-inch cast-iron skillet or shallow baking dish

METHOD

Prepare the dough:

In a bowl, sift together the dry ingredients and work in
the butter with your fingertips or with an electric
mixer until the mixture is a mealy consistency.

A little at a time, add the ice water until the dough
sticks together. Do not over-mix.

Shape into a ball, wrap in waxed paper, and refrigerate for 15 minutes.

Preheat the oven to 425°.

Prepare the filling:

Peel and slice the peaches and toss with the lemon
juice and sugar.

Place the peaches in an ovenproof skillet or shallow
baking pan.

On a floured surface, roll out the dough to fit the pan.

Place the dough over the peaches.

Dust with the sugar.

Bake for 45 minutes, or until golden brown.

Serve warm, with heavy cream or vanilla ice cream.

Serves 4 to 6

Hopping John Dinner

GRILLED OYSTERS*

GLAZED COUNTRY CURED HAM*

ONION VINAIGRETTE*

HOPPING JOHN*

GLAZED SWEET POTATOES*

COLLARD GREENS*

HOT CURRIED FRUIT*

POUND CAKE*

NAVARRO VINEYARDS
GEWÜRZTRAMINER

The oyster roasts of the colonial South developed into huge feeds at electioneering time, the various candidates holding elaborate feasts who would win popular favor more or less depended on the food served—the amount, the selection. It is a subtle, hidden, but important fact of post-colonial life, that the American politician got to the voter through his stomach. Hopping john is always served on New Year's Day. A coin thrown into the pot, and whoever found it was assured of good luck. A locally cured ham presided over the hopping john and a variety of vegetables and sweet potatoes in one form or another. Spiced fresh fruits were a luxury. Rich cake, measured out in a pound each of sugar, eggs, butter and flour, was beaten by the sturdy family cook.

GRILLED OYSTERS

INGREDIENTS

10 to 12 oysters per person

TOOLS

Grill with charcoal and hickory or oak

METHOD

Wash and clean the oyster shells thoroughly. Keep the oysters on ice until ready to cook.

Prepare a hickory or oak fire with a lot of kindling.

Set a large rack over the fire.

When the coals are a dusty red glow, place the oysters on the rack and cook.

As the oysters open, remove with long tongs.

Pry open with a knife and eat immediately.

The oysters will have a pungent, smoky flavor.

When cooked, drain off the water.

Preheat the oven to 425°.

Peel back the skin 2 inches below the hock and reserve it for the Hopping John or Collard Greens.

Place the ham on a roasting pan.

Remove the excess fat, leaving a ½-inch covering over the meat. Reserve the fat.

Score the ham and cover with Ham Glaze.

Bake for 20 to 30 minutes, until heated through and browned.

Slice very thinly.

Serves 8 to 10

HAM GLAZE

INGREDIENTS

1 cup dark brown sugar
1 tablespoon dry mustard
⅓ cup bourbon or corn whiskey
¼ cup blackstrap molasses

METHOD

In a bowl, combine the brown sugar with the dry mustard and bourbon. Stir in the molasses.

Coat the ham.

Baste twice while the ham bakes.

Makes about 1¼ cups

ONION VINAIGRETTE

INGREDIENTS

12 medium white onions
1 cup pearl onions
1 cup shelled fresh green peas
Vinaigrette (see Basics, page 345)

METHOD

Slice off the top third of each white onion and cut an "X" at the base.

Place the onions in a steamer and cook for 10 to 15 minutes, or until tender. Reserve.

GLAZED COUNTRY CURED HAM

INGREDIENTS

1 ham (12 to 14 pounds)

METHOD

Scrub off any mold that has developed on the skin of the ham.

Place the ham in a pot with water to cover and allow to sit for at least 8 hours or overnight.

Drain and add fresh cold water to cover.

Bring to a simmer and reduce the heat to just a slight bubble. Cook for 6 hours, replacing any evaporated water with fresh warm water to cover.

Check the meat by piercing it with a skewer. If firm, continue cooking for an additional 2 hours.

Meanwhile, cut an "X" on the bottom of each pearl
    onion and poach in boiling, salted water for
    5 minutes.
Drain and peel.
Blanch the peas in salted boiling water for 4 minutes.
    Drain and mix with the pearl onions.
Peel off the outer skin and scoop out the heart of the
    larger onions to make onion shells.
Coat the pearl onions and peas with vinaigrette and
    spoon into the hollowed onions.
Serve at room temperature.

Serves 12

HOPPING JOHN

INGREDIENTS

1 pound dried black-eyed peas
Ham hock or Country Cured Ham skin and
    fat trimmings
1 medium onion, finely chopped
1 bay leaf
¾ cup long-grain rice
Salt and freshly milled pepper

METHOD

Soak the peas overnight in several quarts of water.
Dice the ham fat and render it in a large pot over
    moderate heat.
Add the onions and cook until wilted.
Drain the peas and add them along with the bay leaf

and cold water to cover.
Add the ham hock or a large piece of ham skin.
Bring to a boil and reduce the heat to a simmer.
Cover and cook for 45 minutes, or until the peas are
    almost tender.
Add the rice, cover, and cook for 20 minutes, adding
    more water if necessary, until the rice is tender.
Season to taste with salt and pepper and serve.

Serves 8 to 10

GLAZED SWEET POTATOES

INGREDIENTS

6 sweet potatoes or yams
1 cup packed brown sugar
¼ cup bourbon
4 tablespoons butter, melted
Grated zest of 1 lemon

METHOD

Boil the potatoes until almost tender.
Preheat the oven to 350°. Butter a shallow ovenproof
    baking dish.
When cool enough to handle, peel the potatoes and cut
    into ½-inch-thick slices. Place in the prepared
    baking dish.
In a small saucepan, dissolve the brown sugar in the
    bourbon over moderate heat.
Add the melted butter and lemon zest.
Pour the glaze over the potatoes and bake for 15 to
    20 minutes, until glazed and heated through.

Serves 8 to 10

COLLARD GREENS

INGREDIENTS

3 pounds collard greens, stalks removed
Ham hock with reserved ham skin
1 tablespoon sugar
Salt and freshly milled pepper

METHOD

Wash, drain, and chop the greens. Set aside.

Place the ham hock and skin in a large kettle, and add about 3 quarts cold water to cover. Bring to a boil over high heat.

Simmer over moderate heat for 30 minutes.

Add the greens and sugar and simmer for 2 hours.

Drain the "likker" and serve it with the greens and spooned over corn bread.

Serves 8 to 10

HOT CURRIED FRUIT

INGREDIENTS

12 firm ripe pears

About 3½ cups sugar (depending on the sweetness of the fruit)

3 small cinnamon sticks

10 whole cloves

Juice of 2 lemons

12 oranges

1 winter melon

1 bunch red grapes, preferably seedless, cut into small clusters

1 lemon, sliced

1 tablespoon curry powder

½ cup crystallized ginger, cut into julienne

METHOD

Peel the pears, leaving the stems intact.

Place them in a large nonaluminum pot with enough water to cover.

Add the sugar, spices, and lemon juice.

Cover the pears with a round of waxed paper cut to fit the interior of the pot.

Bring to a boil, reduce to a simmer, and cook until the pears can be easily pierced with a knife.

Meanwhile, slice away the skin and pith from the oranges.

Remove the pears to a serving bowl and add enough syrup to cover.

Place the oranges in the cooking liquid and simmer for 15 minutes, or until tender.

Peel and seed the melon. Cut into long 1-inch strips.

Add the melon strips to the poaching oranges and simmer for 5 minutes. Remove to the serving bowl.

Add the grapes and lemon slices to the poaching liquid, and simmer about 3 minutes. Remove to the bowl.

Add the curry powder to the liquid and whisk to dissolve.

Cook the syrup until reduced by half. Strain through a double thickness of dampened cheesecloth. Drain away any juices that have collected in the serving bowl and pour the syrup over the fruits.

Serve the fruit with a little of the crystallized ginger julienne spooned over each portion.

Serves 8 to 12

POUND CAKE

INGREDIENTS

½ pound unsalted butter

1 cup sugar

5 eggs

2¼ cups all-purpose flour

1 teaspoon baking powder

½ teaspoon salt

½ cup sour cream

Confectioners' sugar

TOOLS

2 medium loaf pans

METHOD

Generously butter the loaf pans.

Preheat the oven to 350°.

In a mixing bowl, cream together the butter and sugar.

One at a time, add the eggs, mixing thoroughly.

Sift together the flour, baking powder, and salt. Add the dry ingredients, alternately with the sour cream.

Divide the batter between the loaf pans.

Bake for 40 minutes, or until the loaves pull away from the sides of the pans.

Allow the cakes to rest for 10 minutes, remove from the tins, and cool on a rack.

Dust with confectioners' sugar.

Makes two 1-pound loaves

STREET FOOD

Crab Cakes

Crab cakes, a variation on croquettes, make a very pleasant meal. They join the common ranks of lobster salad and oysters just slapped on a hamburger bun. The perpetual accompaniment is little paper cups of creamy cole slaw and tartar sauce.

CRAB CAKES

INGREDIENTS

THE CRAB CAKES:

1 pound (about 2½ cups) flaked crab meat, picked over
1 small onion, finely chopped (about ¾ cup)
1 teaspoon dry mustard
¼ teaspoon cayenne pepper
¼ cup homemade Mayonnaise (see Basics, page 345)
1 egg, beaten with 3 tablespoons heavy cream
¼ cup fresh bread or cracker crumbs

FOR FRYING:

Vegetable oil
1 cup dried bread crumbs

METHOD

In a bowl, combine all of the crab cake ingredients and shape into 8 cakes.
In a heavy skillet, heat 1 inch of oil over moderately high heat.
Lightly coat the cakes in the dried bread crumbs and fry in the hot oil until golden brown.
Serve with Tartar Sauce (see Basics, page 345).

Makes 8 crab cakes

Mint Julep

How to make a julep: crush the mint, bruise the mint; freeze the glass, freeze the silver chalice; make it with rye, make it with bourbon. These are the disputes. I offer my julep—I make it with scotch.

MINT JULEP

INGREDIENTS

½ cup packed fresh mint sprigs
¼ cup Simple Syrup (see Basics, page 348)
2 to 2½ cups shaved ice
6 ounces scotch

TOOLS

Blender
Two julep cups
Glass straws

METHOD

In a blender, combine the mint and Simple Syrup, mixing until puréed thoroughly.
Place half of the mint mixture and 1 straw in each julep cup. Packing the ice around the straw, fill the cup almost to the top with shaved ice. Set the cups in the freezer for at least 30 minutes.
Touching the outside as little as possible, remove the cups from the freezer and pour scotch over the shaved ice.
Decorate with mint sprigs and sip in the shade.

Makes two 12-ounce drinks

Deep South

"The heavy firing gives us showers every day and nature is more lovely than usual. The flowers are in perfection, the air heavy with the perfume of cape jasmin, and honeysuckle, and the garden bright and gay with all the summer flowers. The fruit is coming to perfection, the apricots more abundant and more beautiful than I ever saw them. Nature is all fair and lovely—'all save the spirit of man seems divine.'" —from the diary of
Emma Balfour, of Vicksburg, Mississippi, Monday, May 25, 1863

The extraordinary yield of southern rice fields was the result of backbreaking labor, for rice was planted by hand from soil "loosened first with a kitchen spoon." Rice fields, abutting the stately plantations, might be tended by as many as 2,100 slaves for every 500 acres. Fields of last year's stubble were burnt after the first killing frost, then lightly plowed and ditched, and the soil clods crushed. Seeds were sown at the end of March or in early April, at first by hand, and later by ox- or mule-drawn drills. The months after sowing saw the fields alternately flooded and dried, painstakingly coaxing the rice to germinate and thrive. Rice-tending is a year-round vigil, from clearing the irrigation ditches (60 miles of ditch to every 500 acres of field!) of clogging grasses to a long winter's work of threshing in the mills. The Civil War marked the decline of the plantation. Slaves were freed and the countryside ravaged, and only a handful of plantations returned somewhat to their former glory during Reconstruction. Most blacks, newly homeless, looked for work far from the plantation, taking with them their skill at operating the trunks, ditches, canals, levels, floodgates, and banks attendant to the rice fields. Deprived of their usual help, the field foremen hired immigrant workers, for the most part Irish and Italians from the brickyards on the Hudson River, but the labor was neither cheap nor as satisfactory. Rice culture declined rapidly at the beginning

of this century, and by 1920 there were no more than 500 acres of aggregated fields along the river. The great Carolina rice industry, sprung from one small bag of Madagascar rice carried by an English sea captain into Charlestown harbor, flourished nearly 200 years before falling away to a single, stately plantation. Beyond the swamps and up the grand oak-lined drives that lead to once-proud mansions, one is hard put to imagine that there was once a way of life modeled on that of England's feudal lords.

Today, rice fields flourish in the small towns of southern Louisiana, on Bayou Teche and down to the intercoastal water route. No longer the domain of the gentleman farmer but of the working land farmer, Louisiana is one of this country's great rice producers. Though Louisiana shares the export market with other states, her people consume as much rice at their tables as do most Asians. Rice and hominy are the staples of the low country and on through the Deep South. Hominy is for breakfast, a foundation for breads and batter. Rice is for dinner, passed at the table hot and fluffy with gumbos, jambalayas, vegetable soups, okra soups and stews, the backbone of vegetable and meat pilafs. (Servants saved the starchy rice water for pressing household linen and cotton, just as the frugal New England housewife saved the water in which she'd soaked beans to clean her kerosene lamps.) Rice is the cornerstone of any southern kitchen, the basis of elegant dishes and humble ones (rice cakes, puddings, and tarts, and of course red beans and rice) alike. Flooded fields make perfect crawfish farms. Louisiana produces more than 20 million pounds annually, keeping three-quarters of the catch for herself. The rest is shipped throughout the country. (Crawfish, undoubtedly to be followed by catfish, will soon be as standard as production-line chicken.) During the crawfish season, flat-bottomed pirogues, some still made from hollowed cypress logs, are poled through the swampy bayou like Venetian gondolas, the navigator emptying wire traps until he is boot-deep with crawling, tiny-clawed monsters. Cranes, herons, and egrets nest in the trees of the bayou, where alligators and turtles wait below in the hope that an egg or chick will fall their way. Crawfish, or "mud-bugs" (so-called because they burrow into the mud when their watery environment goes dry), like soft-shell crabs, must be shipped live. Cooked crawfish will keep only a short while, and if frozen with its own fat the meat spoils quickly. Crawfish fat is a critical if luxurious ingredient in many dishes.

On Good Friday, picnickers take to the levees by the tree ponds and boil up hundreds of crawfish in sawed-off gasoline drums, generously figuring about seven pounds for every man, five for every woman. Folk are very practical when it comes to this type of cooking, best done out-of-doors because of smoke and smell. (Blackened redfish, the infamous redfish, pompano, or tile fish that is charred in a white-hot cast-iron skillet, is also done outside. Only some trend-happy urbanite would attempt this smoking inferno in an apartment kitchen!) In this country one feasts on jambalaya, crawfish bisque and crawfish étouffé, frogs, turtle soups and turtle stews, crabs, alligator steaks and fried alligator sausage, and definitive Cajun gumbo thickened with filé (powdered native sassafras leaf). In winter, there are rabbits, deer, raccoons, possums, snipe, grouse, wild ducks, turkey, and geese.

The Cajuns left their Atlantic coast of France in the 1600s, settling in Acadia (in Nova Scotia, near the St. Lawrence River). "Cajun" (slurred from the word "Acadian") is a language closer to French than to any other, though removed by 300 years and further spiked with Indian, Spanish, and English. The Cajuns concerned themselves with fishing, trapping, and farming, and adamantly refused to swear British allegiance. When banished from this territory in 1755, the Cajuns crept down the St. Lawrence to the Great Lakes, across the plains and down the Mississippi, settling, between 1760 and 1785, in the waterlogged parishes of southern and western Louisiana. As a society they have kept their customs, trades, and language, although the language is now in danger of dying out. Slapdash and impulsive, Cajun cooks use more spices, herbs, and hot peppers than their Creole brothers and sisters in the city. Filé is very much a part of Cajun cooking, and was long known to the Choctaw Indians who would dry the young sassafras leaves and grind them to powder. A small amount thickens and seasons gumbo. Okra also is used to thicken gumbos and soups. (Okra and filé must not be used together or the intended soup would turn to sludge. Filé must be added off the heat, because, if boiled, it turns stringy.)

This area has a worldwide reputation for *hot* food. There are more peppers grown and used in Louisiana than in any other region, including the Southwest. Anaheim chiles, Louisiana sports, serranos, torridos, jalapeños, Bahamian reds, powdered peppers for cayenne, crushed red pepper flakes and seeds, red and green tabascos (combined in a secret formula for the bottled sauce of that name), as well as countless other types of peppers are grown in the parishes of Vermilion, Lafayette, New Iberia, and St. Mary. Hot sauce in one form or another is in nearly every home and on the bar of nearly every restaurant across this land. Louisiana exports paprika even to Hungary! Natives have a sweet way of referring to black pepper as "aromatic," white as "bright," and red as "a burn." Pepper sauces range from hot, to hot hot, to the colloquial "Hot Damn!," and an evening in a local barroom will more likely end in a hot pepper-eating

contest than in a brawl. There are as many gumbos as there are peppers and cooks: chicken, ham, Andouille sausage, tomato, shrimp, and "tasso," a peppery ham similar to Texas jerky, and they are rich with peppers and myriad spices. Gumbo always begins with a roux, not in the classic manner of blending flour and butter, but using fat instead and cooking it until nearly burned. A devoted Cajun may "carry" her roux for close to an hour, wanting it rich and dark, just shy of scorched. This roux has a pronounced flavor, preferred to the lighter golden roux of the city. Cajuns rarely cook with wine; with such flavor, why would they want to!

One neighbor's variation on another's dish often comes about simply because one uses what is available. The local parishes are close-knit, and nearly all the locals are aware of the presence of a visitor in the neighborhood. A visitor at lunch or dinnertime is reason enough for celebration, the folk from nearby bringing fresh gifts from their gardens, or fish or alligator hooked and shot that morning. The people here have managed well by exchanging and sharing what they have. "We still live in an area where someone gives you their beans and you give them some of your crab."

Unlike jazz, which can sustain itself with but a few players, Cajun gumbo offers a full orchestra of ingredients. The recipes that follow tend to complement a featured ingredient, embellishing it and weaving supporting themes. This isn't necessarily typical of the character of gumbos made locally, served alongside heaping plates of sweets and sours. And just as local cooking neatly suits local taste, local technique is the cook's own vision of inherited tradition. A native of New Orleans or from down on River Road is likely to credit her recipes from "my old black mammy," but efforts to coax from a local just how she works out a dish may be rewarded with vague logic: "How long do you cook the okra?" "I put it on when I do the rice." "How long do you steam the rice?" "'Til dinner's ready." There is, somehow, a certain magic, a voodoo, in the fingers of cooks devoted to their work, and it is mystifying to observe the nonchalance of a Savannah cook who can stand, one hand on hip, trading tales and laughing a mile a minute while turning chicken and gesturing with a dripping two-pronged fork, casually bringing forth a mouthwatering masterpiece.

Eighteenth-century Louisiana acquired a diverse and unusual populace, and yet somehow managed to assimilate them all. At that time, Paris was clearing out her prisons and houses of correction, and many of these inmates flocked to the territory claimed by LaSalle for France in the 17th century. It was a dubious group that furthered settlement of this malaria-ridden backwash. By 1721, a German contingent had established itself on the west side of the river, and later, aristocrats fleeing the French Revolution sought refuge here (as did some footloose Parisian chefs, having seen their less fortunate employers carted off to the guillotine). New Orleans' *Vieux Carré* architecturally flaunts her Spanish ancestry (reflecting the change of hands when the French ceded their colony) with extravagant wrought-iron balconies from one end of the old city to the other. And with the Spanish came the spices and hot peppers of the pre-Columbians. By the mid-18th century, these various contributions were spawning yet another style, Creole, which emerged with the addition to Louisiana society of Haitians. By 1810, there were more than 100,000 French-speaking *gens de couleur,* and today French is taught throughout the Bayou, in part subsidized by the French government.

If Cajun is country food, then Creole is the food of the city. Creole society blossomed until the Civil War, and New Orleans-Creole fortunes were made and lost in cotton, sugar, and rice. Elegant town houses were fully staffed and stood ready for the merchant's visits to town, but the flavor of this era has been brought to our century more by the legacy of restaurants than of homes. Creole food is very sensual by comparison to the comforting, homey dishes typical of most of this country, and New Orleans jazz halls and turn-of-the-century restaurants are living reminders of a lush life.

New Orlean's old market runs parallel to Decatur Street and the River, and supplies most of the vendors and restaurants in the Quarter. Farmers arrive at dawn, having driven from as far as 150 miles away, and the array of their produce stalls reads like a recipe for gumbo: big red and green bell peppers, little baskets of yellow onions, strings of garlic, tin tubs of fresh herbs mingling the pungent fragrances of thyme, rosemary, mint, basil, cilantro, fennel, dill, tarragon, even cardoons (a member of the artichoke family, rarely seen in American markets). And the Creole tomatoes! Vine-ripened and bursting with juice, one plunge in hot water and these large, sweet-acid tomatoes slip obligingly out of their skins.

Fresh fishes and shellfish are the province of New Orleans dining. Descendants of Yugoslav immigrants continue to fish these coastal waters, where New

Orleans oysters, culled from the beds of Lac Barre and Barataria Bay, were as famous as the Chincoteagues of the Chesapeake, the tiny Culcaines of Puget Sound, and the Wellfleets of Cape Cod. It is tragic that many of the local beds have been lost, not to over-fishing, but to pollution, so that now oysters are farmed down on the lower Mississippi and shipped from Houma and Morgan City. Many of the oysters are farmed in the salt marshes and brackish waters of the Bayou, and when the spats reach maturity they may be moved four or five times to waters nearer to the Gulf, in order to take on the distinctive saline taste associated with good oyster eating. New Orleans offers oysters year-round, but it is in spring that the coast's oyster shacks and the city's oyster bars boast the most utterly luscious oysters; the females are plump with millions of eggs and the wobbly flesh just bursts on the tongue. (One must be wary, for not all oyster bars offer local bivalves, but rather serve up an Eastern imposter.) Quick to follow the oyster in season are the celebrated lake and river shrimp that find their way into gumbos and jambalayas, grilled in hot sauces, barbecued in unthinkable amounts of crushed black pepper and oceans of butter, stuffed into artichokes, dipped into rémoulades, coupled with merlitons in salads, or rolled into filleted catfish with capers and pecans, or with rockfish *en papillote*.

The fish markets are a feast of pompano, Spanish mackerel, grouper, redfish, speckled trout and fresh-water green trout, dainty croakers, soft-shell and blue crabs, green turtles, and sweet, ugly catfish. Catfish, the highest-priced fish in their markets after pompano, are in demand nationwide. Frog's legs are

conspicuous, often as heavy with meat as chicken legs. These bull frogs are as sweet and tender as any trio of *cuisses* that could be found in France's Loire valley.

Florida doesn't really feel like part of the Deep South; in fact, it seems more like a state of mind than a state at all. Parts of Florida, especially around the Keys, are very Hemingway-with-his-gin-and-lime—it's the heat, the humidity, the gingerbread Victoriana, the spark and danger of the drug trade, the palms. The interior is a green maze of swamps and rivers, miles of cattle ranches, citrus groves, and farm communities that supply much of this country with salad greens from November to June.

The northern part of Florida smacks of southern cooking, with its biscuits, corn breads, muffins, and pies. The Gulf shore, though, has a Caribbean feel to it—paellas, conch stews and chowders, coquina soups swimming with tiny shellfish no bigger than a fingernail, thick bean soups and chorizo sausages. And, naturally, rum was being drunk here before it reached New England. Cuba has a strong influence, and the yard-long, pale and crusty loaves with their fluffy interiors set a high standard. Because the dampness encourages mold, particularly in yeast breads, this Cuban custom of flour, salt, and water as a bread base is still the tradition. These Gulf Coast meals hark back to the Spanish-Cuban influence with such romantically named dishes as *Morros y Christianos,* Moors and Christians, made of black beans and white rice. Their fruit salads are served not as dessert but as part of the meal, composed of guava, mango, loquat, mammee-sapota, coconut, papaya, and cabbage palmetto. The favorite dessert remains the flan, many preferring a short-cut version produced by boiling an unopened can of condensed milk (what some of us fondly remember as a nursery treat).

The joy of a key lime pie is the key lime itself. The explosively-flavored zest and astringent juice combine to punch right through the sweetened cream. A facsimile of the key lime pie can of course be tried with ordinary limes, but the resulting flavor will be only a ghost of the original. And, the true pie has *always* been made with condensed milk.

A Red Dinner

BOILED CRAWFISH*
SHRIMP BOIL*
CAJUN RED RÉMOULADE SAUCE*
HOT PICKLED RED PEPPERS
CREAMERS
STRAWBERRIES WITH
BOURBON AND WHIPPED CREAM*

BEER or
SANFORD WINERY SAUVIGNON BLANC

Louisiana's lust for the spice and heat of pepper culminates in this red hell of a dinner. Natives are willing to eat river and lake shrimp and crawfish for breakfast, lunch and dinner. Boiled up in hot peppery shrimp and crawfish boil, they are eaten with this Cajun rémoulade, fiery red peppers, and creamers spiced with the same pungent boil—all washed down with beer, the only beverage that will quench the heat of all these spices. Local strawberries—their season lasts but a few weeks—are the most fragrant berries and taste the way strawberries should taste.

BOILED CRAWFISH

INGREDIENTS

4 cloves garlic, unpeeled
3 lemons, thinly sliced
1 cup chopped celery leaves
4 sprigs fresh parsley
3 medium yellow onions, sliced
1 package (3 ounces) shrimp or crab boil
7 pounds live crawfish

METHOD

Fill a large stockpot one-third full of cold water.
Add all of the ingredients except the crawfish and boil for 20 minutes.
Meanwhile, soak the crawfish in salted cold water for about 15 minutes; rinse.
Strain the stock and discard the vegetables.
Place the crawfish in the liquid and add water to cover, if necessary.
Bring to a rolling boil, reduce the heat and simmer for 15 minutes.
Drain and serve.
Note: The crawfish will become spicier the longer they sit in the liquid.
To make Boiled Shrimp, use 5 pounds shrimp instead of the crawfish and remove the shrimp as soon as they come to a boil.
Creamers (baby new potatoes) are the usual accompaniment, cooked in the same crawfish liquor.
Serves 5

CAJUN RED RÉMOULADE SAUCE

INGREDIENTS

½ sweet red bell pepper, roasted and peeled (see Basics, page 349)
1 cup homemade Mayonnaise (see Basics, page 345)
1 scallion, including some of the green, minced (about 2 tablespoons)
1 tablespoon minced lemon zest
¼ cup minced dill pickle
2 tablespoons chopped fresh or pickled hot peppers such as serranos, tabascos, or cayennes

1 tablespoon freshly grated horseradish
1 tablespoon capers—washed of brine, dried,
    and chopped
¼ cup chopped fresh parsley

TOOLS

Food processor

METHOD

Purée the roasted pepper with the mayonnaise in the
    food processor.
Add the remaining ingredients and purée until smooth.
Do not overbeat.
Chill for 30 minutes before serving.

Makes about 2 cups

STRAWBERRIES WITH BOURBON AND WHIPPED CREAM

INGREDIENTS

2 quarts ripe strawberries, with stems
½ cup bourbon
½ cup confectioners' sugar
1 cup heavy cream, whipped

METHOD

Wash the strawberries and leave the stems attached.
Drain.
Place the berries, bourbon, and confectioners' sugar in
    separate bowls.
Dip the berries in the bourbon and then in the sugar.
Serve, accompanied with the whipped cream.

Serves 5 to 6

Ghost Mansion Picnic

CREAMED CRAWFISH BISQUE*

ROAST CHICKEN WITH CORN BREAD
AND OYSTER STUFFING*

RICE SALAD WITH CORN

CHARLOTTE DU PLESSIS*

KISTLER VINEYARDS CHARDONNAY

This is not at all a traditional crawfish bisque. Usually the crawfish heads are stuffed with a mixture of spicy bread crumbs and crawfish fat and set adrift in the soup, but this is a nit-picking preparation that adds little to the essence of the dish. Crushed crawfish shells infuse the bisque with flavor, and the tail meat, fat, and tomalley enrich this cool, elegant soup. The ghost chicken (unphotographed) invisibly follows the bisque; it's really not a figment of the reader's imagination, and, indeed, a recipe follows. It is stuffed with seasoned corn bread, moistened with enough oyster liquor to keep the oysters plump. The elaborate Charlotte pays homage to a stately past. The suggested California sparkling wine is a delightful thirst-quencher, but a Creole undoubtedly would quaff quantities of French, and only French, Champagne.

CREAMED CRAWFISH BISQUE

INGREDIENTS

7 pounds live crawfish, cooked (see page 143)
¼ pound unsalted butter
1 medium yellow onion, finely chopped
1 celery heart, finely chopped
¼ teaspoon cayenne pepper
2 quarts heavy cream
Salt

TOOLS

Food processor

METHOD

Break the cooked crawfish in half and remove the
    tail meat and fat.
Reserve the shells and meat separately.
In a stockpot, melt the butter and sauté the onion and
    celery until wilted.
Add the cayenne, heavy cream, and reserved crawfish
    shells, heads, and fat.
Simmer over low heat for 45 minutes.
In a food processor, blend the shells with the cream.
Pass the soup through a fine sieve; discard the solids.
Add the reserved tail meat and chill until ready
    to serve.

Note: The bisque may be served hot.
The crawfish heads hold the fat which enriches
    the bisque.

Serves 6

ROAST CHICKEN WITH CORN BREAD AND OYSTER STUFFING

INGREDIENTS

STUFFING:
¼ pound unsalted butter
1 small yellow onion, finely chopped
2 celery ribs, finely chopped

2 cups crumbled Corn Bread (see recipe, omitting the
    vegetables page 250)
1 teaspoon finely chopped fresh sage
½ teaspoon chopped fresh thyme
½ teaspoon chopped fresh rosemary
¼ cup heavy cream
1 dozen oysters, shucked and drained with about ½ cup
    oyster liquor reserved
1 egg
Salt and freshly milled black pepper
2 whole chickens (each about 3½ pounds)

METHOD

Preheat the oven to 450°.
In a medium skillet, melt the butter and sauté the
    onions and celery until wilted.
Turn into a bowl and add the remaining stuffing
    ingredients.
Stuff and truss the chickens and set them on a rack in
    a large roasting pan.
Roast for 45 minutes, or until the thigh juices run
    clear. Serve at once.

Serves 6

CHARLOTTE DU PLESSIS

INGREDIENTS

CAKE:

Follow the recipe for Coconut Cake (page 121), sub-
    stituting ½ cup buttermilk for the coconut milk

FILLING:

3 cups heavy cream
6 egg yolks
6 ounces semisweet chocolate, grated
1 cup confectioners' sugar
¼ pound dry macaroons, crushed
¼ cup ground blanched almonds
¼ cup grated citron
1 cup sweet sherry
2 cups heavy cream, lightly whipped for the icing
Wild strawberries for decoration

METHOD

Make the cakes.
The fillings:
In a large heavy saucepan, bring the heavy cream to a
    boil over moderate heat.
Whisk the egg yolks until velvety and smooth and add
    to the cream, stirring continuously until the mixture
    thickens, about 5 minutes. (If the mixture sepa-
    rates, remove from the heat and beat in an addi-
    tional ¼ cup cream.)
Divide the mixture between 2 saucepans.
In one saucepan, mix in the grated chocolate, ⅓ cup
    of the confectioners' sugar, and the crushed
    macaroons.
Stir until well-blended and thick; set aside to cool.
In the other saucepan, add the ground almonds, citron,
    and the remaining ⅔ cup confectioners' sugar.
    Cook over moderate heat, stirring until thickened.
    Set aside to cool.
To assemble:
Divide the cakes into four ½-inch layers, trimming the
    bottoms and tops evenly.
Brush each layer with the sherry.
Set one layer on a platter and top it with half of the
    almond filling. Set the second layer in place and top
    with half of the chocolate filling. Alternate fillings
    and cake until all are used.
Frost the entire cake with the whipped cream and chill
    until ready to serve.
Decorate with wild strawberries.

Serves 8 to 10

Breakfast

CALAS *
CAFÉ AU LAIT

Calas was an early morning New Orleans snack, a hot, sweet-spiced rice cake fried crispy and served with the morning's café noir, or café au lait (that wonderful combination, half rich coffee and half hot milk). As New Orleans was going through her growing pains, this great breakfast drink was not only thought to be good for the health, but also a preventative for such infectious diseases as malaria. These Creole fritters were sold at the marketplace and at the railroad platform by ladies in gingham dresses with starched white aprons, who carried them in baskets, singing their vending song, "Belle Calas!"

CALAS

INGREDIENTS

½ cup long-grain rice
Salt
½ ounce fresh cake yeast or 1 package active dry yeast
3 tablespoons lukewarm water
2 eggs, separated
4 tablespoons sugar
⅛ teaspoon freshly grated nutmeg
⅛ teaspoon ground allspice
¼ teaspoon cinnamon
Grated zest of ½ lemon
½ cup all-purpose flour, sifted
Vegetable oil, for deep frying
Confectioners' sugar, for decoration

TOOLS

Deep-frying thermometer

METHOD

Boil the rice in salted water until soft and mushy.
Drain thoroughly and mash the rice until soft and creamy.
Dissolve the yeast in the lukewarm water and add to the rice.
Cover with a clean cloth and allow to sit overnight.
In a mixing bowl, beat the egg yolks until thick and creamy, gradually adding 2 tablespoons of the sugar.
Fold in the spices and lemon zest.
In another bowl, beat the egg whites with the remaining 2 tablespoons sugar until stiff and glossy.
Combine the egg yolks with the rice.
Sift the flour into the mixture and mix well.
Fold in the egg whites and mix just until no streaks show.
In a large deep heavy skillet, bring 1 inch of oil to about 365°.
One at a time, drop the mixture by teaspoonfuls into the hot oil and fry until golden, 5 to 7 minutes.
Drain on paper towels.
Dust the calas with confectioners' sugar and serve in batches of one or two dozen.

Makes 5 dozen calas

Boudin Lunch

TURTLE SOUP*
BOUDIN BLANC*
HOT SLAW*
STEWED TOMATOES
WITH OKRA*
PECAN PIE*

BEER or
AU BON CLIMAT CHARDONNAY

Turtle soup, or terrapin stew, is on a par with all of the gumbos—it is most popular and best when it comes to the table seasoned with the same generous hand, and after the same long simmer. It goes back to the 17th century when the area was settled, and they called it "mi-jeute," meaning "slowly cooked." Local turtles are brought live to the fish markets of New Orleans. As turtle meat is illegal in many states, one can substitute chicken, since the dish is a gumbo. Boudin is one of the most gossamer of all sausages, usually a blood sausage or veal sausage, with the consistency of clotted cream. The Louisiana translation substitutes a variety of meats and rice, so hotly spiced that it resembles the French version of boudin in name only. Rather than getting entangled with sausage casings, the simplicity of plastic wrap is an easy and effective alternative. Pecan pie is the quintessential end to this Southern meal.

TURTLE SOUP

INGREDIENTS

STOCK:

3 quarts Chicken Stock (see Basics, page 343)
2 pounds turtle meat
4 celery ribs, coarsely chopped with the leaves
2 medium carrots, coarsely chopped
2 cloves garlic, chopped
1 large onion, coarsely chopped
2 bay leaves
8 peppercorns, crushed
1 teaspoon fresh thyme leaves
1 teaspoon fresh rosemary leaves

SOUP:

¼ cup plus 1 tablespoon Clarified Butter
 (see Basics, page 344)
¼ cup plus 1 tablespoon all-purpose flour
1½ cups chopped celery
1½ cups chopped onions
1½ cups chopped green bell pepper
2 cloves garlic, minced
4 large tomatoes—peeled, seeded, and chopped with
 juice reserved (about 4 cups)
4 bay leaves, crushed
½ teaspoon ground allspice
½ teaspoon fresh thyme leaves
½ teaspoon chopped fresh rosemary leaves
Salt, freshly milled black pepper, and cayenne pepper
1½ to 2 tablespoons gumbo filé powder
Dry sherry

METHOD

The stock:

In a soup kettle, combine all of the stock ingredients
 and bring to a boil over high heat.
When the liquid begins to boil, reduce the heat and
 simmer, skimming the surface from time to time,
 for 1 hour.
Remove from the heat and reserve.
The soup:
When the meat is cool enough to handle, remove it
 from the liquid.
Strain the stock and return it to a clean soup kettle.
 Discard the solids.

With a sharp boning knife, remove any gristle or fat from the turtle meat. Finely dice the meat.

Add the meat to the strained stock and place the kettle over moderately low heat. Allow the soup to heat through but do not let it bubble. Reduce the heat if necessary.

In a heavy saucepan, heat the clarified butter over moderately low heat and whisk in the flour.

Continue to whisk until the mixture becomes thick and a rich brown color, about 7 minutes, adjusting the heat so the roux does not burn.

Add 1 cup of the simmering stock to the roux and continue to whisk until the mixture is smooth and thick. (Add a little more stock if necessary.)

Add the roux mixture to the stock and stir to blend.

Add the chopped vegetables and herbs. Season to taste with salt, pepper, and cayenne pepper.

Bring the soup to a low boil, reduce the heat, and simmer for 2 hours.

Check for seasonings and remove from the heat.

Just before serving, stir in the filé powder and serve in heated bowls, accompanied with dry sherry to be poured into the soup by the guest.

Note: Filé gumbo powder is a matter of taste. It should be added off the heat to prevent its becoming stringy.

A soup spoon of sherry is sufficient for each bowl of soup.

Fresh boiled or steamed rice quite often accompanies this dish.

Place the rice in each individual bowl and ladle the soup from a tureen at the table.

Serves 6 to 8

BOUDIN BLANC

INGREDIENTS

½ pound rabbit meat
½ pound lean pork
⅓ pound pork fat
1 cup heavy cream
1½ to 2 teaspoons cayenne pepper (depending on desired hotness)
¼ teaspoon dried rosemary, chopped
¼ teaspoon ground sage
¼ teaspoon dried thyme
⅛ teaspoon ground cumin
1 allspice berry, crushed
1 tablespoon chopped fresh parsley
1 teaspoon salt
½ cup packed soft-cooked rice
⅓ cup finely chopped onion
2 egg yolks
4 to 5 tablespoons butter

TOOLS

Meat grinder

METHOD

Grind the meats and pork fat together in a meat grinder.

Place the cream in a heavy saucepan and cook over very low heat until reduced by half.

Add all the spices and seasonings to the meat mixture and mix well.

Add the reduced cream, rice, onions, and egg yolks and mix again thoroughly.

In a large skillet over low heat, lightly simmer the boudin mixture for 10 minutes, stirring constantly.

Cool the mixture and stuff into lamb casings, or use the easy method that follows.

Place ⅓ cup of the mixture on a 7-inch square of plastic wrap.

Roll up the boudin mixture to make a 3½-inch-long sausage. Tie tightly with string at each end.

In a large pot of lightly boiling water, poach the boudin for 15 minutes. Remove and chill thoroughly. Remove the plastic wrap "casings."

In a skillet, heat the butter over moderate heat and gently cook the boudin until brown.

Serve immediately.

Note: Substituting plastic wrap for hard-to-find casings works very effectively. Test one boudin if you have not tried this method before.

The mixture may also be used to make small patties. If you choose this method, shape the patties after mixing all the ingredients and brown in the butter. It is not necessary to poach the mixture.

Turkey, chicken or partridge may be substituted for the rabbit.

Makes 12 small boudins

HOT SLAW

INGREDIENTS

2 cups heavy cream
¼ pound butter
1 small head white cabbage, cored and thinly sliced
  (about 4 cups)
½ red bell pepper, cut into julienne
1½ tablespoons Creole mustard
Salt and freshly milled pepper
1 tablespoon chopped parsley

METHOD

Place the cream in a saucepan and reduce by one
  half over moderate heat.
In a large pot, melt the butter over moderate heat.
Add the cabbage and toss to coat with the butter.
Fold in the red pepper julienne.
Continue to cook until the cabbage begins to wilt.
In a bowl, whisk the mustard into the reduced cream.
Season the cabbage with salt and pepper to taste.
Fold in the cream mixture and sprinkle with the
  chopped parsley.

Serves 8

STEWED TOMATOES WITH OKRA

INGREDIENTS

8 large ripe tomatoes—peeled, seeded, and coarsely
  chopped with the juices reserved
6 small okra, trimmed and quartered lengthwise
1 teaspoon sugar
Salt and freshly milled pepper
¼ teaspoon chopped fresh rosemary

METHOD

Place all of the ingredients in a medium saucepan over
  low heat and simmer for 15 minutes.

Serves 8

PECAN PIE

INGREDIENTS

PASTRY:

¼ pound plus 4 tablespoons unsalted butter
3 cups all-purpose flour
3 tablespoons sugar
2 egg yolks, lightly beaten
About ¼ cup ice water

FILLING:

5 whole eggs
1 egg yolk
1 cup packed light brown sugar
2 tablespoons butter, melted
2 teaspoons vanilla extract
2 to 3 tablespoons bourbon
3 cups pecan pieces, lightly toasted

1 cup heavy cream, whipped, for serving

TOOLS

9-inch pie pan

METHOD

The crust:
In a mixing bowl, cut the butter into the flour until it
  reaches the consistency of fine meal.
Sprinkle on the sugar and add the egg yolks and ice
  water.
Lightly blend together.
Form the dough into a ball, wrap in waxed paper, and
  chill for at least 20 minutes.
The filling:
Preheat the oven to 350°.
In a bowl, mix together all of the filling ingredients
  except the pecans.
Blend well.
Roll out the pastry on a lightly floured surface and fit it
  into the pie pan.
Evenly coat the pastry with the pecan pieces.
Pour the filling mixture over the nuts.
Bake for 1 hour, or until golden brown.
Cool to room temperature before serving with the
  whipped cream.

Serves 8

Creole Dinner

CREOLE OYSTERS*

SAUTÉED FROG'S LEGS*
MUSTARD GREENS AND CREAMERS

BREAD PUDDING SOUFFLÉ
WITH WHISKEY SAUCE*

DOMAINE LAURIER CHARDONNAY

This simple stew is nothing more than a reduction of cream and oyster liquor, with the addition of cayenne pepper to give it a Southern jolt. Cardoons are a Mediterranean vegetable. If you ever come across a cardoon, for heaven's sake buy it and think of a way to cook it; "Creole Oysters" was a dish inspired by the unexpected appearance of this vegetable in a New Orleans market. Jumbo frog's legs are as tender as butter and are accompanied with peppery mustard greens, blanched and sautéed in butter. Creamers, baby potatoes that, like the culls of New England, have been left in the fields after the harvest, usually are served with sour cream (which is how they came to be called "creamers"). Bread pudding is one of the favorite desserts of the Deep South, always served hot with a whiskey sauce or vanilla cream. In soufflé form it is lightened and airy.

CREOLE OYSTERS

INGREDIENTS

10 stalks cardoons, cut into 2-inch julienne
Juice of 1 lemon
6 cups heavy cream
4 dozen oysters, shucked with 1 cup of their liquor reserved
½ teaspoon cayenne pepper
2 teaspoons filé gumbo powder

METHOD

Peel and clean the cardoons. Set aside in cold water to cover with the lemon juice.
In a heavy saucepan, reduce the cream by half over moderate heat.
While the cream reduces, cook the cardoons in salted boiling water until tender.
Drain and keep warm.
Strain the oyster liquor into the reduced cream and reduce the mixture by one-third to about 2½ cups.
Add the cayenne.
Poach the oysters in the cream for 3 minutes.
Off the heat, stir in the filé gumbo powder or add a pinch to each serving at the table.
Drain the cardoons thoroughly and arrange them on a heated deep platter.
Pour the oysters and cream over the cardoons.
Serve in heated soup plates.

Serves 8

SAUTÉED FROG'S LEGS

INGREDIENTS

½ pound unsalted butter
Salt and cayenne pepper
16 frog's legs (each about 4 ounces)
1 cup all-purpose flour
2 tablespoons chopped fresh rosemary
1 cup dry white wine

METHOD

Preheat the oven to 250°.

Melt ¼ pound of the butter in a large heavy skillet.

Lightly salt half the frog's legs and sprinkle with cayenne.

Dredge lightly in the flour.

Sauté the floured frog's legs over moderately high heat until golden.

Sprinkle with half of the rosemary.

Keep warm in the oven.

Repeat the process with the remaining frog's legs and keep warm.

To deglaze the pan, add the wine and cook over high heat, scraping up the brown bits that cling to the bottom of the pan until the liquid is reduced by half.

Strain the sauce over the frog's legs and serve.

Serves 8

BREAD PUDDING SOUFFLÉ WITH WHISKEY SAUCE

INGREDIENTS

SOUFFLÉ:

Butter and sugar for the mold

4 eggs, separated and at room temperature

1 cup sugar

1 teaspoon vanilla extract

¼ teaspoon cinnamon

¼ teaspoon freshly grated nutmeg

4 cups milk

Pinch of salt

½ cup sultanas, soaked in enough dark rum to cover

½ cup chopped pecans

5 cups day-old French bread (from a large loaf, not a baguette), cut into 1-inch cubes

WHISKEY SAUCE:

1 cup heavy cream

2 egg yolks, at room temperature

2 tablespoons sugar

¼ cup bourbon

METHOD

The soufflé:

Preheat the oven to 350°. Butter and sugar a large deep baking dish.

In a mixing bowl, beat the egg yolks with ¾ cup of the sugar, the vanilla, and spices until thick, creamy, and lemony in color. Mix in the milk.

Place the cubed bread in a large bowl and pour the yolk/milk mixture over the bread. Set aside for 45 minutes.

In a bowl, beat the egg whites with the salt and the remaining ¼ cup sugar until stiff, glossy peaks form.

Stir the sultanas and pecans into the soaked bread and fold in the meringue.

Turn the mixture into the prepared mold and bake for 35 to 40 minutes, until puffed and golden.

The whiskey sauce:

Heat the cream over simmering water in a double boiler.

In a bowl, whisk the egg yolks with the sugar until thick. Off the heat, whisk the yolks into the heated cream.

Return the mixture to the double boiler and cook over simmering water, whisking constantly, until thickened enough to coat the back of a spoon.

Slowly add the bourbon and continue to cook until lightly thickened and smooth.

Serve warm with the soufflé.

Serves 8

Oyster Lunch

OYSTERS ROCKEFELLER *

IRON HORSE VINEYARDS BRUT
SPARKLING WINE

The less you cook an oyster, the more delicious it will be. Blanketing an oyster with crumbs or cream results in a smothered oyster. Of the many ways to serve oysters in the South, Oysters Rockefeller remains the most famous. It was invented around 1900 by Jules Alciatore, son of the founder of Antoine's Restaurant. With a glass or two of Champagne, it makes a delightful lunch or supper.

OYSTERS ROCKEFELLER

INGREDIENTS

FILLING:
1 pound spinach, washed and stemmed
4 tablespoons unsalted butter

3 scallions, chopped
2 large shallots, minced
1 clove garlic, minced
1 cup chopped fresh parsley
2 tablespoons dry vermouth
1 tablespoon heavy cream
1 tablespoon fresh lemon juice
1 tablespoon Herbsaint or Pernod
Few dashes of hot sauce
¼ cup fresh bread crumbs (optional)

Rock salt or kosher salt, for the oyster pans
2 dozen oysters, shucked and left in the half shell

TOOLS

2 large ovenproof pans or jelly roll pans
Food processor

METHOD

Preheat the oven to 400°.
Bring a large pot of lightly salted water to a boil.
Submerge the spinach in the water and drain
    immediately.
Melt the butter in a large skillet and sauté the
    scallions, shallots, and garlic over moderate heat
    until wilted.
Press any excess liquid from the spinach and add
    it to the pan.
Fold in the parsley and the remaining filling
    ingredients.
Purée the mixture in a food processor.
To assemble:
Cover 1 or 2 ovenproof pans with ½ inch of rock salt.
Nestle the oysters in the salt; it will keep them level.
Spread 1 tablespoon of the spinach mixture over
    each oyster.
Bake for 10 minutes, or until the edges of the oysters
    begin to curl.
Serve immediately.

Note: Do not wash the oysters after shucking
    in order to keep the saline flavor.
    Rock salt keeps oysters level and
    helps retain the heat.

Serves 2 to 3

Mackerel Dinner

BARBECUED SHRIMP*

BAKED SPANISH MACKEREL*

BURNT ALMOND AND
APRICOT ICE CREAM*

PEDRONCELLI VINEYARDS
ZINFANDEL

Barbecued shrimp is a simple dish, just a butter bath infused with quantities of pungent, freshly crushed black pepper—nothing more, nothing less. The shrimp are cooked in their shells and peeled at the table, the aromatic butter sopped up with hot, crusty bread and washed down with rich red wine. A Spanish mackerel, one of the Gulf fishes that is available in profusion, is an inelegant creature. Doctored up in this fashion, it's pretty tasty. And, for dessert, burnt almonds and apricots make an unearthly ice cream.

BARBECUED SHRIMP

INGREDIENTS

40 medium shrimp, in their shells
¼ cup crushed black peppercorns
1 pound butter, cut into bits and chilled
Juice of 2 lemons

METHOD

Preheat the oven to 400°
Wash the shrimp and dry with paper towels.
Spread on paper towels and let stand for 1 hour to dry out.
Place the shrimp in an ovenproof casserole and toss with the peppercorns.
Top with the butter.
Bake for 4 minutes.
Toss gently and bake for another 4 minutes.
Remove and place the shrimp under a hot broiler for 1 minute.
Remove, squeeze the lemon juice over the shrimp and serve.

Serves 4

BAKED SPANISH MACKEREL

INGREDIENTS

3 to 4 tablespoons melted butter
One 4-pound or two 2-pound Spanish mackerel, cleaned and gutted with head and tail intact
4 strips lemon zest
4 strips orange zest
1 sprig fresh rosemary
1 tablespoon chopped fresh rosemary
2 ripe tomatoes—peeled, seeded, and thinly sliced
2 dozen green and black Italian or Greek olives
Freshly milled black pepper
4 large scallions, thinly sliced
Two 2-ounce cans anchovy fillets, drained and patted dry

METHOD

Preheat the oven to 375°.

Place a piece of aluminum foil large enough to envelop the fish on a baking sheet. Line the foil with a large sheet of parchment paper.

Brush the bottom of the parchment with melted butter and place the fish on top.

Stuff the cavity with the citrus zest and sprig of rosemary.

Scatter all of the remaining ingredients except the anchovies on and around the fish.

Arrange the anchovies on top of the fish in herringbone fashion.

Tightly wrap the fish in the parchment and foil and bake for 10 minutes for every inch of thickness.

Place on a platter and serve.

Note: If you have two fish, place them side by side and cook together, in one package.

Serves 4

BURNT ALMOND AND APRICOT ICE CREAM

INGREDIENTS

1 quart English Cream (made with ⅓ cup sugar; see Basics, page 348)
2 cups dried apricots
⅓ cup bourbon
½ cup sugar
1 cup slivered blanched almonds

TOOLS

Food processor
Ice cream machine

METHOD

Chill the English Cream.

Place the apricots in a small saucepan. Cover with the bourbon and enough cold water to cover.

Simmer over moderate heat until the apricots plump up and soften. Cool.

Place the sugar in a small heavy skillet and melt over moderate heat, stirring with a wooden spoon just until it starts to caramelize.

Immediately remove from heat.

Fold in the almonds and pour onto a sheet of waxed paper.

Place the apricots in a food processor with ½ cup of the bourbon liquid and process, turning the machine on and off 5 or 6 times. The apricots should be chunky.

Place a sheet of waxed paper over the almonds and lightly crush with a rolling pin.

Stir the apricots and almonds into the English Cream and place the mixture in an ice cream machine.

Freeze according to the manufacturer's directions.

Makes 1½ quarts

Jambalaya

SHRIMP JAMBALAYA*
RICE TART*

LOUIS MARTIN WINERY
ZINFANDEL

Jambalaya, similar to a Spanish paella, is as famous a Creole-Cajun dish as gumbo. Howard Mitcham, who wrote a wonderful entertaining book entitled Creole Gumbo and All That Jazz, *suggests that the word "jambalaya is probably derived from 'jambon,' which means ham in both Spanish and French. The 'a-la-ya' is probably an African expletive which can be interpreted as either acclaim or derision." Though the tendency is to include a mess of spices, sausage, ham, and tasso as well as okra, I prefer this simple version which plays up the shrimp. Rice is traditionally incorporated and cooked into the jambalaya. I like it served on the side. The rice tart is entirely fabricated, a nice way to avoid yet another rice pudding!*

SHRIMP JAMBALAYA

INGREDIENTS

¼ pound unsalted butter
1 medium yellow onion, minced
4 medium cloves garlic, minced
1 cup very thinly sliced celery
3 green or red bell peppers—seeded, deveined, and cut into long julienne
4 to 5 semi-hot yellow finger peppers—seeded, deveined, and cut into long julienne
3 medium tomatoes—peeled, seeded, and thinly sliced
2 pounds medium shrimp, peeled and with tails intact
1 cup Fish Stock (see Basics, page 344), or shrimp stock
Salt and cayenne pepper

METHOD

In a large skillet, melt the butter over moderate heat.
Wilt the onions in the butter. Add the garlic and all of the vegetables and simmer over low heat.
When the vegetables are still slightly crisp, add the shrimp and the stock.
Bring to a simmer, season to taste, cover, and cook for about 5 minutes, until the shrimp are just cooked through.
Do not overcook the shrimp.

Serves 6

RICE TART

INGREDIENTS

PASTRY:
2½ cups all-purpose flour
3 tablespoons granulated sugar
⅛ teaspoon salt
¼ pound unsalted butter, chilled and cut into bits
About ¼ cup ice water

FILLING:
⅓ cup long-grain rice
4 cups milk
¼ teaspoon vanilla extract
About 1 cup heavy cream

4 eggs, beaten

¼ cup granulated sugar

Grated zest of 1 lemon

2 tablespoons grated citron

2 tablespoons peach preserves

3½ ounces marzipan

1 tablespoon confectioners' sugar

TOOLS

Electric mixer

12-inch fluted loose-bottomed tart pan

Aluminum baking weights (optional)

METHOD

The pastry shell:

Place the flour, sugar, salt, and butter in a
medium bowl.

Using an electric mixer on low speed, mix for about 8
minutes, or until all the butter is incorporated.

Slowly add the ice water until the pastry pulls away
from the sides of the bowl and adheres to the beater.

Shape the pastry into a ball, wrap in waxed paper, and
refrigerate for 30 minutes.

Preheat the oven to 375°.

Roll out the dough on a lightly floured surface.

Place the dough in the tart pan, fitting it evenly over
the bottom of the pan and pressing it against the
inside edges.

Roll a rolling pin over the pan to trim off the
excess dough.

Prick the dough all over with a fork.

Cover the pastry with aluminum foil and weigh down
with dried beans, rice, or aluminum baking weights.

Bake for 18 to 20 minutes, until the edges start to
turn golden.

Remove the beans and foil and bake 8 more minutes, or
until the pastry is lightly browned.

Remove to a rack and cool.

The filling:

In a small saucepan, cook the rice with the milk and
vanilla until tender.

Strain the milk and rice through a sieve into a large
measuring cup.

Add enough heavy cream to the milk to equal 2 cups.

Stir the eggs and sugar into the cream mixture.

Add the rice, zest, and citron to the cream. Set aside.

Evenly coat the bottom of the tart shell with the
preserves.

On a lightly dusted surface of confectioners' sugar, roll
out the marzipan to fit the bottom of the tart shell.

Place the marzipan over the preserves.

Fill the tart shell with the rice mixture.

Bake for about 50 minutes, or until the center is firm.

Remove from the oven and dust with 1 tablespoon
confectioners' sugar. Place under a hot broiler for 1
to 2 minutes, or until the surface is golden.

When cool, remove the sides of the tart pan.

Serve at room temperature.

Serves 10

Green Trout Dinner

BLACK BEAN SOUP*
SKILLET-BAKED GREEN TROUT*
TOMATO RICE PILAF*
SAUTÉED GREEN BEANS
CORN STICKS*
ORANGE AMBROSIA*
PRALINES*

LOUIS HONIG CELLARS
SAUVIGNON BLANC

Black bean soup and hot buttered corn sticks are a rich beginning to a meal. The Southern penchant for using sherry to flavor soups is their little signature of elegance. Sherry in soup is not everyone's preference; use it with a light hand or serve it on the side. Not every Southern fish is doused with sauce. This white, flaky fish is not a true trout, but a member of the weakfish, croaker, and redfish family, and any of these fishes may be substituted. Pralines are the sweet addiction of the South—as habit-forming as sipping lemonade while rocking away the afternoon on the porch. They should be served creamy soft and

fresh. A cool, citric ambrosia is a perfect foil for this Southern sweet.

BLACK BEAN SOUP

INGREDIENTS

1 pound dried black beans
6 ounces smoked bacon, diced
2 medium yellow onions, finely chopped
3 quarts Chicken Stock (see Basics, page 343)
⅛ teaspoon ground cloves
⅛ teaspoon ground mace
¼ teaspoon cayenne pepper
1 cup washed, chopped, and packed mustard greens
1 lemon, thinly sliced
Dry sherry

METHOD

Wash the beans thoroughly in cold water.
In a large pot, render the bacon until golden. Drain the bacon on paper towels.
Add the onions to the fat and cook until wilted.

Add the stock and beans, bring to a boil, and reduce
the heat to a simmer.

Add the spices and simmer for 2 to 2½ hours, until the
beans are soft.

Add the mustard greens and cook for 1 hour more.

Serve in warmed soup bowls with a thin slice of lemon.

Top with a soup spoonful of dry sherry at the table.

Serves 6 to 8

SKILLET-BAKED GREEN TROUT

INGREDIENTS

2 green trout (each about 3 pounds), gutted with heads
and tails intact and gills removed

Salt and freshly milled pepper

½ pound unsalted butter

METHOD

Preheat the oven to 375°.

Wash and dry the fish with paper towels.

Salt and pepper trout.

In two ovenproof skillets, melt the butter and set one
trout in each pan, stomach-side down, curling the fish
to fit the pan.

Baste with the butter and cook for 5 minutes over
moderate heat.

Baste the trout again and place in oven to cook for 15 to
20 minutes, until moist and tender.

Place on a heated platter with the pilaf and beans.

Serves 6

TOMATO RICE PILAF

INGREDIENTS

3 tablespoons butter

1 medium onion, chopped

2 cups long-grain rice

1 quart Chicken Stock (see Basics, page 343)

3 ripe tomatoes—peeled, seeded, and chopped

1 lemon, halved

¼ cup pecan pieces, toasted and salted (see Basics,
page 349)

METHOD

Preheat the oven to 350°.

Melt the butter in an ovenproof skillet and sauté the
onions until wilted.

Add the rice and stir.

Add the stock, tomatoes, and lemon.

Bring to a boil over high heat.

Cover and bake for 40 minutes. Let the rice rest five
minutes, or until the liquid is absorbed.

Serve sprinkled with the toasted pecan pieces.

Serves 6

CORN STICKS

INGREDIENTS

1 cup all-purpose flour

1 cup yellow cornmeal

1 tablespoon baking powder

1½ teaspoons salt

1½ teaspoons sugar

1 cup buttermilk or milk

2 tablespoons butter, melted

2 eggs, lightly beaten

Bacon fat

TOOLS

Cast-iron corn stick mold

METHOD

Preheat the oven to 400°.

In a large bowl, mix together the dry ingredients. Stir in the buttermilk, butter, and eggs.

Generously grease the corn stick mold with bacon fat and place in the oven for 5 minutes, or until smoking.

Remove the mold from the oven and spoon batter into each mold until one-third full.

Return the mold to the oven and bake for 12 to 15 minutes, or until golden.

Remove the cornsticks, regrease the mold with bacon fat and repeat until all of the batter is used.

Makes 1½ dozen cornsticks

ORANGE AMBROSIA

INGREDIENTS

12 navel oranges
½ cup Grand Marnier
1 cup shredded unsweetened coconut

METHOD

Slice the ends off of each orange, and remove all the peel and pith.

Slice each orange ¼ inch thick and arrange on a platter.

Sprinkle with the Grand Marnier.

Cover tightly with plastic wrap and refrigerate for at least 1 hour.

Remove 15 to 20 minutes before serving. Uncover and sprinkle with the shredded coconut.

Serves 6

PRALINES

INGREDIENTS

2 cups sugar
½ cup heavy cream
1 cup pecan pieces, toasted (see Basics, page 349)

TOOLS

Candy thermometer

METHOD

In a heavy saucepan, combine 1½ cups of the sugar and the cream over moderately high heat.

Stir the mixture until the sugar begins to melt.

Place the thermometer in the mixture and cook until it registers 220° or the soft ball stage.

Meanwhile, place the remaining ½ cup sugar in a heavy saucepan and stir constantly over moderately high heat until the sugar melts and begins to turn a golden caramel color.

Pour the hot cream mixture into the caramelized sugar and stir in the pecans.

With a large soup or dessert spoon, immediately spoon out the mixture onto a cool marble surface or onto a sheet of parchment paper.

Allow to cool.

Note: Pralines will keep for a week in an airtight container.

They are best served when fresh.

Makes 2 to 2½ dozen

Soul Food

CATFISH WITH SESAME SEEDS*

WHITE RÉMOULADE*

HUSH PUPPIES*

WATERMELON

PRESTON VINEYARDS
SAUVIGNON BLANC

Blacks ate differently from everybody else. From the "largesse" of their owners, and with the wild greens and roots they scavenged, they defied the meagerness of these offerings and created a cooking of their own, calling it "soul." The best catfish are the firm, sweet bullheaded ones from the channels of Louisiana. It's the ugliest fish in the fish kingdom but it fillets well and is close to sole in texture and flavor. Catfish has caught the fancy of the American public, and catfish farms from Texas to Arkansas are flourishing. Hush puppies are yet another corn bread invention of black cooks, a bread so rustic that it didn't make it into the formal lexicon of plantation recipes.

CATFISH WITH SESAME SEEDS

INGREDIENTS

1 pound catfish fillets
½ cup yellow cornmeal
½ cup all-purpose flour
Salt and freshly milled black pepper
¼ pound lard or unsalted butter
¼ cup sesame seeds, toasted in a dry skillet

METHOD

Wash and pat the fish dry with paper towels.
Cut the catfish diagonally into 1-inch strips.
In a shallow pan, combine the cornmeal, flour, and salt and pepper to taste.
Lightly dredge the fish in the cornmeal mixture.
Melt the lard in a large skillet and pan-fry the catfish until golden brown. Drain on paper towels.
Sprinkle the fish with the toasted sesame seeds.
Serve with White Rémoulade.

Serves 2 to 3

WHITE RÉMOULADE

INGREDIENTS

2 cups homemade Mayonnaise (see Basics, page 345)
1 clove garlic, finely chopped
4 scallions, including some of the green, finely chopped
1 tablespoon capers—washed, drained, and chopped
¼ cup finely chopped sour gherkins
½ teaspoon Worcestershire sauce
¼ teaspoon cayenne pepper
¼ cup finely chopped fresh parsley
3 anchovy fillets, mashed
Juice of ½ lemon

METHOD

In a bowl, whisk together all of the ingredients and chill for 1 hour before serving.

Makes about 2½ cups

HUSH PUPPIES

INGREDIENTS

½ cup white or yellow cornmeal
½ cup all-purpose flour
½ teaspoon salt
1 teaspoon baking powder
½ teaspoon sugar
1 egg beaten
About ¼ cup milk
1 jalapeño pepper, finely chopped
4 scallions, including some of the green, finely
   chopped
⅛ teaspoon cayenne pepper
Vegetable oil, for frying

METHOD

Sift the dry ingredients into a mixing bowl.
Add the beaten egg and enough of the milk to make a
   light paste.
Add the jalapeño pepper, scallions, and cayenne and
   blend thoroughly.
In a large heavy deep pot, heat at least 2 inches of the
   oil until it begins to smoke.
Drop the batter by tablespoonfuls into the hot fat and
   fry until golden.

Serves 2 to 3

Stone Crab Lunch

STONE CRAB CLAWS

MUSTARD MAYONNAISE*

GREEN SALAD

CUBAN BREAD

FRESH FRUIT SHERBETS*

KEENAN WINERY CHARDONNAY

Winter stone crabs, looking like bright red parrot heads with jet black beaks, are bought fully cooked because they are steamed and refrigerated aboard ship as soon as they are caught or at local crab houses. Only the claw of the crab is kept, and this crustacean is often thrown back into the sea to grow another. They are at their best served simply with the traditional mustard mayonnaise. Yard-long loaves of crusty Cuban bread are very much a part of Florida cookery, where the Cuban influence has been especially strong since the early 20th century. By and large, the cookery here is simple. In the sticky heat, what could be more refreshing than ripe, luscious fruits transformed into cooling jewels of sherbet.

MUSTARD MAYONNAISE

INGREDIENTS

4 egg yolks, at room temperature
1 teaspoon Dijon-style mustard
Salt and freshly milled pepper
1 tablespoon dry mustard
¼ teaspoon cayenne pepper
¾ cup mild olive oil
¾ cup vegetable oil
2 tablespoons fresh lemon juice
1 tablespoon boiling water

TOOLS

Electric mixer or food processor

METHOD

Place the egg yolks, mustard, salt, pepper, dry mustard, and cayenne in the bowl of a mixer or food processor and beat at high speed for 2 minutes, or until the mixture is creamy.

In a thin stream, gradually add the oils, beating all the while.

Add the lemon juice and adjust the seasonings to taste.

Add the boiling water and mix for 2 to 3 seconds, just until incorporated.

Refrigerate the mayonnaise in a covered container.

Serve the mayonnaise with very well chilled stone crabs.

Makes about 1½ cups

FRESH FRUIT SHERBETS

INGREDIENTS

FOR ORANGE OR GRAPEFRUIT SHERBET:

3 cups fresh squeezed juice
⅔ to 1 cup light Simple Syrup (see Basics, page 348, quantity will depend on the sweetness of the juice)

FOR LEMON OR LIME SHERBET:

1 tablespoon grated zest
1½ cups fresh squeezed juice
2¼ to 2½ cups light Simple Syrup (see Basics, page 348)

METHOD

In a bowl, combine the juice and syrup and chill
thoroughly.
Pour the mixture into the container of an ice cream
maker and freeze according to the manufacturer's
directions.

INGREDIENTS

*FOR PULPY FRUITS, SUCH AS MELONS,
MANGOES, OR PAPAYAS:*

2 to 4 ripe mangoes, papayas (or 1 melon)
¼ cup superfine sugar
Juice of ½ lemon

METHOD

Peel, pit, and seed fruit.
Cut the pulp into small pieces and toss with the sugar
and lemon juice. Chill for 20 minutes until softened.
Using a blender or food processor, purée the fruit
mixture; there should be about 4 cups of purée.
Chill for 20 minutes.
Pour the purée into the container of an ice cream
maker and freeze according to the manufacturer's
directions.

INGREDIENTS

FOR RASPBERRY OR STRAWBERRY SHERBET:

1 quart of berries: strawberries hulled and halved, or
raspberries left whole
Juice of 1 lemon
¼ cup superfine sugar

METHOD

In a nonaluminum saucepan, combine the berries with
the lemon juice and sugar over moderate heat. Bring
to a simmer, stirring from time to time, just until
the fruit begins to give off its juice.
Remove from the heat and purée in a food processor or
blender.
Pass the pulp through a sieve to remove the seeds.
Chill for at least 20 minutes.
Pour the purée into the container of an ice cream
maker and freeze according to the manufacturer's
directions.
Makes 1 quart

The Oyster Bar

There was a time when oyster bars offered up a platter of these succulent bivalves for the price of a five-cent beer. Times have changed, but the good oyster bars, scattered throughout the old quarter of town, serve forth these plump refreshers on shells still coated with the salty mud from the oyster beds. From morning until night you can step up to the counter and indulge in these luscious oysters, saucing them to suit your taste. Ketchup, horseradish, hot sauces, and lemons are set out on the bar to allow patrons to stir up their own concoctions.

Mandiche's Po' Boy

The po' boy was known as the peacemaker. After a night of hooch and jazz, the typical wayward husband brought home this toasted loaf of French bread filled with succulent fried oysters as an early Sunday morning peace offering to his wife.

MANDICHE'S PO' BOY

INGREDIENTS

SAUCE:

1 cup olive oil
1 head of garlic, peeled and finely chopped
3 scallions, including some of the green, chopped
1 teaspoon salt
¼ teaspoon freshly milled pepper
1½ teaspoons cold water
2 tablespoons dry sherry

SANDWICH:

½ loaf of French bread, halved lengthwise
3 tablespoons unsalted melted butter
1 quart vegetable oil, for deep-frying
1 dozen oysters, shucked
2 eggs, beaten
1 cup all-purpose flour
1 tablespoon chopped fresh parsley

TOOLS

Deep-frying thermometer

METHOD

The sauce:
Combine all of the ingredients except the sherry in a

medium saucepan and bring to a boil.

Reduce the heat and simmer until the garlic is soft.

Remove from heat and stir in the sherry. Set aside.

The sandwich:

Preheat the oven to 400°.

Generously brush the French bread with melted butter and place it on a baking sheet.

Bake for 10 minutes, or until the edges are brown.

In a deep pot, heat the oil to 365°.

Dip the oysters in the beaten eggs and pat them lightly in the flour.

Deep-fry until golden and crispy.

Drain on paper towels.

Quickly dip the oysters into the sauce and place on the bottom half of the French bread.

Sprinkle with the parsley and serve hot.

Serves 1

METHOD

Swirl the Herbsaint around the glass and discard any excess.

Place 6 to 8 ice cubes in a pitcher and pour in the rye, simple syrup, and bitters.

Stir briskly and strain into the glass. Add 1 ice cube.

Twist the lemon zest over the top of the liquor.

Serves 1

Sazerac

Of all the drinks to come out of the watering holes of the Delta and the Quarter—the fizzes, the punches, the café brulôts and café diablos—the Sazerac is without doubt one of the world's great mixtures, on par with the Negroni for taste and the Martini for the skill required to make it right. Originally the recipe called for the Sazerac glass to be lightly coated with absinthe (which of course is not available any longer) and Peychaud bitters, a Creole creation of Antoine Amedea Peychaud who brought his recipe from Haiti. The Sazerac was invented at the Sazerac Bar.

SAZERAC

INGREDIENTS

4 drops Herbsaint or Pernod
Ice cubes
3 ounces rye or bourbon
½ to 1 ounce Simple Syrup (see Basics, page 348)
4 to 5 dashes Peychaud bitters
Small strip of lemon zest

TOOLS

Cocktail pitcher and stirrer
1 double Old Fashioned glass

TOASTED PECANS

INGREDIENTS

1 pound shelled pecan halves
6 tablespoons butter, melted
About 1 tablespoon kosher salt

METHOD

Preheat the oven to 325°.

Toss the pecans with the melted butter and spread out on a baking sheet.

Toast, stirring, for about 10 minutes, or until the nuts begin to turn golden brown.

Remove and place in a paper bag.

Add the salt and shake.

Serve warm.

Makes 1 pound

"A mighty porterhouse steak an inch and a half thick, hot and sputtering from the griddle; dusted with fragrant pepper; enriched with little melting bits of butter of the most unimpeachable freshness and genuineness; the precious juices of the meat trickling out and joining the gravy, archipelagoed with mushrooms; a township or two of tender, yellowish fat gracing an outlying district of this ample county of beefsteak; the long white bone which divides the sirloin from the tenderloin still in its place." – from the writings of Mark Twain, while touring Europe in 1878.

America is commonly thought of as a nation overrun with cattle and gorged on wheat. Our anthem invokes "amber waves of grain," but the early years of the Midwest saw neither wheat nor beef. Instead there were patches of Indian maize, and waves of buffalo blackened the Plains. Wheat drifted to this region from the Atlantic coast in the early 1780s (Jesuits brought it to California as early as 1769) and it took vigorously. By the mid-19th century, the prairies of Illinois, Indiana, and Wisconsin were the great wheat producers; by 1870 the hard, matted grass of Kansas and Nebraska had turned to gold. Man can indeed live nearly by bread alone (although luxurious butter and wine do much to help). Entire nations depend on bread, and this country's Plains states remain, as they have been for more than a century, the "bread basket of the world." Many civilized cultures consider bread not a mere supplement to a meal, but the meal itself; wheat has always been the premier grain for bread baking here, containing as it does gluten, which helps the action of yeast to make a light, leavened bread. (Commercial wheat is grown principally for flour: common or "bread" flour, cake or "club" flour for pastries, and durum for noodles.) Wheat keeps well and travels well, and so was carried whenever possible by

settlers bound for wheat-scarce lands. Wheat was something the Puritans had missed, and was a prestigious addition the southern gentry insisted on adding to the menu. Pioneer wagons rolling over the grazing fields of the buffalo carried as much as 200 pounds of flour per family for their journey. The simple meal settlers ate when they paused along the trail was "journey" or "johnnycake." A sack of flour (wheat or corn flour) was "X-ed" with a knife, and water was poured in; as much flour as had absorbed the water was used immediately, baked on boards set next to an open fire (a variation on the "hoe" cake method of coastal settlers) or in hastily-assembled Dutch ovens (cast-iron pots with fitted lids, set right among the coals, like makeshift ovens). These various breads, the product of Indian and coastal settler know-how, would eventually travel the length and breadth of this country.

Wheat flour is our luxury grain and we have refined it more than any other. Huge quantities of the other cereal grains, such as corn, soybeans, oats, and barley, nourish us less directly as fodder for the animals on which we feed. Barley attracts particular attention, about one-quarter of the 500 million bushels grown every year used to produce alcoholic beverages. Barley is the base of beer, and malt (sprouted barley), the base of whiskey. We as a nation would sooner have one or the other than a bowl of barley soup, with or without the fillip of a lamb bone.

For the 19th-century American, the Western horizon seemed endless. The population of the East grew dramatically, the slave controversy in the South escalated all the while, and families of modest means were lured West in search of land and better lives. The Kansas-Nebraska Act of 1854 caused a homesteading fever that swept the country through every New England town and through every southern city. Wagons were loaded with carpetbags and trunks, supplied with tins of crackers, dried apples, pounds of flour, cornmeal, sugar, rice, and salt pork, and were drawn by ox or mule. No corner of the wagon was left empty, and some pioneers used even the family wooden washtub to plant little fruit trees for tending along the way. Indispensable for a family with children were live chickens and perhaps a cow. Babies screamed themselves to sleep to the bump of the wagon, and women often walked the entire journey, boarding the wagon now and again to churn butter to the heaving rhythm of the cart. As perilous as the journey was, the calamities in store for homesteaders were daunting—Indian raids, droughts, fires, hail storms, cyclones, rattlesnakes, wolves, outlaws, and nightmarish locust plagues. Farming has always had to contend with disaster. Kansas became a homestead focal point, the North wanting it "free" and the South hoping for another "slave" state. After the Civil War, the earlier pioneers were joined by the destitute, by freed slaves, and by widows with money to invest in land—all of them eager to start life anew, to build new homes and towns. Alexis de Tocqueville wrote on October 2, 1831, "Sparks said to me today: 'Landed estates in Massachusetts are no longer being divided up. The eldest always inherits the whole of the land'. 'And what happens to the other children?' I asked. 'They emigrate to the West'."

The life perfected by pioneer men and women was "making do", and many of the women transplanted from the cities to the plains found a very different life. "Woman's work" included seeding fields, herding cattle, tending animals, and washing, nursing, and feeding their young. The prairie woman became an expert marksman, not only to hunt, but to protect her brood as well. If married, her life was a partnership that equally shouldered the fearsome burdens of prairie survival. If alone, it was a partnership of one. The early Midwest diet was high in salt pork, fried beef, eggs, milk, butter, buckwheat cakes, potato cakes, johnnycakes, and sometimes a good dose of mercury from wells dug in the developing mining areas. Here again, corn was king, and every pioneer table served it as bread, mush, grits, or pudding (white flour so hard to come by that when available, its price was gold). Sorghum, the "sugar of the plains", was a sweetener, sometimes boiled down to syrup. In the mid-19th century this cereal ranked fourth after wheat, rice, and maize, and in time was used to fatten cattle before they were driven from the Texas Panhandle to Kansas.

In 1874, thirty-four Russian Mennonites were given free transportation by the Santa Fe railroad to Kansas, where the government had set aside an 8,000–acre tract to farm and build on. Among their few belongings was a jar of drought-resistant winter wheat

called "Turkey Red," later to become one of the most valuable strains of wheat farmed in this country. Other European immigrants would settle the Plains states: Germans flocked to Ohio and into Missouri, the Swiss to Wisconsin, the Dutch to Michigan, and the Swedes and Norwegians to Wisconsin as well as deeper into the Northern Regions. For some, emigration to the Midwest was merely a stop on the long haul to the very end of the continent. By the end of the 19th century, the United States was in an unprecedented state of flux. The railroads had opened the country, and with them came industrialization: huge corporations, assembly lines, wealthy developers, factories, and the lunch pail.

The same railroad that brought kegs of salted mackerel and barrels of fresh oysters to enhance the tables of the Midwestern well-to-do returned East with smoked buffalo tongues for restaurants and later for export to Europe as novelty food. The dairymen of Iowa and Wisconsin had overstocked cheese sheds filled with cheddars, blues similar to those of Scandinavia, and

wonderful imitations of Swiss, and so cheese veined the country following the railroad lines. By the close of the century, refrigerator cars, modeled after home iceboxes, were swiftly transporting perishables in every direction.

This was a new age of advertising. Packaged cake mixes found a ready market. Flour mills and baking powder and chocolate companies offered recipes with every purchase, appealing to the sweet tooth of their countrymen. American cookbooks proliferated, and Fannie Farmer was the cooking bible until Rombauer & Becker took her place in the 1930s. The American housewife was much taken with desserts, and her repertoire included dozens of versions of rich Devil's Food cake, marble cake, tea cake, spice cake, Angel Food cake, coconut and cream pies made only with thick cream and sugar. There were taffies, puddings, and junket transformed into countless gelatin salads (the *"pièce montée"* crowning the tables of a thriving middle class). The kitchen hearth was replaced by cast-iron, nickel trimmed cookstoves. Visitors to the

1893 Chicago World's Fair were dazzled by the first electric kitchen and by a "snack" called Crackerjacks. German wurst makers from Wisconsin put forth the frankfurter on a roll with mustard, and the hamburger on a bun was introduced at the 1904 St. Louis Fair.

In rural areas, the main meal was still usually served at home, at noontime. In the thriving cities (such as Chicago, the grain-receiving center for wheat farmers and on its way to becoming the meat-packing and shipping metropolis of the country) the custom became the lunch pail for the worker and dining out for the wealthy. Chop houses, restaurants, oyster bars, and saloons had a booming lunch business. With a nickel beer or shot of whiskey, the customer was offered "free lunch" and stuffed himself from a display of hams, ribs, beef roasts, sausages, herring, pickled eggs and pig's feet, stews, beans, and potato salad. From Boston to Denver, baronial luncheons were served from silver trays and tureens in oak-paneled halls resplendent with linen, china, crystal, and service to match. Equally plush were the dining cars featuring the fresh delicacies from the regions the trains crossed: crab imperial, oysters, and bisques on the Boston-Ohio, terrapin stews and barons of beef served up with potatoes on the Kansas and Pacific lines.

By 1850, the Kansas-Pacific line offered daily excursions into buffalo country, including refreshments and a guaranteed kill. An efficient sporting party could kill 20 to 50 buffalo in a day, and with the development of a Smith and Wesson rifle...the rest is history. Buffalo

were occasional nuisances to the railroads, which encouraged these excursions (sometimes trains had to wait three hours for a herd to pass over the tracks). But it was the buffalo that gave the Indian independence, a source of food, clothing, bedding, saddlebags, tepees, shields, utensils, and ornaments. Native Americans used every bit of the animals: the marrow-filled bones were roasted, the tongues smoked, flesh "jerked" (cut into long strips and sun-dried for winter use), and pemmican made with the addition of berries and nuts (just as natives of the East and North made pemmican with venison, elk, and moose). With dances and prayers preceding the hunt, they would kill with lances, knives, and bow and arrows only what was needed. The hunt ended with a feast of thankful celebration, honoring the beast which was God's gift to mankind.

When white hunters traveled to the Plains, it was to hunt buffalo. Four great herds once grazed as far north as Montana, down through Wyoming and Nebraska to Colorado and Kansas, to the Texas Panhandle. The U.S. Army encouraged white hunters with free ammunition. For expansion's sake, the buffalo or the Indian had to go, and it was easier to shoot the buffalo. A large beast of small intelligence, the buffalo must have been a pathetically docile target. When threatened, the bulls would encircle their cows and calves, facing their enemies and snorting and pounding the grass with their hooves. Heads bowed and facing away from the protected cows, they were an easy kill, dead center in the forehead. (Most of the buffalo skulls and horns that decorate homes of the Plains bear witness to this.) As each bull fell, his fellows would tighten their protective circle until all had been killed, leaving the defenseless cows for the final slaughter. The creature's hides were sold to tanners for lap throws, and buffalo steaks were more fashionable than the beef T-bone in the East. Taking only a haunch or two for their own provisions, the hunters left most of the dead buffalo to the wolves and vultures. When the hunting season of 1883 came to a close, the northern herd was wiped out. The remaining herds perished soon after. Gradually herds of cattle took their place in huge numbers, and land not used for grazing gave itself up to the farmer and his crops.

Breakfast

This simple child's breakfast is reminiscent of trips to my grandmother's, when she and I would go out to the hen house. We'd shoo the hens away and pull eggs from the nests, absolutely warm. They went straight to the kitchen and were boiled up for me. The memory of this creamy, rich, orange-yellow yolk is difficult to capture today except from the eggs of a free-range chicken. So-called free-range chickens demand a hefty price. It seems ridiculous; we pay more for a chicken that scratches around in the dirt, just as chickens have been doing for centuries, than for the factory-raised variety sold in supermarkets. Hot blueberry muffins are a delight for children of all ages, accompanied with a good glass of ice-cold milk.

JASON'S BLUEBERRY MUFFINS

INGREDIENTS

2 tablespoons butter, for coating the muffin tins
2 cups all-purpose flour
1 cup blueberries
1 tablespoon baking powder
1 teaspoon salt
⅓ cup sugar
2 tablespoons butter, melted
2 eggs
1 cup buttermilk
1 teaspoon grated lemon peel
1 teaspoon vanilla extract

TOOLS

12-cup muffin tin

METHOD

Butter the muffin tin with the 2 tablespoons butter. Set aside.

Preheat the oven to 400°.

In a small bowl, toss ¼ cup of the flour with the blueberries and set aside.

In a large mixing bowl, combine the remaining 1¾ cups flour, the baking powder, salt, and sugar.

Blend in the melted butter, eggs, and buttermilk. Mix until the flour is dampened. Add the grated lemon peel and the vanilla extract.

Fold in the blueberries and fill the muffin cups two-thirds full.

Bake for 20 minutes.

Allow the muffins to set for 2 to 3 minutes before removing from the pan.

Eat them while they are hot.

Makes 1 dozen

Steakhouse Meal

STEAK*

CHOPPED SALAD*

SARATOGA CHIPS*

FRENCH FRIED ONIONS*

CHEESECAKE

JORDAN VINEYARDS
CABERNET SAUVIGNON

Meat and potatoes were the sustenance of the Midwest. "We ate meat, lots of meat—always cooked to death. Potatoes, mashed or boiled, and a vegetable—never broccoli—beans! They were real cooked. The meat was right in front of you, facing your stomach—just set out like those divided plates." By the beginning of the 20th century, the Midwest had graduated from the frugal pork barrel to this: steak and potatoes, the most solid meal in American repertoire, simple American cooking at its best.

STEAK

Club steak, T-bone, porterhouse, shell, and sirloin steaks can be adequately pan-fried over high heat in cast-iron skillets with a little oil or butter. This method, however, is very smoky and tends to toughen the meat. The best method I have found for home cooking is to choose a well-marbled steak that is 2 to 2½ inches thick. Remove the meat from the refrigerator at least 45 minutes before cooking. Preheat the broiler and lightly brush the grill with oil. If the broiler is fueled by gas, set the rack 5 inches from the flame; if electric, the meat should be 3 inches from the heat source. Likewise, if cooking over charcoal, the coals should be a dusty red glow, and the grill lightly brushed with oil and set 5 inches above the coals. Sear the meat for 4 to 5 minutes on each side or until the cooked side is a rich light crusty brown. Do not allow to char or the meat will toughen. Place the meat in a preheated 325° oven and cook for 5 to 10 minutes, or until done to your preference. Experienced cooks can test for doneness by pressing the index finger into the center of the steak; for those less experienced, the best, but not most efficient way is to cut into the center with a sharp paring knife.

CHOPPED SALAD

INGREDIENTS

1 head garden lettuce, such as buttercrunch,
  loose-leaf, or oak leaf
1 medium-size red bell pepper—cored, seeded,
  deveined, and finely diced
2 ears fresh sweet corn, cooked and kernels removed
2 ripe tomatoes—peeled, seeded, and chopped
1 small cucumber—peeled, seeded, and chopped
1 celery heart, finely chopped
8 red radishes, chopped
1 tablespoon capers—washed, drained, and chopped
6 anchovies—drained and chopped
¼ cup olive oil
3 tablespoons high quality red wine vinegar
Salt and freshly milled black pepper

METHOD

Place the vegetables in separate bowls, cover, and
  refrigerate until ready to serve.
When ready to serve, combine the vegetables in a
  large mixing bowl with the capers and anchovies
  and toss with the oil and vinegar. Season to taste
  with the salt and black pepper. Serve cold.

Serves 4 to 6

SARATOGA CHIPS

INGREDIENTS

4 Idaho potatoes

1 quart vegetable oil
Salt

TOOLS

Deep fryer and basket

METHOD

Wash the potatoes under cold running water.
Peel off the skin and discard it.
Thinly slice the potatoes ⅛-inch thick.
Place the slices in a bowl of ice water and set aside for
  30 minutes.
Drain and dry thoroughly with paper towels.
Pour the oil into a deep fryer. Heat the oil to 360°.
Place about 1 cup of the potatoes into the oil and
  stir lightly.
Cook until the potatoes become a crisp golden brown.
Remove the potatoes and drain on paper towels.
Repeat with the remaining potatoes.
Sprinkle lightly with salt.
Place on a serving plate and serve hot.

Serves 4

FRENCH FRIED ONIONS

INGREDIENTS

4 medium-size Spanish onions, sliced paper-thin
½ cup all-purpose flour
1 quart vegetable oil
Salt

TOOLS

Deep fryer and basket

METHOD

In a large bowl, toss together the onions with the flour.
Pour the oil into a deep fryer and heat to 360°.
About 1 cup at a time, add the onions and fry until
  golden brown.
Drain the onions on paper towels and repeat the
  process with the remaining onions.
Serve hot.

Serves 4

Barbecued Ribs

Eating fast in the West is eating big and hearty. Even food-on-the-run is a substantial lunch, and no cool, dainty sandwich appears here. Connoisseurs maintain that the best barbecued meat is served in Texas, but the best barbecued ribs are in Kansas. Cole slaw, beans, or potato salad and a slice of white bread fill up the plate, and jalapeño pepper is a likely Southwestern garnish.

HANK COLEMAN'S BARBECUE SAUCE

INGREDIENTS

4 cups Ketchup (see Basics, page 346)
Grated zest of 1 large lemon
Juice of 2 large lemons
¼ cup Creole mustard (such as Zatarain's from Baton Rouge)
2 tablespoons Trapees Louisiana Red Sauce or 1½ tablespoons Tabasco sauce
¼ cup Worcestershire sauce
2 tablespoons molasses
2 tablespoons sugar
1 clove garlic, chopped
2 tablespoons red wine vinegar

TOOLS

Grill with mesquite charcoal, soaked chips, or wood
Tongs and basting brush

METHOD

In a large nonaluminum saucepan, combine all of the sauce ingredients and warm through over low heat. Do not allow to simmer or bubble.

Remove the sauce from the heat and set aside to cool until ready to use.

Prepare the grill and ignite the charcoal.

Place the sauce in an old metal pot and set close to the smoking fire to absorb the smoke flavor.

Note: The covered sauce on the side of the fire will continue to absorb the smoke which acts as a preservative. Stored airtight in the refrigerator, the sauce will keep for weeks.

The sauce may be used for 4 pounds of ribs (single or rack), a 4-pound brisket, or 3 halved or quartered chickens.

Makes about 5 cups

BARBECUED RIBS OR CHICKEN

METHOD

When preparing ribs for a grill, weave the cut ribs on a spit and if using a rack of ribs, coat the meat with the sauce before placing the rack directly on the grill.

Baste the meats frequently during cooking. The ribs should be placed about 6 to 8 inches above the coals and grilled for 40 to 45 minutes, or until evenly browned. Watch carefully and do not overchar, adjusting the level of the grill accordingly.

When grilling chicken follow the basting method above.

Evenly brown the cut chicken for 7 to 8 minutes on each side. Place the chicken pieces in a preheated 350° oven for 10 to 15 minutes, depending on the size of the pieces.

To "barbecue" in the oven:

Preheat the oven to 325°.

Place the ribs in a shallow baking pan and cover with half the sauce.

Bake the ribs in the center of the oven for 45 to 60 minutes, depending on the size of the ribs.

Baste frequently and serve with the remaining barbecue sauce.

OVEN-BRAISED BARBECUED BRISKET

INGREDIENTS

4 to 5 pound brisket, covered with ¼ inch of fat
Kosher salt and freshly milled pepper
¼ cup vegetable oil
2 cups Chicken or Beef Stock (see Basics, page 343)
Hank Coleman's Barbecue Sauce

METHOD

Preheat the oven to 325°.

Let the brisket come to room temperature.

Salt and pepper the meat.

In a large heavy skillet, heat the oil over moderately high heat.

Brown the brisket, fat side down, for 3 or 4 minutes, or until a crust is formed.

Turn and brown the other side.

Place the brisket in a shallow baking pan with the chicken stock and bake for 2 hours.

Coat the brisket on both sides with half of the sauce.

Return to the oven and continue to bake for 2 to 3 hours, or until tender.

Remove and let the brisket rest for 10 minutes before slicing.

Serve with the remaining barbecue sauce.

Lemonade

Lemonade is probably the most refreshing thirst-quencher I can think of for the hot months of July and August. It is something I associate with summers, laziness, reading a book, or doing nothing—a part of civilized life. It should always be made with pure lemon juice and sugar syrup—tangy and not sweet. The tongue should smart with more sour than sweet and the jaw should squeak a little when you drink it.

LEMONADE

INGREDIENTS

1 cup Simple Syrup (see Basics, page 348)
Juice of 6 to 7 lemons (1½ cups lemon juice)
Soda water (optional)

METHOD

In a pitcher, combine the simple syrup and lemon juice and chill until ready to serve.

Add 3 cups of soda water or ice water to the mixture and pour over ice in tall glasses.

Makes about 6 glasses

Thanksgiving

CHATEAU STE.
MICHELLE SEMILLON

SCALLOP STEW*
(see page 53)

STONY HILL CHARDONNAY

ROAST TURKEY WITH PAN GRAVY*

ALEXANDER VALLEY VINEYARDS
CABERNET SAUVIGNON

CREAMED ONIONS

HARGRAVE VINEYARDS
WHOLE BERRY PINOT NOIR

RUTABAGA AND APPLE PURÉE

MASHED POTATOES

CRANBERRY AND KUMQUAT
CONSERVE*
(see page 199)

NUT CONSERVE*

HEITZ CELLARS BELLA OAKS
CABERNET SAUVIGNON

YOUNG RED CHARD CHIFFONADE
SALAD WITH VINAIGRETTE AND
TOASTED SHAVED HAZELNUTS

MAYTAG BLUE CHEESE

VELLA DRY JACK CHEESE

NEW JERSEY GOAT CHEESE

AGED SHARP VERMONT CHEDDAR

ESSENSIA BY QUADY
(ORANGE MUSCAT)

PUMPKIN MOUSSE WITH
CRYSTALLIZED GINGER*

ELYSIUM BY QUADY
(BLACK MUSCAT)

HOT MINCEMEAT*
(see page 210)
WITH RUM HARD SAUCE*
(see page 348)

SCHRAMSBERG VINEYARDS
BLANC DE NOIRS

COFFEE

The tying of a few ears of maize to our doorways is a homey touch passed on to us by the Indians, symbolizing the celebration of the harvest. Every year, our country stops to reflect and give thanks and we do it all with family and friends, more often than not dining on a big turkey. I like to think of those comforting smells wafting through the house. It is the one day when most of us are usually eating the same celebratory meal, and usually too much of it. I love the idea of the proud golden bird brought to the table in all its succulent splendor. I like even more turning the turkey into sandwiches, hash, and soup. This meal is a rather odd assemblage of foods: root vegetables, creamed and puréed, sweet relishes and savory pies. Trying to match it with wines that complement the changing tastes of all these dishes is often difficult for the host. I suggest choosing one of the wines for each course if your guests number up to 12, and if you are entertaining a crowd, two wines for each course. One can safely avoid the problem and serve a sparkling wine throughout the entire meal.

ROAST TURKEY WITH PAN GRAVY

INGREDIENTS

12- to 14-pound turkey
6 to 8 cups stuffing (see page 46, or page 145)

FOR MAKING STOCK:
2 celery ribs, chopped
1 medium carrot, chopped
½ onion, chopped
2 parsley sprigs

FOR ROASTING THE TURKEY:
Vegetable oil, for basting the bird
2 celery ribs, cut in half
1 medium carrot, washed and cut lengthwise
1½ onions, peeled and halved

FOR THE GRAVY:
¼ cup all-purpose flour
Salt and freshly milled pepper

METHOD

Singe, wash, and dry the turkey thoroughly.

Remove the wing tips, and chop the gizzard and heart.

In a small saucepan, combine the wing tips, neck, gizzard, and heart, along with the vegetables for the stock. Add water to cover.

Bring to a boil over high heat, skim, and reduce the heat to a simmer. Continue to simmer for 1½ hours, or until the neck and bones have fallen apart. Add water as necessary to keep the ingredients covered with liquid. When the stock is cooked, strain, discarding the solids. There will be about 2 cups of stock.

Meanwhile, stuff and truss the turkey.

Preheat the oven to 450°.

Coat the bird with oil and place on a rack in a roasting pan and surround it with the roasting vegetables.

Place in the oven and immediately reduce the heat to 325°.

After the first 30 minutes, baste the bird every 15 to 20 minutes with the pan drippings and cover with a large sheet of foil when you begin basting.

Cook for 15 to 20 minutes per pound, or until the internal temperature reaches 180°, or until the juices run clear after piercing the leg joint with a kitchen fork. Remove the foil during the last 30 minutes to brown the bird.

Remove the bird from the oven and let rest while you prepare the pan gravy.

Pour off all but 2 tablespoons of fat from the roasting pan and place over moderate heat.

Blend in the flour and cook for 1 minute.

Add 2 cups of strained stock and cook, whisking constantly until the gravy is smooth, 8 to 10 minutes. Season to taste with salt and pepper.

Strain the gravy into a saucepan and keep warm until ready to serve with the bird.

Note: For a 12- to 14-pound turkey you will need 6 to 8 cups of stuffing. If making the corn bread stuffing, triple the recipe; if making the sausage stuffing, double the recipe. This menu works nicely for 12 to

24 persons. Rather than preparing an enormous bird, two smaller birds of 12 pounds each are more delicious and give you a choice of two stuffings. As time consuming as it is, a well-basted bird will be the tenderest bird.

Serves 10 to 12

NUT CONSERVE

INGREDIENTS

9 navel oranges, cut in half and thinly sliced
2 lemons—cut in half, thinly sliced, and seeds removed
1½ cups sultana raisins
4 cups chopped walnuts
1¾ cups white grape juice
¼ cup bourbon

TOOLS

Food processor

METHOD

Combine all the ingredients in a large heavy saucepan.
Bring to a boil and immediately reduce the heat to a simmer.
Cook, stirring from time to time, for 1¼ hours, or until the mixture is the consistency of marmalade.
Purée the conserve briefly in a food processor, about 6 turns on and off, to produce a chunky texture. Serve as an accompaniment to game meats and birds.

Makes about 2 quarts

PUMPKIN MOUSSE WITH CRYSTALLIZED GINGER

INGREDIENTS

1 teaspoon unflavored gelatin
¼ cup dark rum
4 egg yolks
½ cup sugar
1 cup pumpkin purée (a 2- to 3-pound pie pumpkin will yield 2½ to 3 cups of pumpkin purée)
¼ teaspoon cinnamon
¼ teaspoon ground mace
⅛ teaspoon ground cloves
2 egg whites
1 cup heavy cream, whipped
¼ cup crystallized ginger, cut into julienne, for decoration
Whipped heavy cream, for decorating and serving

TOOLS

3½- to 4-cup serving bowl
Electric mixer
Pastry bag with star tip (optional)

METHOD

In a double boiler, dissolve the gelatin in the rum over simmering water.
Remove from the heat and set aside.
Whisk the egg yolks with ¼ cup sugar until lemony in color and the mixture falls in ribbons from the whisk.
In a mixing bowl, combine the purée, the dissolved gelatin and rum, and the spices.
Blend well and fold in the yolk mixture.
Beat the egg whites in an electric mixer. When they begin to stiffen, gradually add the remaining ¼ cup sugar, continuing to beat until the whites form stiff glossy peaks.
Fold the meringue into the purée mixture.
    Gently fold in the whipped cream.
    Do not overblend.
Turn the mixture into the serving bowl and freeze for 10 minutes, or until set.
Place the bowl in the refrigerator for 2 hours, or until thoroughly chilled.
When ready to serve, sprinkle with the ginger julienne or decorate with additional whipped cream, piped on in a lattice fashion and dusted with the ginger.
Serve with additional unsweetened whipped cream.

Serves 6 to 8

Northern Regions

"After they had smoked the pipe, my father took a kind of drum which is used in charming (the antelope) and made music with it. It was our only kind of musical instrument which my people have, and is only used for antelope charming. Then two men who were messengers went out to see the antelopes. They carried torches (made of sage brush bark) in their right hands, and one carried a pipe in his left hand. This was done every day for five days and after the first day all the men and women and boys followed the messengers, and went around the circle where the antelopes were to enter. On the fifth day the antelopes were charmed and the whole herd followed the tracks of my people and entered the circle where the mounds were, coming in at the entrance, bowing and tossing their heads, and looking sleepy under a powerful spell. They ran round and round inside the circle just as if there were a fence all around it and they could not get out, and they stayed there until my people had killed every one."
—*Sarah Winnemucca, a member of the nomadic tribe of Paiutes* (WOMEN OF THE WEST, 1982)

The promise of big game was an irresistible lure to trappers and fur traders. These mountain men moved north, leaving behind them the buffalo of the Great Plains. The mountains of the northern regions were rife with beaver, porcupine, rabbit, hare, black bear, elk, antelope, and moose, and when the Lewis and Clark expedition reached the Yellowstone River in the spring of 1805, Lewis recorded, "we can scarcely cast our eyes in any direction without perceiving deer, elk, buffalo or antelopes." In the warmer months a mountain dweller could neatly dine on trout, fiddlehead ferns (from which they made, oddly enough, a sort of bread), and an abundance of wild mushrooms. The territory was brilliant with summer's currants—red, yellow, black, and purple grew sweet in the valleys and the tarter mountain currants grew along the craggy cliffs. Summer was an explosion of wild raspberries, blackberries, and choke-cherries, and apple and plum branches were heavy with fruit. Pioneers dried as many foods as they could to supply the long winter months ahead—fruits, of course, were saved and the walnuts, hazelnuts,

and butternuts that were to be found. In lean times the dried cherries, apples, and nuts either were mixed with a little flour and boiling water to produce a rude fruitcake or to dress a boiled bird or hare. Many folk sustained themselves on roots alone, among them the wild artichoke (similar to the Jerusalem artichoke) and the prairie turnip (or "prairie potato"), eaten raw or cooked. Elk and antelope were dried and jerked like the Plains buffalo, and early explorers found it excellent, if leathery, for strengthening teeth, though they rarely commended the taste.

The Great Lakes offered walleyed pike, whitefish, chub, lake herring, perch, eel, and catfish; the Snake, Clearwater, and Salmon Rivers, stretching from Wyoming to Idaho, ran with trout, bass, and salmon. (The parasite lampreys wreaked havoc in the Great Lakes, introduced to these waters by clinging to the hulls of ships entering the St. Lawrence Seaway. Elvars killed most of the Lakes' Mackinaw trout and cutthroat trout. Today these trout thrive in Jenny Lake, just outside Jackson Hole, where they were stocked as a precaution after their alarming decline in the Great Lakes. They are a chief delight of that seasonal sport, ice fishing. The success of these transplanted trout is similar to that of the coho salmon, native to the Pacific northwest, introduced to Lakes Michigan and Superior in the late 1960s, where it has done very well indeed.) Waterfowl and game birds once included all mannner of ducks, geese, grouse, pheasants, quail, woodcock, snipe, larks, and the sage hen or sage chicken. Some of the best sage hen hunting remains in Wyoming today. Larger than a chicken, smaller than a turkey, this bird feeds principally off wild sage. As soon as the sage hen is killed, the entrails as well as the feathers of this fragrant bird must be removed, else the flavor will be too high; in this respect the sage hen should be treated differently from other game birds, where hanging improves the taste, intensifies the flavor, and makes the meat more tender. Later Scandinavian and middle European settlers would marinate shore birds in sour milk or yogurt, which not only tenderizes the meat but also removes the fishy taste, a natural result of the birds' diet.

The "good berry" is the Chippewa Indian name for what is known as wild rice, one of North America's great luxuries. Wild rice is actually not rice at all, but rather a kernel from aquatic grasses that grow in shallow lake water. Minnesota became a preeminent reaper of this grain, and 90 percent of Minnesota wild rice is harvested just as the Indians have done for centuries. Skiffs and canoes slide through the tall grasses; the berries ripening at the tops of the reeds are hit with sticks, and the loose grains shower into the boats. Many fall back into the marsh, seeding next year's crop as well as feeding fish and fowl. Nowadays, wild rice farms use mechanical harvesters, equipped with wooden flails which knock the kernels into motorized skiffs. Perishable wild rice must be processed immediately. Roasting the grains gives them a dark, nutty color after the chaff has been separated by the polishing process. And because the grains ripen first at the very top of the stalk, the same plants must be harvested several times. It is no surprise, considering time and labor, that wild rice is perhaps the dearest grain.

Early trappers were a fearless breed, whose wanderlust drove them into the mountain regions for whole years at a time. Their comforts didn't exceed the usual supplies of flour, sugar, meal, coffee, whiskey, and tobacco, and they relied on their guns to provide meat. In summer, most trappers traveled down to the plains of Idaho and Utah, and to Jackson Hole, to sell their accumulated bundles of pelts to the fur merchants who journeyed from St. Louis to buy from them. The 1840s saw a wave of German immigrants fleeing one of the European potato famines; their first stop was Ohio, with many continuing on to Wisconsin and to the harsher climes of Minnesota and the Dakotas. The Germans were followed by the Scandinavians, Austrians, and Swiss. These immigrants brought with them a penchant for simple meals of potatoes: boiled, steamed, fried, or spooned into dumplings, and flavored with parsley, onion, and chopped bacon. They brought their sauerkraut to accompany a variety of wursts (which by 1910 would accommodate the growing American popularity of the "meal on the run"). Wisconsin has more varieties of excellent bratwurst and sausage than anywhere else in the nation, and wurst cook-offs attract as many devotees as Texas chili competitions. The Swiss made a variation of their *rösti* potatoes, cakes of moist shredded potatoes, caramelized with the smoky, dark maple syrup made by New Englanders gone west. The Swedes of Wisconsin would dish out *pitti panna* (a highly-seasoned hash of round ham and beef served with a raw yolk cradled in its shell), taking it with them as far as the Northwest coast.

About 1850, the occasional log cabin appeared in the foothills of these mountain ranges, and the plains of Nebraska and the Dakotas sprouted sod houses built with blocks of matted grass, roots, and mud. Some of these primitive domiciles were built into hillsides, incorporating the natural embankment as one or more walls. Since settlements were far removed from one another, isolation was a way of life and winter survival demanded self-sufficiency. One young pioneer woman commented on her life, "While I'm young this sort of life will be exciting, and when I get old I'll be used to it." Three generations later another young woman said, "Life in this part of the world has its rewards. We don't get to see many people. We will get in a car on a good day and drive 400 miles to the nearest French restaurant, just for a change."

The grasses of spring and summer have always produced prime quality beef for market. Lush grass and abundant water make the northern valley a natural haven for cattle and other livestock, but life in river country above the plains could be as devastating as in any other part of the wilderness. Spring's high-running waters were a constant threat to farms, livestock, homesteads, and the settlers themselves. The rushing waters pulled out bridges and tore away protective dams. Rivers and streams could change their course practically overnight, settlers finding themselves abruptly islanded, their livelihood demolished.

Ranchers along Wyoming's Snake River buy their calves in early spring. Today, vaccinated, branded, and fed on hay as winter recedes, the calves are turned out to feed on grass before sale in the fall. The cattle are rounded up before dawn, as quietly as possible so as not to excite them; once their adrenalin's going, they lose weight. The cattle are weighed, four or five at a time, at the ranch weighing shed. Buyers and sellers drink hot coffee and eat doughnuts, joking with one another and betting on the weight of the cows as the

animals are prodded onto the scales. The cattle are trucked off to Idaho feed lots, where they will be fattened on corn. (Grass-fed steer is tougher and less fatty than grain-fed, and though American taste runs to the grain-fed variety, these steer have a sweet, distinctive flavor.) Thus there really is no "local" beef eating in Wyoming, for to have native beef the animal would have to be sent to Idaho, slaughtered there, and shipped back. The rancher would do better to slaughter the cow himself for his own family needs.

Fall is the season to pickle and preserve summer's harvest. The growing season is short; spring rushes into summer, and by September winter is back. Thimbleberries, gooseberries, huckleberries, and plums are speedily put up in jams and conserves, along with sweet and pickled cherries, and Utah's peaches and pears. Garden vegetables and tomatoes are blanched, salted, and packed, and the wild mushroom hunter lays by a stock of cèpes, chanterelles, and morels.

An important source of food for many who live here, perhaps as much so today as in the past, is big game. Many a family lives off the elk, antelope, moose, black bear, mountain sheep, and deer that were bagged in autumn. (Elk is native to Wyoming and Montana and is eaten most often there.) Snow has already covered the ground when the hunting season begins. The hunter makes his way through the woods on cross-country skis; it's easier going for the hunter, but easier too for the prey to hear the approaching danger. Perhaps this makes for an even match at the outset, but carting home the kill is exhausting. The good hunter rarely shoots his game if he has seen the animal run more than 100 feet; fear causes an animal's adrenalin to peak, and to kill it then, would lend the meat a sour or "gamey" taste. There is more to hunting than proper aging and butchering! The elk herd is one of the greatest single sights in the northern valleys. On the drive from the airport to Jackson Hole during the winter, one might glimpse the herd of some 8,000 elk on the range, fed by the Fish and Game Preserve. The Preserve became a necessity because so many elk perished during the bitter winters. The starving creatures moved into the range, and the kindness of many a 19th-century farmer kept some of their number alive. It is not rare, either, for a moose to come lumbering

through the snow and up to a kitchen window, sniffing for a meal.

Big game is dressed immediately after shooting. Heart and liver are drained and cooled, then usually prepared and eaten fresh; the livers are roasted or made into sausages and pâtés, and the hearts grilled, or perhaps stuffed with dried fruits and nuts and roasted with a rich game sauce. Deer, elk, moose, and mountain sheep carcasses are aged for about a week before cutting and wrapping for the freezer. (Animals under a year old don't require aging.) Bull elk and bull moose are aged for a period of two weeks, and antelope prepared within three days of the kill will avoid the mushy texture typical of this meat. Immediate butchering and freezing are necessary of course for carcasses shot in warm weather, as well as for animals stressed prior to shooting or having suffered extensive wounds.

In butchering, virtually all fat is trimmed from the animal to avoid a "turn". (The meat can later be larded with pork fat.) Wild game fat quickly turns rancid, and this in part accounts for the "gamey" tang people seem to find so objectionable, but in game that has been properly butchered this needn't occur. There is a "best cooking method" for every cut of meat. As with game birds, marinades tenderize these meats and can enhance or even disguise (if that should be desired) the flavor. Big game cuts should be cooked according to the principles applied to the cow; the cuts are similar, if not the same. The shank, neck, and shoulder for stewing; the chuck, shoulder, leg, and breast for braising; rib steaks and loin chops for broiling, pan sautéing and grilling; and the whole loin and rib roasts for roasting. Braising and stewing should be done on low heat or low temperature for two to three hours to achieve a tender dish. Steaks and chops need only be browned and basted, and roasts need to be basted frequently at a temperature of 300° to 350°. Choice cuts such as these are best served very rare (when the internal temperature reaches 105° on a meat thermometer). Game flesh is tougher and leaner than domestic, and cooking these princely cuts rare will result in a tastier and juicier dish. Always defrost game meat in the refrigerator, and always serve it very hot or very cold. Small game birds are treated in the same way as big game. Hunters freeze the viscerated birds with feathers intact, just as they freeze fish in water with scales still on and, more often than not, ungutted; the result is a fresher taste. For the devoted hunter who loves to eat his "bag", this remains the best way to retain freshness and taste. The tradition of the trapper lives on in these regions. Bearskins and beaver pelts still bring in good prices, and local artisans make jackets, gloves, and shirts from deer, elk, and antelope hides.

Breakfast

FLAPJACKS*

MAPLE SYRUP

CRANBERRY AND
KUMQUAT CONSERVE*

COFFEE, HONEY, AND CREAM

The flapjack was breakfast food that traveled from New England straight across the country with the pioneers. Cranberries and the maple tree were not indigenous to New England only, but thrived in the northern regions, especially around Minnesota. Cranberries are served with the flapjacks as a winter fruit.

FLAPJACKS

INGREDIENTS

1½ cups all-purpose flour
1 teaspoon salt
2 tablespoons sugar
2 teaspoons baking powder
1¼ cups milk
2 eggs, lightly beaten
3 tablespoons melted butter

Butter, for cooking
Unsalted butter, warmed maple syrup, and Cranberry
   Kumquat Conserve, for accompaniments

METHOD

In a large mixing bowl, combine all of the dry
   ingredients.
Add the milk, eggs, and melted butter, and mix
   together. Set aside.
Melt 1 tablespoon butter in a large skillet, tilting to coat
   the entire bottom of the pan.
Using a two-ounce ladle, pour circles of pancake
   batter into the pan.
When the pancakes bubble, flip them over with a
   spatula and brown the other side.
Serve with additional butter, warmed maple syrup, and
   Cranberry Kumquat Conserve.

Makes sixteen 4-inch pancakes

CRANBERRY AND KUMQUAT CONSERVE

INGREDIENTS

20 medium kumquats, seeded and thinly sliced
1 pound fresh cranberries, washed and drained (about
   4 cups)
¾ cup maple syrup

METHOD

Combine all the ingredients in the heavy saucepan and
   bring to a simmer over moderate heat.
When the berries begin to pop, reduce the heat to very
   low, cover, and continue to cook, stirring from time
   to time to prevent sticking, for 10 minutes.
Remove from the heat and serve the relish warm with
   flapjacks, buckwheat cakes, game meats, birds, or
   sausages.

Makes about 3 cups

Rabbit Shortcake Supper

POTATO, LEEK, AND HAM SOUP*

RABBIT SHORTCAKE*

LA CREMA VINERA VIN GRIS

Long before the Idaho strain became prince of all potatoes, mountain settlers relied on the prairie potato, wild turnips, burdocks, cattails, ramp grass, and wild onions to make soups and flavor dishes. This creamy stew with bits of ham in it is a Swedish variation. Although rabbit has more nutritional value than chicken, it is quite often met with resistance. It can be a sweet, tender meat if properly cooked. Perhaps our fondness for Beatrix Potter gets in the way of our appreciation. I like rabbit, but when that first plate was set down in front of me I suddenly saw all my childhood dreams shot to hell.

POTATO, LEEK, AND HAM SOUP

INGREDIENTS

4 cups milk

1 ham bone or ham knuckle with ham

3 cups diced potatoes (use a combination of Idaho, Maine, and new-red potatoes)

¼ pound butter or ½ cup bacon fat

4 leeks—washed, split, and the white part cut into 2-inch julienne

1 cup chopped celery and celery leaves

2 tablespoons mustard seed, crushed

Salt and freshly milled black pepper

2 tablespoons all-purpose flour mixed with 2 tablespoons softened unsalted butter

METHOD

In a stockpot, simmer the milk with the ham bone and potatoes for 30 minutes, or until the potatoes are almost tender.

Meanwhile, melt the butter in a large sauté pan or skillet over moderate heat.

Add the leeks and cook until wilted.

Add the leeks to the milk mixture.

Add the celery and mustard seed to the soup and cook for 15 minutes.

Season to taste with salt and pepper.

Whisk in the flour and butter.

Remove the ham bone and flake off the ham.

Fold it into the soup and stir.

Continue to simmer for 10 minutes, or until the flour is completely dissolved.

Serves 4 to 5

RABBIT SHORTCAKE

INGREDIENTS

DOUGH:

4 cups all-purpose flour

2 teaspoons salt

2 tablespoons baking powder

2 scant teaspoons sugar

2 cups heavy cream

RABBIT:

1 large rabbit (about 5 pounds)
½ cup all-purpose flour
Salt and freshly milled black pepper
12 shallots, halved
1 cup fresh cranberries
4 medium parsnips, peeled and cut into
    2-inch julienne

SAUCE:

1 cup dry vermouth
2 cups Brown Sauce (see Basics, page 344), reduced
    to 1 cup
3 cups sour cream
½ cup heavy cream
¼ cup plus 1 tablespoon honey mustard
Freshly grated nutmeg
Salt and freshly milled black pepper
¼ cup chopped fresh parsley

METHOD

The dough:

In a mixing bowl, sift together the dry ingredients and
    fold in the cream.

Cover in waxed paper and chill until needed.

Preheat the oven to 350°.

The rabbit:

Cut the rabbit into small serving pieces.

Remove all of the fat and place it in a shallow ovenproof
    casserole. Place in the hot oven to render the fat.

Season the flour with salt and pepper and dredge the
    rabbit pieces in it.

Pour the rendered fat into a large heavy skillet set over
    moderate heat.

When the fat is hot, add the shallots and rabbit pieces
    and cook until browned on all sides. Transfer the
    rabbit and shallots to the shallow casserole.

Add the cranberries and parsnip julienne.

The sauce:

Remove any excess fat from the skillet and place it over
    moderate heat.

Add the vermouth and deglaze the pan, scraping up the
    browned bits that cling to the bottom.

Add the reduced brown sauce, sour cream, heavy
    cream, and honey mustard. Blend well and simmer.

Season to taste with nutmeg and salt and pepper.

Cook the sauce until reduced slightly and pour over the
    rabbit.

Sprinkle with the parsley.

Assemble the shortcake:

Either spoon the dough over the rabbit and sauce to
    cover, or on a floured surface, use your fingers to
    pat out the dough ½-inch thick, shaped to fit the
    casserole, and set the dough in place.

Bake for 45 minutes, until golden, and serve.

Serves 8 to 10

Game Pie Dinner

SMOKED LAKE TROUT WITH
SAUTÉED PEPPERS*

GAME PIE*

PICKLED SOUR CHERRIES

PEAR SNOW*

CHOCOLATE POTATO CAKE*

CLOS DU VAL CABERNET SAUVIGNON

Any old campaigner or trapper knew more about the art of survival and cooking in the wild than most hunters do today. At the end of the day, it was the fault of the hunter or his gun if he had not bagged a brace of birds. The smart hunter dried the spring morels, boletus, and chanterelle mushrooms in the fall, packing them alongside his provisions of dried fruits, salt, lard, and whiskey or rum. This is a genuine woodsman's game pie, following the hunter's adage that game is best put forth with the foods the animal himself eats. A brown sauce rich with the addition of game bones is added after the pie is baked, avoiding yet another soggy crust. Fluffy pear snow is complemented by brilliant put-up fruits from the last of summer's harvest. The cake is rich, dense, and very chocolatey, using potatoes, a traditional extender for the white flour that was expensive and so hard to come by.

SMOKED LAKE TROUT WITH SAUTÉED PEPPERS

INGREDIENTS

4 sweet green frying peppers
8 small yellow hot peppers
Olive oil
Salt and freshly milled black pepper
4 smoked trout, preferably boned with head and tail
    intact (each 6 to 8 ounces)
2 to 3 lemons, halved
Freshly grated horseradish

METHOD

Preheat the oven to 300°.
Cut both types of peppers lengthwise and remove the
    seeds and veins.
Lightly coat a heavy skillet with olive oil.
Sauté the peppers until they give off their juices
    and wilt.
Season to taste with salt and pepper.
Place the trout on a baking sheet and heat in the oven
    for 10 minutes.
Serve with the peppers, fresh lemon wedges, and
    freshly grated horseradish.

Serves 4

203

GAME PIE

INGREDIENTS

DRIED INGREDIENTS:
1 cup dried morels
½ cup dried cherries

BIRDS:
4 partridges (each about 1½ pounds) or 6 pounds of
    pheasant, quail, or Canadian goose breast
Salt and freshly milled black pepper
¼ pound unsalted butter

STOCK FOR GAME PIE:
2 quarts Brown Sauce (see Basics, page 344), reduced
    over moderate heat by half
Necks, gizzards, and hearts, from the birds
1 celery rib, coarsely chopped
1 carrot, coarsely chopped
1 bay leaf
6 peppercorns, crushed
5 juniper berries, bruised

VEGETABLES AND FRUIT:
1 leek, including some of the pale green—washed, split,
    and cut into 2-inch julienne; reserve the dark green
    stalks
24 pearl onions
2 large carrots, peeled and sliced diagonally
    ¼ inch thick
2 small white turnips, peeled and cut into
    ½-inch cubes
2 hard pears—peeled, cored, diced into ½-inch cubes,
    and tossed in the juice of ½ lemon
2 recipes Pie Dough, made with lard (see Basics,
    page 346)
1 egg, beaten with 2 tablespoons cold water, for
    egg wash

TOOLS

Poultry shears
Large chef's knife or cleaver
Boning knife
9-inch loose-bottomed tart pan with 2-inch sides

METHOD

The dried ingredients:

In a bowl, soak the dried morels in warm water for about 2 hours.

In another bowl, soak the dried cherries in warm water for about 1 hour.

The birds:

Wash the birds and pat dry with paper towels.

Lightly salt and pepper the cavities of the birds.

Melt the butter in a large heavy ovenproof skillet.

Brown the birds evenly on all sides. The meat will be rare. Set aside to cool.

Remove and allow to cool.

Using poultry shears, cut the birds lengthwise in half, splitting the breast.

Cut away the backbone.

Remove the wing tips and feet with a chopping knife or cleaver.

Remove the upper wing bone from the breast portion.

Remove the thighs and legs from the frames with a sharp boning knife.

Cut the legs from the thighs.

Remove the breast meat from the frame.

Reserve all the bones and cut the meat into bite-size pieces: do not remove the meat from the legs. Cover and reserve the meat.

The game stock and vegetables:

Place the bones in a stockpot with all the remaining stock ingredients. Add ¼ cup of the water from the soaking morels and ¼ cup water from the soaking dried cherries. Add the reserved dark green leek stalks and salt and pepper.

Bring to a boil. Skim, reduce the heat, and simmer for 1 hour.

Strain the sauce through a fine sieve into a saucepan; discard the solids and reserve the sauce.

In a saucepan filled with boiling water, blanch the vegetables separately for 1 minute each. Start with the leeks first, then the onions, then the carrots, and end with the turnips. Cool under cold running water. Set aside with the pears.

To assemble the pie:

Preheat the oven to 400°.

Divide the pie dough in half.

On a floured surface, roll out one half about ¼-inch thick.

Line the tart pan with the dough.

Toss the meat with the blanched vegetables, drained morels and cherries, and the pears.

Fill the pan with the mixture.

Roll out the top crust. Moisten the sides of the dough with egg wash and set the top crust in place. Trim and crimp the dough, pressing down lightly on the edges of the pan.

Roll the pastry scraps and make a braid to fit around the exterior rim. Make leaves and berries to decorate the top.

Brush the top of the pie with the egg wash and cut a small round hole in the center of the pie. Decorate the hole with more braid and coat the decoration with egg wash.

Set the pie on a baking sheet and bake for 50 minutes, until golden. If the crust browns too quickly: cover loosely with foil.

To serve, remove the sides of the pan, leaving the pie on the false bottom. Reheat the game sauce. Set the pie on a serving platter and funnel hot game sauce through the opening on top.

Serves 6

PEAR SNOW

INGREDIENTS

5 cups peeled, cored, and cubed pears, preferably
    Anjou (about 5 large pears)
Juice of ½ lemon
½ cup sugar
12 peppercorns—crushed, wrapped, and tied in a
    double thickness of cheesecloth
1 tablespoon unflavored gelatin
2 tablespoons Aquavit or peppered vodka
3 egg whites, at room temperature

TOOLS

Electric mixer
5-quart decorative mold
Food processor

METHOD

Place the pears in a large nonaluminum pot with the
    lemon juice and enough cold water to cover.
Add the sugar and peppercorns and simmer over
    moderate heat until tender. Allow to cool thoroughly.
Meanwhile, place a 5-quart mold in the freezer
    to chill.
In a double boiler over hot water, combine the gelatin,
    Aquavit, and 2 tablespoons of the pear liquid. Cook
    until the gelatin dissolves. Set aside to cool.
Drain the pears of their liquid. Remove and discard the
    peppercorns and purée the pears in a food pro-
    cessor until velvety and smooth.
In a bowl, beat the egg whites until stiff, but not dry.
With an electric mixer, beat the gelatin mixture into
    the pear purée and fold in the beaten egg whites.
    Turn the mixture into the chilled mold and freeze for
    15 minutes, until set.
Refrigerate the snow for 4 hours.
Unmold and serve with the Chocolate Potato Cake and
    the put up fruits.

Serves 10

CHOCOLATE POTATO CAKE

INGREDIENTS

Butter and flour, for the loaf pans
½ pound unsalted butter, at room temperature
2 cups sugar
¼ cup unsweetened cocoa powder
4 ounces unsweetened chocolate, melted
3 eggs
1 cup cooked mashed potatoes (about 2 medium
    potatoes)
1 teaspoon vanilla extract
1 cup milk
2½ cups all-purpose flour, sifted
2 teaspoons baking powder

TOOLS

2 medium loaf pans
Electric mixer

METHOD

Butter 2 medium loaf pans and dust with flour, shaking
    to discard any excess.
Preheat the oven to 350°.
In a mixing bowl, cream the butter and sugar with an
    electric mixer.
Add the cocoa powder and blend. Stir in the melted
    chocolate.
One at a time, add the eggs and beat until smooth.
Add the mashed potatoes and blend well.
Add the vanilla and blend well.
Alternately add the milk and dry ingredients until the
    mixture is smooth.
Divide the batter between the prepared loaf pans.
Bake for 35 to 40 minutes, or until the cake pulls away
    from the sides of the pans. Unmold onto a rack and
    allow to cool thoroughly before slicing. Cover and
    refrigerate any leftovers.

Makes 2 loaves

Hunters' Dinner

FRESH FRIED TROUT

ELK ROAST WITH WILD RICE

**CRANBERRY AND
JERUSALEM ARTICHOKE FRITTERS***

WILD CURRANT JAM

**VENISON MINCEMEAT WITH
CANDIED FRUITS***

RUM HARD SAUCE
(see Basics page 348)

PORT AND COFFEE

**STERLING RESERVE
CABERNET SAUVIGNON**

or **GRGICH HILLS
CELLAR CHARDONNAY**

Game supports many a northern family, and is put away in freezers or sometimes frozen outside and used as the winter wears on. Fresh-caught trout deserve a quick fry in butter. Catching a 5- to 6-pound trout is not unusual here, and it's such a meaty fish that it often is served as a main course. The finer cuts of elk, antelope, moose, or deer should be served rare; short cooking time results in a more tender meat. It's difficult to get a good head of lettuce up here in winter, but with put-up fruits, vegetables and preserves, you're not as limited as you might think. The Jerusalem artichoke is a versatile tuber that can be shaved directly into salads or boiled and dressed with hollandaise; here, it's grated into a fritter batter with cranberries. Homemade mincemeat is sturdy enough to last a season or two under refrigeration, and homemade candied fruit retains more zest than any store-bought variety.

CRANBERRY AND JERUSALEM ARTICHOKE FRITTERS

INGREDIENTS

FRITTER BATTER:

2 eggs, separated
¼ teaspoon salt
2 tablespoons granulated sugar
¾ cup milk
1⅓ cups all-purpose flour
3 to 4 gratings of nutmeg

2 cups fresh cranberries
Confectioners' sugar, to coat the berries
1 Jerusalem artichoke—peeled, grated, and soaked in
    water with 2 tablespoons lemon juice
Vegetable oil, for frying
Granulated sugar, for serving (optional)

TOOLS

Deep-frying thermometer

METHOD

In a mixing bowl, beat the egg yolks until creamy.
Add the remaining batter ingredients but not the egg
    whites and mix well. Set aside for 1 hour.
Coat the berries in confectioners' sugar.
When ready to make the fritters, beat the egg whites
    until soft peaks form and fold into the batter
    mixture.
Drain the artichoke and dry thoroughly.
Stir the berries and grated Jerusalem artichoke into
    the batter.
In a large heavy skillet, heat 1½ inches of oil until
    almost smoking (365°).
Using a teaspoon, drop the fritter batter into the hot
    vegetable oil and cook for 3 to 4 minutes, or until
    golden brown.
Sprinkle with granulated sugar if desired, and serve.

Makes 2½ to 3 dozen fritters

VENISON MINCEMEAT WITH CANDIED FRUITS

INGREDIENTS

VENISON AND STOCK:

4 pounds neck or shoulder of venison
1 bay leaf
8 to 10 whole cloves
8 peppercorns
4 juniper berries
1 small cinnamon stick
3 cups apple cider
1 cup cider vinegar

CANDIED CITRUS PEEL:

Peel of 6 oranges
Peel of 8 lemons
Peel of 8 limes
4½ cups sugar

MINCEMEAT:

1 pound suet, minced or ground
1 quince—peeled, cored, and diced
4 apples—peeled, cored, and diced
2 pounds sultana raisins
2 pounds currants
½ pound candied lemon peel, reserved from above
½ pound candied orange peel, reserved from above
4 cups dry sherry
1 cup Cognac
1 tablespoon ground cloves
1½ teaspoons freshly grated nutmeg

TOOLS

Meat grinder
Ceramic or glass crock

METHOD

The venison:
In a large stockpot, simmer the venison with all of the
    stock ingredients and water to cover until tender,
    about 1½ hours.
Drain, reserving the liquid. Shred the meat or grind
    through the fine blade of meat grinder.

The citrus peel:

Cut the orange peel into ¼-inch squares.

Place the peel in a saucepan with water to cover and boil for 15 to 20 minutes.

Drain and repeat the process 3 more times.

In a medium saucepan, combine ¾ cup water and 1½ cups of the sugar. Cook until the sugar dissolves and add the orange peel. Cook for 15 minutes, or until translucent.

Remove the peel with a slotted spoon to a sheet of waxed paper. Allow to cool.

Reserve the sugar syrup for the mincemeat mixture.

Repeat the process with the remaining fruits and peels.

When all of the peels are dry, reserve ¼ cup of each to serve with the completed mincemeat.

Make the mincemeat:

In a heated bowl or pot, combine the shredded or ground venison with the suet, 3½ cups of the reserved meat juice, and the remaining mincemeat ingredients.

The mixture should be loose; if necessary, add an additional cup or two of Cognac.

Place the mixture in a large, or makeshift, double boiler and cook over boiling water for 4 hours, until thick.

Place the mincemeat in a crock and cover or put up in sterilized jars.

Allow to stand in a cool or refrigerated place for a month or longer before using.

Check the mincemeat from time to time.

If too much liquid is absorbed and the mincemeat is dry, add additional sherry or a combination of sherry and Cognac.

To serve, heat in a double boiler and serve with Rum Hard Sauce and candied fruit peels, or serve hot in miniature tart shells.

Note: Tart Shells, see Basics, page 346. Rum Hard Sauce, see Basics, page 348.

Makes about 6 quarts

Festive Dinner

GAME SOUP WITH PEARS*

ROAST PHEASANTS WITH
BUFFALO SAUSAGES AND
SPARKLING CIDER SAUERKRAUT*

MICHIGAN POTATO CAKE*

CARAMEL DUMPLINGS*

ROBERT HUNTER BLANC DE NOIRS
SPARKLING WINE

It's a foolish cook who throws the carcass in the garbage. Crush the bones and store them in the freezer until you have enough to make a good, rich stock—basic for a variety of game soups and sauces. Though the sauerkraut can be prepared with cider, sparkling cider is drier and less sweet. A handful of ranchers raise buffalo, and the meat of grass-fed buffalo cows is as sweet and lean as that of grass-fed cattle before they've been sent to corn feedlots. This sausage makes a nice change from pork. Dumplings here, again reflect the influence of the northern Europeans, are flour dumplings, steamed with sugar and spices, coated with caramel syrup, and with a grating of lemon and orange zest for relief; it's a nice lift, if a desperate one.

GAME SOUP WITH PEARS

INGREDIENTS

STOCK:

3 pheasant cacasses or 6 partridge carcasses
3 celery ribs, roughly chopped
3 carrots, roughly chopped
10 peppercorns, crushed
2 bay leaves
1 teaspoon dried thyme
1 teaspoon dried sage
1 teaspoon dried rosemary
8 juniper berries, bruised
4 sprigs fresh parsley
3 quarts Chicken Stock (see Basics, page 343)
Salt
2 medium onions, halved

SOUP:

3 carrots, peeled and cut into 2-inch julienne
3 medium leeks, washed well and cut into 2-inch julienne
2 hard winter pears, such as Bosc or Seckle

METHOD

The stock:

Break up the carcasses of the birds and place them in a large soup kettle.

Add all of the remaining stock ingredients except the onions and bring the stock to a boil over high heat.

Place a black cast-iron skillet over high heat. Add the halved onions, flat side down, and cook until blackened. Remove the skillet from the heat and add the onions to the soup kettle.

Reduce the heat to low and simmer for 1 hour.

Strain the soup into a large pot.

Simmer the stock over moderately high heat.

Add the carrots and the leeks.

Thinly slice the pears from stem to base.

Add the pear slices to the soup. Simmer for 3 to 4 minutes, or until the pears begin to wilt. Serve hot.

Note: The game stock can be prepared in advance and can also be frozen.

Serves 6

ROAST PHEASANTS WITH BUFFALO SAUSAGES AND SPARKLING CIDER SAUERKRAUT

INGREDIENTS

6 pounds sauerkraut, washed in cold water to remove brine and squeezed dry
3 thick slices smoked bacon
1 medium-size yellow onion, diced
1 tart apple, diced
2 quarts sparkling cider
1 tablespoon caraway seeds
2 pheasants (each about 3 pounds)
¼ pound unsalted butter
8 juniper berries, bruised
2 fresh or dried sage sprigs
2 pounds buffalo sausage links
¼ cup finely chopped fresh parsley

METHOD

Preheat the oven to 325°.
When the sauerkraut is washed and the moisture removed, fluff the sauerkraut strands and reserve.
In a large skillet or saucepan, render the bacon fat but do not allow the bacon to crisp or brown.
Remove the bacon to an ovenproof casserole.
Add the onions to the rendered fat and sauté until wilted. Add the apple and sauerkraut.
Pour in the sparkling cider and bring to a boil over moderate heat. Mix in the caraway seeds.

Transfer the sauerkraut mixture to the casserole with the bacon. Cover the casserole and bake for 3 hours, tossing the mixture every hour.
Remove and keep covered.
To cook the pheasants:
Preheat the oven to 425°.
Melt the butter in a heavy ovenproof skillet.
Divide the juniper and sage between the cavities of both birds.
Truss the birds.
Brown the birds evenly on all sides.
Place the skillet in the oven and roast for 30 to 40 minutes, until the juices run pale pink.
While the birds are cooking, prick the sausages and cook them in a heavy skillet with about ½ cup water until browned.
To serve, cut up one or both pheasants.
Arrange the meats attractively over the sauerkraut and dust with the chopped parsley.
Note: The sauerkraut can be prepared up to a day in advance. Bring to room temperature and reheat on stove top.

Serves 6

MICHIGAN POTATO CAKE

INGREDIENTS

10 large Idaho potatoes
1 pound unsalted butter, clarified, (see Basics, page 344), or a combination of butter and lard
Salt and freshly milled black pepper
½ cup maple syrup
¼ cup chopped fresh parsley

METHOD

Boil the potatoes in their skins in lightly salted water.
Cook for about 15 minutes, or until a paring knife easily pierces the outer part and the knife meets resistance about ½ inch into the potato.
Drain, cool, and refrigerate.
Peel the potatoes and shred on a grater.
Pour half of the butter into a large 15-inch skillet.
Heat the butter over moderately high heat and add the shredded potatoes.

Sprinkle liberally with salt and pepper.

Push the stray shreds in from the rim of the pan and pat the top into a large pancake.

Reduce the heat and cook, shaking and rotating the pan to loosen the potatoes.

Drizzle a few tablespoons of butter around the inner rim of the pan.

Continue to cook for 15 minutes. Invert the skillet and slide the potatoes out of the pan onto a large plate.

Slide the pancake into the skillet, cooked side up, and drizzle the remaining butter around the inner rim. Drizzle in the syrup in the same manner.

Continue to cook until golden.

Use a rubber spatula and lift from the edge when checking for doneness.

Sprinkle with the parsley and serve.

Note: This recipe is virtually the same as *rösti* potatoes, with the addition of maple syrup.

Serves 6 to 8

CARAMEL DUMPLINGS

INGREDIENTS

DOUGH:

1 cup all-purpose flour, sifted
2 teaspoons baking powder
⅛ teaspoon salt
Grated zest of 1 lemon
1 egg, beaten
⅓ cup milk
1 tablespoon unsalted butter, melted

POACHING LIQUID:

1½ cups brown sugar
2 tablespoons unsalted butter

CARAMEL SAUCE:

1½ cups granulated sugar
½ cup heavy cream
3 tablespoons unsalted butter
Grated zest of 1 lemon
Grated zest of 1 orange

METHOD

The dumpling dough:

In a mixing bowl, combine the dry dough ingredients with the lemon zest.

Mix in the egg, milk, and melted butter and beat just until the batter is smooth.

The poaching liquid:

In a large saucepan, dissolve the brown sugar and butter in 2 cups water and bring to a simmer over moderate heat.

The caramel sauce:

Place the granulated sugar in a heavy saucepan and melt over low heat, stirring constantly with a wooden spoon until the sugar is dissolved and becomes a golden brown.

Add the heavy cream, stir in the butter, and mix until smooth.

Reserve.

The dumplings:

Working in batches if necessary, use a large oval soup spoon to drop the dough by spoonfuls into the poaching liquid.

Cover and cook for 5 minutes.

Turn the dumplings over and cook, covered, for 3 to 5 minutes more.

Remove with a slotted spoon, place one dumpling on each serving plate, spoon the caramel over, and sprinkle with the lemon and orange zests.

Makes 8 to 10 dumplings

Winter Picnic

WILD MUSHROOM SOUP*
SMOKED TROUT SCONES*
CHOCOLATE SNOW*
APPLES AND RAT CHEESE
LENA'S GLÖGG*

Expeditions into the woods by dogsled, skis, snow-shoes, and snowmobiles can become pretty elaborate. Fires are built, steaks are grilled, potatoes are fried; but I prefer not cooking at all and find packing up scones flecked with smoked trout, thermoses of hot spiced wine and wild mushroom soup, some apples and dependable store-bought rat cheese equally satisfying. Chocolate snow is one of winter's pleasures, not unlike the hot maple syrup New Englanders drizzle into snowbanks where the syrup hardens into crystalline webs.

WILD MUSHROOM SOUP

INGREDIENTS

1 pound fresh morels or boletus mushrooms (American cèpes), or substitute 2 ounces dried morels, 2 ounces dried cèpes and ¾ pound fresh button mushrooms
3 cups Chicken Stock (see Basics, page 343)
1 cup heavy cream
2 tablespoons all-purpose flour mixed with 2 tablespoons softened unsalted butter
Salt and freshly milled pepper

TOOLS

Food processor

METHOD

If using dried mushrooms, plump them in the stock for about 1 hour before cooking.
In a large heavy saucepan, place the stock and the mushrooms over moderate heat.

Bring to a simmer and continue to cook for about
15 minutes.

Drain the mushrooms, reserving the stock. Strain the
stock through a double thickness of dampened
cheesecloth and return it to the saucepan.

Coarsely chop the mushrooms in a food processor,
pulsing 4 or 5 times. Do not purée; they should be
chunky.

Return the chopped mushrooms to the stock and add
the cream.

Bring to a simmer over moderatly low heat and whisk
in the flour-butter mixture.

Season to taste with salt and pepper and cook for
about 10 minutes, or until the flour dissolves.

Serve immediately.

Serves 4 to 5

SMOKED TROUT SCONES

INGREDIENTS

8 ounces smoked trout, finely flaked
¼ cup finely chopped scallions, including scme
of the green
Grated zest of 2 lemons
2 cups all-purpose flour
2 tablespoons baking powder
2 tablespoons cold unsalted butter
2 eggs, lightly beaten
½ cup heavy cream
1 egg, beaten with 1 tablespoon cold water, for egg wash

TOOLS

Electric mixer (optional)

METHOD

Preheat the oven to 400°.

In a bowl, combine the trout, scallions, and half of the
lemon zest. Set aside.

Sift the flour and baking powder into a mixing bowl.

Cut the butter into bits and rub it into the flour by hand
or with an electric mixer.

Combine the eggs, cream, and the remaining zest and
mix into the flour mixture. Do not overmix.

Divide the dough in half.

On a lightly floured surface, roll out each portion of
dough ⅓-inch thick.

Cut one piece of dough into triangles that measure
3 inches a side.

Place 1 tablespoon of the trout mixture in the center of
each triangle.

Paint the edges of each triangle with the egg wash.

Cut the remaining dough into triangles.

Top each of the filled triangles with dough and crimp
the edges with a fork.

Brush the top of each scone with the egg wash.

Place the scones 2 inches apart on one or two baking
sheets and bake for 15 to 20 minutes, or until
golden.

Makes 8 scones

CHOCOLATE SNOW

INGREDIENTS

8 ounces semisweet chocolate

TOOLS

Double boiler

METHOD

Chop the chocolate into small pieces and place them in
the top of the double boiler. Fill the bottom of the
double boiler with water and set the top in place.

Set over moderately high heat and bring the water to a
  simmer.

When the chocolate melts, remove from the heat.

Dip a fork into the chocolate and flick the chocolate
  over the snow in a back and forth motion. Do this
  several times to make a lattice of chocolate over the
  snow. Carefully pick up the lattice from the top of
  the snow and eat.

Note: This may be prepared over a camp fire.

LENA'S GLÖGG

INGREDIENTS

2 quarts dry red wine
8 cardamom pods
5 whole cloves
1 small cinnamon stick
Zest of 1 lemon cut into strips
Zest of 1 navel orange cut into strips
1 cup sugar
12 to 18 whole blanched almonds
¼ cup raisins
6 to 8 ounces Aquavit

TOOLS

1 dozen 4-ounce glasses
1 dozen small silver spoons

METHOD

In a nonaluminum kettle, combine the wine with the
  cardamom, cloves, cinnamon, orange zest and
  lemon zest. Stir to mix and set aside to steep
  overnight.

Next day, add the sugar and warm the mixture over
  very low heat until the sugar has dissolved and the
  mixture is hot, about 15 minutes.

Place 1 almond and 2 or 3 raisins in each glass.

Add about 1 tablespoon of Aquavit to each glass and
  place a silver spoon in each.

Pour the hot wine into the glass and serve.

Makes 12 to 18 servings

RANGE FOOD

Beef Jerky

*Jerky was never meant to be incorporated into a
dish. The meat (elk, antelope, deer, or beef) is cut
into ribbons, salted and left out in the sun to dry.
Dishes such as creamed dried beef came along
later, using meat cured by a process much less
severe. This was saddlebag food that sustained the
woodsman from the North and the cowboy of the
Panhandle. When you hold a piece of this meat in
your hand, you say to yourself, "My God, how
unappealing," and then as you actually begin to
chew it, it all juices up, becomes quite delicious,
and makes a lot of sense.*

Southwest

"When they left the rock or tree or sand dune that had sheltered them for the night, the Navajo was careful to obliterate every trace of their temporary occupation. He buried the embers of the fire and the remnants of food, unpiled any stones he had piled together, filled up the holes he had scooped in the sand. Since this was exactly Jacinto's procedure, Father Latour judged that, just as it was the white man's way to assert himself in any landscape, to change it, make it over a little (at least to leave some mark of memorial of his sojourn), it was the Indian's way to pass and leave no trace, like fish through the water, or birds through the air.

"It was the Indian manner to vanish into the landscape, not to stand out against it. The Hopi villages that were set upon rock mesas were made to look like the rock on which they sat, were imperceptible at a distance. The Navajo hogans, among the sand and willows, were made of sand and willows. None of the pueblos would at that time admit glass windows into their dwellings. The reflection of the sun on the glazing was to them ugly and unnatural—even dangerous. Moreover, these Indians disliked novelty and change. They came and went by the old paths worn into the rock by the feet of their fathers, used the old natural stairway of stone to climb to their mesa towns, carried water from the old springs, even after white men had dug wells."— DEATH COMES FOR THE ARCHBISHOP *by Willa Cather. 1927, Alfred A. Knopf*

The old-time cowboy was a rough-and-tumble loner who smelled of his horses and cattle, and whose sweaty life was romanticized until it became the stuff of children's dreams. He was a different breed of settler, drawn west by the promise of work, inheriting horse and longhorn steer from the Conquistadors before him. In the 1830s, the cowboy worked miles from the ranch, making his home with the herd on a range millions of acres across. He packed his saddlebags well with *charqui* (Spanish for the leathery Indian jerky that passed for countless meals) and carried among his staples of coffee, tobacco, and ammunition a treasured keg of sourdough starter. Sourdough traveled well, and the starter could take the pounding abuse of long days in the saddle. These basics sustained the lone horseman until he rejoined his outfit. A chuckwagon followed the

herd, a veritable pantry on wheels stocked with flour, cornmeal, salt, cured pork, lard, sugar, coffee, cane sugar syrup, and one vegetable: dried beans. The round-the-clock beverage was coffee, made black and strong enough to "float a horseshoe." Meals offered pretty much the same unchanging bill of fare, whether they were breakfast, lunch, or dinner: bacon, steaks from a steer slaughtered on the range fried in lard, and chicharrones (fried pork rinds which today are packaged like potato chips).

Chuckwagon cooks could manage to drum up some variety for the boys, after the best cuts of meat went to the foremen and owners. A notorious fiery stew was made from beef tripe, marrow, brains, kidneys, lungs, and heart, boiled together with spicy chiles. It was a very Texan dish, called "cowboy" stew in polite society, though cowhands knew it only as "son-of-a-bitch." There were beans *ad infinitum*—pinto, red, pea, and lima—often all cooked up into a heavy porridge and sopped up with biscuits or corn breads produced in makeshift Dutch ovens. At meal's end, a keg of smoky

cane sugar syrup was passed around to be poured over the last of the bread, a habitual quick dessert still common. A rare "real" dessert might be put forth, perhaps an egg pie, sweetened with molasses, in a sourdough crust. Stick-to-the-ribs meals answered the demand of heavy work in 115° heat. Most dishes reflected, if only subtly, the influence of the Spanish and the Indians. The barbecue, one of many Latin American methods adopted by the Spanish, would become popular on the range, as the cowboys often worked too far away to get back to the ranch.

The longhorns were driven from the grasslands of southern Texas to market in the Panhandle, Oklahoma, and southwestern Kansas, a journey that took months. The more slowly the steer crossed these territories, grazing on rich summer grasses as they went, the fatter they would be when they reached the rowdy cow towns of Wichita, Dodge City, and Abilene. This trip was perilous, with every likelihood of ambush by rattlesnakes, Indians, cattle rustlers, and horse thieves, and the cowboy valued his gun as dearly as he did his outfit's chow cook. Dangers notwithstanding, the demand for beef in the East spurred Texas to achieve an even stronger foothold as the nation's cattle domain. The cowboy's long cattle drive ended with the sale of the herd in one of the legendary cow towns, where most hands squandered their hard-earned wages on drink and roughhousing to celebrate the end of the trail. By 1900, the heyday of the cattle drive was over, and railroads were shipping cattle-on-the-hoof to Chicago and New York where demands for meat verged on gluttonous. The cattle barons were rolling in wealth, and wherever they went were trailed by bank robbers, cattle thieves, horse thieves, train robbers, and gun fighters who found the waistcoated entrepreneurs easy targets.

Texas can be thought of as one big country pieced together from four sections: east, central, south, and west Texas. Every section champions its own ways in the kitchen, so it's easy to see how a Texan might get into a heated argument when a supposedly "authentic" barbecue or chili is announced. Almost everyone has the "only" recipe. Most agree that typical barbecue meats include pork back ribs, short beef ribs, brisket, chicken, sausage, pork loin, and baby pig, but as for method, accompaniments, and sauces—the field is open to dispute. In east Texas, they like a thick, sweet barbecue sauce brushed on the meat before cooking over oak and hickory, smacking of the South particularly when accompanied by black-eyed peas, baked beans with ham hocks, or beans cooked to a mush with hot sauce à la Creole. Central Texas favors mesquite and charcoal in addition to oak and hickory, and their beans-and-sausage comes to the table with sliced tomatoes, onions, and pickles. Mesquite is currently something of a buzzword; like green oak, it gives off extraordinary heat. The wood comes from a succulent tree, whose roots pull nearly every drop of water from the surrounding soil. Mesquite fuel results in a moist heat that flavors meat distinctly but doesn't dry it out. The wood is taken for granted in Texas, regarded simply as a local convenience, but it is prized as a status fuel in the restaurants of the East. Fortunately there are not enough barbecue pits in the country to exhaust the supply. South Texas likes her barbecue cooked only on mesquite, with the sauce spicy and hot and not too thick. Her beans are spicy Mexican brown beans or Ranch beans, served with *pico de gallo*, a combination of tomatoes, onions, garlic, and jalapeños chopped in oil. (Beans are of humble repute. At one hastily called White House dinner given by President Johnson for a rather celestial group of cabinet members, the President tucked a napkin under his chin and put away a bowl of black-eyed peas while the others waited for the meal to "commence.") South Texas serves barbecue with tortillas and guacamole, capping it with grapefruit and oranges from the nearby Rio Grande valley. West Texas does up a sauce thick with tomatoes and spiked with signature New Mexico chile peppers. Cole slaw might accompany barbecues, prepared in any number of ways. There's "pig" slaw (green cabbage chopped with onions and carrots in sugary mayonnaise), "honky" (green and red cabbage with green onions, garlic, paprika, sugar, and mayonnaise), and "trash" (cabbage chopped fine with carrots, sugar and oil, made lively with vinegar and lemon). Roadside barbecue comes with packaged soft white bread, because that's the habit and that's the way they like it. The barbecue has served the cowboy and the rancher well, and from the early 19th century has often been a celebrated social event sometimes associated with politics and vigorous electioneering.

Texas boasts an eclectic bounty, her rivers running thick with trout, perch, and catfish, and the Gulf waters from Padre Island to Port Arthur supply abundant red snapper, king mackerel, speckled sea trout, redfish, shrimp, flounder, crabs, and oysters. Pecan producers here are second only to those in Georgia, and the pralines of south Texas and pecan pies of east Texas bespeak a southern influence. The lower Rio Grande valley grows some of the finest pink grapefruits in the land, in addition to juicy fragrant honeydews, cantaloupes, and watermelons. Tiny figs thrive as far north as the irrigated gardens of Dallas and Fort Worth and are made into tarts and rich, syrupy conserves with thick slices of lemon and whole figs the size of shooting marbles.

Tex-Mex is a cookery hybrid that developed in San Antonio and Austin, spun out of the far western corner of El Paso where they serve the best Mexican food in the state. Tex-Mex started out as cheap and trashy food, using inexpensive cuts of meat, chicken parts, cuts of old cows and goats, and poor cuts of pork smothered in spices to seem more appealing. In early

days, the meats were shredded and spooned into corn tortillas with hot sauces, but by the 1930s, ground meats were being used in fillings, and today there is a tendency to glamorize the food with inappropriately expensive cuts of meat. The food remains best and truest eaten from a street cart.

Southwestern style finds its heritage in the food known to native American tribes. The Southwest's endless horizon reaches over rock, mesas, desert, and the verdant vein that runs along the Rio Grande as it weaves through New Mexico. For millenia people have lived here in caves and cliff dwellings on the face of the mesas. Tiered level on level, the dwellings were connected with wooden ladders, making a sort of primitive cityscape that afforded a 360 degree view of possible attack. Pueblo Indian culture sprang up in near-total isolation. Their handmade objects of silver, turquoise, pottery, and wool are among the most exquisite designs dreamed up by any civilization.

Maize was the grain that sustained this native agrarian society, so much so that young men were admonished by their elders to love and cherish their corn as they love and cherish their women. Understandably fearful of droughts, they built dams and irrigated the Rio Grande valleys as far north as Taos. Their maize was many-colored: red, white, blue, yellow, purple, black. Breads and tortillas were made from meal of ground kernels. *Posole* was their version of hominy, the tough corn casings removed with a lye made from wood ash. The Pueblos made a pleasant, fresh-tasting dish from dried sweet corn kernels (*chicos*); nowadays these kernels are salted and packaged as a crunchy snack. When the Coronado expedition reached Pueblo country in 1540, they came upon fields standing crowded with maize and storerooms stocked to bursting with a seven-year supply from just one season's harvest. Archeologists are still sweeping fragments of ancient kernels and cobs from the cliff and cave dwellings.

Native Americans of the Southwest, like their Eastern brothers, told their own corn myths. The Navajos believed that when the wild turkey hen came flying from the direction of the Morning Star, she shook her feathers and freed an ear of blue corn which fell to earth. The Hopis of Arizona believed that the color of corn they planted was an indication to the corn god of the color wanted back; if blue and white corn were planted close together, the mixed colors that grew on some of the ears were the result of the deity's confusion. We in turn have almost succeeded in creating a striated red, white, and blue patriotic variety. There was once a feeble, though well thought-out, suggestion made in the 19th century: substitute corn for the olive branch held in the claw of the eagle on the United States seal, in recognition of our debt of gratitude. Like the Indians of New England, western Indians commonly grilled and boiled ears of corn. Everyone loves to eat with his or her hands, and corn on the cob isn't the only such treat. Some folk are shy to use their hands in company. When a Frenchman dines on ortolan, he places a large linen napkin over his head, picks up the minuscule bird by its tiny feet, and consumes it in the privacy of his headdress. The Germans ceremoniously eat the first white asparagus of spring in similar fashion, beginning with the tip. Theirs is an unveiled, almost religious reverence for the vegetable. I suspect the Indians had fun.

When the Spanish arrived they noted with astonishment that the Pueblo Indians were cultivating all manner of beans, squash, melons, wild berries (including strawberries), avocados, and the American plum. The Indians were not great meat eaters but did keep turkeys and prairie hens penned. This tribe rarely bothered with game, excepting the occasional rabbit; big game was left for the warring Apaches. Nuts from the piñon, a native low-growing pine, were used in salads and ground into paste for moles. The piñon wood itself warms the cold desert nights, and as cooking fuel, it imbues meats and fowl with an elusive piney flavor. There is a lovely local habit of lighting a small green piñon branch and walking it through the house, scenting the air more gently than any scented candle ever could. Wild oregano, garlic, and onions lent pungent flavor to many Pueblo dishes, and the river served them with abundant trout that were fried or wrapped in corn husks to be "baked" over hot piñon or mesquite coals. The Pueblo Indian made yeast from fermented wild potato root to raise breads. The *horno* (an outdoor beehive-shaped adobe oven of Spanish-Moorish origin that came with the Spanish) established itself as the preferred way of baking and cooking. Even today the Pueblo bride is trained by her mother in the traditional cooking skills of her ancestors, and prepares foods for the tribe's many feasts. Custom dictates that they must welcome and feed all guests, even those who arrive uninvited (and this presents no small problem when hordes of tourists descend to take advantage and sample the native food as though it were the offering of just another church supper).

The introduction of chiles—fresh and dried, sweet to hot—has brought about a cooking style different from any found elsewhere in the Southwest. It is unlike the Mexican-influenced cookery of the borders of Texas and Arizona and the Anglo-influences of neighboring Colorado and much of the West. Here the exchange of customs with the Indians and the Spanish resulted in a cookery proudly called "New Mexican." The Pueblos use masa prepared from wet kernels of dried, then cooked, corn. Mashed to a smooth paste on a flat metate stone, masa is preferred for tortillas to the dry cornmeal and water preparation of the Mexicans. Tortillas are often made with blue corn masa harina, to be stuffed with fillings for enchiladas, burritos, fried into tostados for scooping salsa and guacamole, and stacked like elaborate club sandwiches layered with tomato, lettuce, avocado, anaheim or bell peppers and topped with mild Chihuahua cheese. Blue corn crêpes filled with chicken and blanketed with cheese and cream are as sophisticated as the dishes highly seasoned with chiles.

By the 18th century, the influential Spanish missions were well established and cultivating their olives and grapes. Spain's political influence was declining, her empire on the wane. Her domination, however, would be felt from the southern coast of California north to San Francisco. The legacy of that influence would change the eating and drinking habits of the entire country two centuries later.

Breakfast

BROILED GRAPEFRUIT WITH HONEY

SOURDOUGH WAFFLES* WITH
CREAMED DRIED BEEF*

COFFEE

DOMAINE CHANDON
BLANC DE NOIRS

Some of the country's best grapefruits come from the orchards of the lower Rio Grande in southern Texas. I doubt any cowboy ever bothered to grill his grapefruit, but halved and sectioned grapefruit smeared with honey and set under the broiler to char makes a warm opening to a meal. Dried beef is an offshoot of Indian preserved meats that have included the elk, the antelope, the buffalo, and finally the cow. The same drying method prevails, and creamed dried beef was often the horror of every soldier's tin plate. What was hell for the enlisted man became a craze in the kitchens of the 1930s, and then a chic dish at New York's "21." Served up on toast, baked potatoes, or waffles, it's a good dish.

SOURDOUGH WAFFLES

INGREDIENTS

1 package sourdough starter
1½ cups cake flour
¾ cup warm milk
⅛ teaspoon salt
1½ teaspoons sugar
1¼ teaspoons baking powder
1 teaspoon baking soda
3 eggs, separated

METHOD

In a bowl, combine the sourdough starter with the
    flour and warm milk.
Cover tightly and set aside at room temperature for
    12 hours.
Store the starter in the refrigerator until ready to use.
Add the salt, sugar, baking powder, and baking soda.
Blend in the egg yolks.
In a bowl, beat the egg whites until they form soft
    peaks.
Fold the whites into the batter.
Ladle the waffle batter onto a hot waffle iron and cook
    until golden.

Makes about 8 waffles

CREAMED DRIED BEEF

INGREDIENTS

1 cup milk
1 cup heavy cream
2 tablespoons bourbon
1 teaspoon Dijon-style mustard
2 tablespoons unsalted butter, at room temperature
2 tablespoons all-purpose flour
2 ounces sharp cheddar cheese, grated
Cayenne pepper
Freshly milled white pepper
1 teaspoon grated fresh horseradish
1 pound dried beef, cut into ½-inch slivers

METHOD

In a heavy saucepan over high heat, bring the milk,
    cream, bourbon, and mustard to a boil. Reduce the
    heat and simmer for 10 minutes.
In a bowl, cream together the butter and flour.
Whisk the paste into the hot milk mixture and bring to
    a boil.
Fold in the cheese and simmer for 5 minutes. Season
    with cayenne and white pepper to taste.
Fold the horseradish and beef into the cream mixture
    and heat thoroughly.

Serves 6

Round-up Lunch I

CHICKEN-FRIED STEAK
AND CREAM GRAVY*

PICKLES

BLACK-EYED PEAS*

LEAH DARBY'S CHOWCHOW*

STEWED CORN*

CANDIED SWEET POTATOES*

MARY PERRY'S
FIVE FINGER CORN BREAD*

CANTALOUPE AND
YELLOW WATERMELON

ICED TEA

Round-up Lunch II

DOUBLE-DUSTED FRIED CHICKEN*

CREAM GRAVY*

PICKLES

MASHED POTATOES

BUTTERED PEAS

TOMATO AND ONION SALAD

GRITS

BANANA BOURBON PUDDING*

ICED TEA

"We don't know how he does it. Every fall, our old foreman sniffs the air one day and then gives us just a week's warning, that on such and such a day the temperature's going to drop, and that will have to be the day to round up the herd." For the next three or four days the cowboys saddle up at four A.M. and break at noon, and the real thrill of their day is to stop in the heat of it all and eat this huge lunch. Typical of many chuckwagon meals, these recipes are actually two days' eating. The chicken-fried steak and the crusty fried chicken are particular specialties of south Texas, where the food smacks more of the South than of the Southwest. Five Finger Corn Bread is yet another expression of the inventive cook. There are end-less corn bread variations, and this recipe might be unheard of just 20 miles away, where the ranch cook learned it from her own great grandmother. She makes a kind of cornmeal mush, scoops up a little cake of it, pats it in the palm of her hand, and fries it. The imprint of her fingers is left on the cake, thus the name. The cowboys eat their beans with forkfuls of chowchow, not the cooked, put-up variety, but fresh chopped vegetables in vinegar. And still, they find room for desserts! The corn bread is sopped up with thick and sticky cane syrup, and they love that Texan specialty, Banana Pudding. You can't beat fresh bananas, and you can't beat vanilla wafers, and I don't see any point in going through the effort of making the wafers yourself; the pudding just wouldn't be the same. Nabisco does just fine.

CHICKEN-FRIED STEAK AND CREAM GRAVY

INGREDIENTS

5 pounds top or bottom round of beef, sliced ½-inch thick
3 cups milk
Salt and freshly milled black pepper
5 cups all-purpose flour
2 eggs, lightly beaten
1 quart vegetable oil, for frying
2 cups heavy cream

TOOLS

Large cast-iron skillet
Meat pounder

METHOD

In a shallow dish, steep the sliced steak in 2 cups of the milk for 1 hour.

Drain and dry with paper towels.

Season the meat with salt and pepper.

Sprinkle lightly with 2 tablespoons of the flour and pound ¼-inch thick with a meat pounder.

In a shallow bowl, combine the eggs and the remaining cup of milk. Lightly dip the meat in the egg mixture.

Dredge in the remaining flour, reserving 2 tablespoons, and dredge twice more, shaking away any excess.

In a large cast-iron skillet, pour in 1 inch of oil.

Heat the oil until hot and fry the steak in batches until golden brown on each side. (The oil will have to be changed at least once for this amount of meat.) Continue frying until all the floured meat is cooked.

When the meat is cooked, pour off all but 1 tablespoon of the oil.

Off the heat, stir in 2 tablespoons flour and mix with the oil.

Return to low heat and add the cream.

Bring to a simmer, stirring constantly and scraping up the browned bits that cling to the bottom of the pan, until the cream gravy thickens.

Season to taste with salt and pepper and serve hot.

Serves 8 to 10

DOUBLE-DUSTED FRIED CHICKEN

INGREDIENTS

3 chickens (each about 3½ pounds), cut into serving
    pieces with livers, gizzards, and hearts reserved
6 cups all-purpose flour
2 tablespoons baking powder
¼ cup salt
2 tablespoons freshly milled black pepper
1 tablespoon paprika
2 tablespoons dried oregano
About 1 quart vegetable oil
2 teaspoons dried thyme
2 eggs, lightly beaten

TOOLS

Deep-frying thermometer

METHOD

Wash the chicken pieces and pat dry with paper
    towels.
Mix the flour, baking powder, and seasonings together
    and divide between two paper bags.
Heat 1½ inches of oil in a large heavy skillet.
Place the chicken pieces in a large bowl and toss with
    the eggs.
Place 4 to 5 pieces in one bag and shake well. Repeat
    until all the chicken has been floured.
Quickly dip the chicken pieces in a bowl of ice water
    and place in the second bag. Shake well.
Fry in the hot oil (365°), turning from time to time,
    cooking slowly until the chicken is golden brown, 10
    to 12 minutes for breasts and thighs, a few minutes
    longer for legs.
Remove the giblets immediately after they turn golden.
Depending on the size of the skillet, the oil will have to
    be changed at least twice.

Note: Cream gravy (see page 232) is often a traditional
    accompaniment to this dish.

Serves 8 to 9

BLACK-EYED PEAS

INGREDIENTS

5 pounds fresh black-eyed peas, shelled
½ pound fresh pork fatback, cut into 1-inch cubes
6 small yellow onions, peeled
Salt and freshly milled black pepper

METHOD

Place the shelled peas, fatback, and onions in a large
    pot and add water to cover.
Bring to a boil, reduce the heat, and simmer for
    several hours, or until the peas are tender.
Season with salt and pepper to taste.
Serve with Chowchow.

Serves 8

LEAH DARBY'S CHOWCHOW

INGREDIENTS

4 medium-size firm tomatoes, seeded and roughly
    chopped
1 medium yellow onion, roughly chopped
2 cucumbers—peeled, cut lengthwise, seeded, and
    chopped
5 tablespoons cider vinegar
Salt and freshly milled black pepper

METHOD

Place the vegetables on a large chopping board.
Roughly chop the vegetables.
Sprinkle with 2½ tablespoons of the vinegar and lightly
    season to taste with salt and pepper.
Continue chopping until the vegetables take on the
    consistency of a relish, adding the remaining vin-
    egar and seasonings.
Spoon the chowchow into a bowl, cover, and chill for
    1 hour.
Serve with the Black-Eyed Peas.

Serves 6 to 8

STEWED CORN

INGREDIENTS

20 ears fresh sweet corn
1 cup milk
¼ pound butter
Salt and freshly milled pepper

METHOD

Remove the kernels from the cobs with a sharp knife.
Reserve in a large nonaluminum pot.
With a soup spoon, scrape the milk from the cobs into
    the pot, over the reserved corn.
Add the remaining ingredients and ½ cup water.
Place the pot over moderate heat and bring to a boil.
Reduce the heat and simmer for 1 hour.
Taste for seasonings and serve hot.

Serves 8 to 10

CANDIED SWEET POTATOES

INGREDIENTS

4 pounds sweet potatoes, peeled and quartered
1½ to 2 cups sugar, depending on the sweetness of the
    potatoes
4 tablespoons butter

METHOD

Place the potatoes and sugar in a large pot and add
    water to cover.
Bring to a boil, reduce the heat, and simmer until
    tender.
Using a slotted spoon, remove the potatoes and place
    in a serving bowl.
Dot with the butter and serve immediately.

Serves 8

MARY PERRY'S
FIVE FINGER CORN BREAD

INGREDIENTS

4 cups white cornmeal
1 tablespoon salt
2 tablespoons sugar
4 to 5 cups boiling water
2 eggs
Vegetable oil, for frying

METHOD

In a large mixing bowl, combine the cornmeal, salt,
    and sugar.
Lightly mix with 4 cups of the boiling water.
If the consistency is dry and lumpy, immediately add
    ½ to 1 cup of cold water.
Add the eggs and mix.
Heat 1½ inches of oil in a large heavy skillet.
When the oil is very hot, dip your fingers into a bowl of
    cold water.
Take about ¼ cup of the cornmeal mixture and pat it
    between your fingers into 3-inch-long ovals. (You
    should see the imprint of your fingers.)

Immediately slip the batter into the hot oil, dipping your hands in the cold water and making more.

Turn the corn bread when golden and continue to cook the other side.

Remove with a slotted spoon and drain on paper towels.

Note: Corn bread is traditionally served with pure cane syrup at the end of the meal. It can be reheated and served with breakfast the next morning.

Makes 2½ dozen

BANANA BOURBON PUDDING

INGREDIENTS

1 cup plus 6 tablespoons sugar
6 cups milk
⅓ cup arrowroot
¼ cup bourbon
8 egg yolks
6 ripe bananas, peeled and sliced ¼ inch thick
3 dozen vanilla wafers
3 egg whites

TOOLS

2½-quart ovenproof bowl
Electric mixer

METHOD

In a large heavy saucepan, combine 1 cup of the sugar and all of the milk and bring to a simmer over moderate heat.

In a small mixing bowl, dissolve the arrowroot in the bourbon.

Whisk the yolks together and add them to the bourbon mixture.

Measure out ½ cup of the simmering milk and whisk it into the bourbon mixture.

Whisk the bourbon mixture into the saucepan of simmering milk.

Stir constantly until the pudding bubbles and thickens enough to coat the back of a spoon.

Remove from the heat, place a sheet of plastic wrap directly on top of the surface, and reserve.

To assemble:

In a large ovenproof bowl, alternate layers of bananas and pudding, lining the sides of the bowl with the vanilla wafers as you fill the bowl.

Cover the pudding with plastic wrap and refrigerate.

Preheat the oven to 400°.

With an electric mixer, beat the 3 egg whites until frothy.

Gradually add the remaining 6 tablespoons sugar and beat until stiff and glossy.

Spread the meringue over the pudding and bake for 10 minutes, or until the meringue is golden brown.

Serves 8 to 10

Mesquite Grilled Duck Dinner

WHITE PUMPKIN SOUP*

MESQUITE GRILLED DUCK*

NOPALES WITH
BLACK AND WHITE BEANS*

SWEET POTATO TART*

SIMI WINERY
CABERNET SAUVIGNON

THOMAS KRUSE
BLANC DE BLANCS
SPARKLING WINE

This white hybrid pumpkin is filled with fruits and vegetables, a combination traditionally loved by the Spanish, celebrated in this recipe perhaps to excess. Wild game abounds in Texas, where it has been protected by law and is available to the hunter only. Local game is not sold in markets, and if it appears on restaurant menus, it is because it's flown in. There are few domesticated game farms, and few game recipes appear in Texas cookbooks. If you're not a hunter, the fatty Long Island duckling, which freezes and transports well, will do. Texans offhandedly use cactus leaves the way Easterners scatter mushrooms in their dishes. The peppery, almost acidic cactus leaf, combined with the beans, is just another pot liquor pulled apart. I've de-sweetened the sweet potato pie, and like all squash tarts and pies, it can use a little lift, hence the pecans and violets. There may be no violets in Texas, but there are people in Texas who go to France and buy candied violets.

WHITE PUMPKIN SOUP

INGREDIENTS

1 large white pumpkin or orange pumpkin (5 to 6 pounds)

1 small orange pumpkin

2½ quarts Chicken Stock (see Basics, page 343)

1 whole chicken breast

½ pound fresh speckled butter beans, fava beans, or lima beans, shelled

6 fresh cornichons, halved, or 1 small Kirby cucumber, cut into 2-inch julienne

8 ears baby sweet corn, husked

1 medium-size hot red frying pepper—stemmed, seeded, deveined, and cut into julienne

1 small yellow bell pepper—stemmed, seeded, deveined, and cut into julienne

1 ripe yellow tomato—peeled, seeded, and coarsely chopped with juices reserved

1 ripe red tomato—peeled, seeded, and coarsely chopped with juices reserved

3 scallions, including some of the green, cut into 2-
inch julienne
1 medium-firm ripe peach, peeled and cut into eighths
3 Seckle pears, thinly sliced
3 fresh figs, cut into ¼-inch slices
Salt and freshly milled black pepper

METHOD

The tureen:

Cut a round "lid" in the top of the large pumpkin. The
stem will serve as the "handle."

Scoop out the seeds and loose fiber.

Return the "lid" and set aside.

The soup:

Seed the smaller pumpkin and dice the flesh into
½-inch cubes. Measure out 1 cup of flesh and
reserve the remainder for another use.

Remove the outer skin; reserve.

In a large kettle, bring 1 quart of the chicken stock to a
boil over high heat.

Reduce the heat, add the chicken breast and simmer
until cooked through.

Remove with a slotted spoon and set aside to cool.

When cool enough to handle, discard the skin and
bones and shred the meat.

Skim off any foam from the top of the stock.

Bring the stock back to a mild boil and cook the butter
beans until almost tender.

Remove the beans with a slotted spoon and reserve.

Bring the stock back to a mild boil and cook the diced
pumpkin flesh until tender.

Remove with a slotted spoon and reserve.

Pour the remaining 1½ quarts chicken stock into
a large pot.

Strain the poaching stock through a fine mesh sieve
into the large pot of stock.

Bring the stock to a light boil and add the cornichons,
baby corn, peppers, and tomatoes.

Simmer for 10 minutes.

Add the scallions, the reserved beans, pumpkin, fruits,
and shredded chicken and simmer for 8 to 10
minutes.

Check for seasonings and add salt and pepper to taste.

Pour the soup into the pumpkin tureen and serve.

Serves 6 to 8

MESQUITE GRILLED DUCK

INGREDIENTS

2 grapefruits
¼ cup sugar
6 boneless whole duck breasts, such as Muscovy,
Canvasback, or Long Island duck, with skin attached
1 quart buttermilk (optional)
Olive oil
Salt and freshly milled black pepper

TOOLS

Grill with mesquite or charcoal, or a combination of
both

METHOD

To prepare the grapefruit:

Using a sharp vegetable peeler, remove the zest from
the grapefruits in long strips.

Cut the zest in long thin julienne; reserve.

Slice the ends off the grapefruits and cut away the peel
and pith.

Segment the fruit and reserve.

Blanch the zest julienne in a small pot of boiling water
for 10 minutes to remove the bitterness.

Drain under cold running water; reserve.

In a small saucepan, dissolve the sugar in ¼ cup of
water over moderate heat.

Add the zest and simmer for 10 minutes. Set aside to
cool.

To prepare the grill and ducks:

If the birds are gamey, soak them in buttermilk for
about 6 hours.

Prepare the grill with mesquite, charcoal, or a combination of charcoal and mesquite chips.

Preheat the oven to 300°.

When the coals take on a dusty red glow, brush the
grill with olive oil.

Pat the duck breasts dry.

Brush with olive oil and season to taste with salt and
pepper.

Place the breasts, flesh side down, on the grill and
cook for about 2 minutes.

Turn and grill on the skin side for 2 minutes.

Remove the duck breasts from the grill, place in a
   baking pan, and bake in the oven for 5 to 7 minutes,
   until rare to medium-rare.

Slice each breast diagonally into 5 or 6 slices.

Arrange the slices on heated dinner plates.

Place 3 to 4 grapefruit sections over and around the
   duck slices.

Remove the julienne from the syrup and sprinkle over
   the slices.

Spoon any pan juices over the duck and serve.

Serves 6

NOPALES WITH BLACK AND WHITE BEANS

INGREDIENTS

6 medium nopales (cactus leaves)

¼ pound butter

¼ pound dried black beans, soaked overnight in water

¼ pound dried navy beans, soaked overnight in water

4 ounces salt pork

2 medium onions

METHOD

To prepare the nopales:

Blanch the nopales in a pot of lightly salted boiling
   water for 4 minutes. Drain and reserve.

When ready to serve, melt the butter in a skillet and
   sauté the leaves briefly on each side.

Remove and cut diagonally into ½-inch strips.

To prepare the beans:

Drain the beans and discard the water.

Place the beans in a large saucepan and add water to
   cover.

Add the salt pork and onions.

Bring to a boil, reduce the heat to a simmer, and cook
   until the beans are tender, about 30 minutes.
   Discard the onions.

To serve, spoon the beans over the nopales.

Note: The beans can be reheated easily and the flavors
   are enhanced on the second day.

Serves 6

SWEET POTATO TART

INGREDIENTS

PECANS:

½ egg white

1 cup pecan halves, broken lengthwise

2 tablespoons sugar

SWEET POTATO MIXTURE:

2 pounds sweet potatoes, peeled and quartered
   (about 3 cups)

¼ teaspoon ground ginger

¼ teaspoon ground cinnamon

Pinch of ground cloves

2 egg whites

⅓ cup sugar

ASSEMBLY:

1 recipe Pie Dough, made with butter and prebaked in
   an 11-inch tart pan (see Basics, page 346)

16 crystallized violets, for decoration

Whipped heavy cream, for serving

TOOLS

11-inch fluted tart pan

Electric mixer

METHOD

Preheat the oven to 300°.

Prepare the pecans:

In a small bowl, lightly beat the ½ egg white until
   frothy.

Add the pecan halves and lightly coat them in the egg
   white.

Remove to a plate and sprinkle with the sugar.

Spread the nuts onto a baking sheet.

Toast the nuts in the oven, shaking the pan occasion-
   ally and watching carefully, until golden, about
   5 minutes.

Remove from the oven and let cool. Set aside 16 pecan
   pieces for decoration.

Prepare the sweet potato mixture:

Place the potatoes in a large saucepan with enough
   water to cover and bring to a boil over high heat.

Cook for 15 minutes, or until fork-tender. Drain.

In a mixing bowl, whip the potatoes and spices with an
   electric mixer until slightly lumpy or completely
   smooth.

Cool in the refrigerator for 20 minutes.

In a large bowl, using an electric mixer, beat the egg
   whites until frothy.

Gradually add the ⅓ cup sugar and continue beating
   until stiff and glossy.

A little at time, fold the meringue into the potato
   mixture.

Fold in the sugared pecans.

Spoon the mixture into the prebaked tart shell and
   smooth the top.

Decorate with the reserved pecan pieces and the
   crystallized violets.

Serve slightly chilled with unsweetened whipped
   cream.

Serves 8

Chili Dinner

CHILI*

GRAPEFRUIT AND CHAMPAGNE
SHERBET*

CULBERTSON
CHAMPAGNE CELLARS BRUT

There are chili recipes, chili cooks, chili contests, chili cook-offs, and people eating quarts of the stuff on those big weekend chili fests all across the state. Some people make it with steak and shun beans; some people say that hamburger meat is even too good for chili and they cook it forever. I'll bite the bullet and give you my own.

CHILI

INGREDIENTS

¾ pound salt pork, diced

7 pounds top round of beef, sliced ¼-inch thick and diced

8 Spanish onions, finely diced

10 cloves garlic, minced

12 ripe tomatoes—peeled, seeded, and chopped with the juices reserved

1 can (6 ounces) tomato paste

¾ cup chile powder

½ cup ground cumin

3 tablespoons crushed red pepper flakes

3 whole dried poblano chile peppers, seeded and chopped

1 tablespoon chopped fresh oregano

2 tablespoons salt

2 tablespoons *masa harina*

2 bunches scallions, including some of the green, thinly sliced

1 pound cheddar cheese, shredded, to accompany the chili

METHOD

In a large heavy skillet, render two-thirds of the salt pork over moderate heat.

Remove the salt pork and place it in a large pot.

Working in batches, brown the meat in the skillet and transfer the meat to the large pot.

When all of the meat has been browned, add the pan juices to the large pot.

Render the remaining salt pork in the skillet.

Add the onions and sauté over a moderately low heat until caramelized.

When caramelized, add the garlic and cook for a few minutes. Turn the mixture into the pot.

Add the tomatoes and their juices and cook for 5 to 7 minutes.

Add the tomato paste and stir it into the meat.

Add the seasonings, chiles, and oregano and salt, and mix thoroughly.

Mix the *masa harina* with 2 tablespoons of water and fold into the chili.

Simmer over moderately low heat for 3½ to 4 hours, stirring from time to time and checking to be sure the chili does not stick to the bottom of the pot.

Before serving, check the seasonings: Depending on the freshness of the chile powder, the strength may vary. You may want additional seasonings.

Serve with the sliced scallions and shredded cheddar cheese.

Note: This chili develops its flavor best over time. Make it ahead of time and chill. Next day, skim off the fat and reheat. The hot chili is served over the cheese and the scallions on top of the chili.

Serves 12

GRAPEFRUIT AND CHAMPAGNE SHERBET

INGREDIENTS

2 cups fresh grapefruit juice, strained and chilled
1 cup Champagne, chilled
½ cup Simple Syrup (see Basics, page 348), chilled
½ cup pomegranate seeds

TOOLS

Ice cream maker

METHOD

In a bowl, mix the grapefruit juice, Champagne, and simple syrup.

Place in an ice cream freezer and chill according to the manufacturer's directions.

When sherbet is frozen, remove, cover, and place in freezer.

When ready to serve, sprinkle with the pomegranate seeds.

Note: Whenever possible, make homemade sherbet close to serving time.

If the sherbet becomes too hard, place it in the refrigerator for 45 minutes to soften up before serving. In fact, fresh sherbet thats have been frozen for a few days or a week may be defrosted in the refrigerator and then refrozen in the ice cream maker to restore a smooth sherbet consistency. This process may be done only once.

Makes about 1 quart

Breakfast

SOPAIPILLAS*
COFFEE

Like pillows of air, these puffed pastries are a New Mexican favorite that have established themselves throughout the Southwest. Like the beignets in the Deep South and the doughnuts in the East, sopaipillas are best served piping hot, with jam, honey or a dusting of powdered sugar. Try them the way the locals do—poke a hole into the pastry and pour a stream of honey into the warm interior.

SOPAIPILLAS

INGREDIENTS

1¾ cups all-purpose flour
2 teaspoons baking powder
1 teaspoon salt
2 tablespoons shortening
1 quart vegetable oil, for frying

TOOLS

Pastry wheel
Deep fryer or deep heavy pot

METHOD

In a mixing bowl, combine the flour, baking powder, and salt.

Cut in the shortening until the mixture resembles the consistency of cornmeal.

Gradually blend in ⅔ cup water.

Knead the dough on a clean surface for 5 minutes, or until smooth.

Divide the dough into 3 equal parts.

Roll out each portion of dough into a ⅛-inch thick circle.

Using a pastry wheel, cut each circle into quarters.

While the dough is resting, heat the oil in a deep heavy pot until it reaches 350°.

Working in batches, fry the sopaipillas, turning with a slotted spoon, for 2 to 3 minutes, or until a pale golden color.

Drain on paper towels and serve hot.

Makes 1 dozen

Menudo Lunch

MENUDO (TRIPE SOUP)*
WITH PIQUANT TAMALES*

GRILLED CHICKEN SALAD*

CANTALOUPE WITH
TEQUILA LIME SYRUP*

JOSEPH PHELPS VINEYARD
SAUVIGNON BLANC

This menu is a cacophony of every spice and herb used in New Mexican cooking. The tripe soup should cook at a lazy bubble on the back of the stove while you prepare the tamales and the salad. Tamales date to the pre-Columbians; practically every culture used stuffed leaves or bark to steam or roast their food. Tamales are little steamed puddings, blue corn flour dough filled with vegetables, tied up like tiny presents. All of the salad components bear witness to the fruitful bounty of the Rio Grande valley, including the sturdy but obliging iceberg lettuce, which becomes quite exotic when shredded. Tequila is New Mexico's wine and liqueur, and combined with limes in a sweet syrup, it enhances ripe melon.

MENUDO (TRIPE SOUP)

INGREDIENTS

2 pounds tripe, cut into ½-inch cubes
1 onion, peeled
3 whole cloves
5 peppercorns
1 clove garlic, crushed
1½ quarts Beef Stock (see Basics, page 343)
¼ cup deveined, seeded, and chopped fresh green chiles
3 large ripe tomatoes—peeled, seeded, and chopped
1 tablespoon chopped fresh oregano
1 tablespoon chopped cilantro
½ cup chopped scallions, including some of the green
Salt

METHOD

Place the tripe in a large stockpot with 2 quarts of heavily salted water.
Bring to a boil over high heat.
Reduce the heat and simmer for 30 minutes.
Drain under cold running water.
Return the tripe to the pot and add the onion, cloves, peppercorns, and garlic.
Add 2 quarts of cold water and bring to a boil.
Cook at a high simmer for 30 minutes.
Add the stock and continue to cook for 2½ hours, or until the tripe is very tender.
Add the vegetables and herbs and simmer for 15 minutes.
Check the seasonings.
Serve immediately in heated bowls.

Serves 6

PIQUANT TAMALES

INGREDIENTS

½ pound dried corn husks
VEGETABLE FILLING:
½ small finely diced eggplant
1 tablespoon salt
3 tablespoons olive oil

¾ cup finely diced onion

1 clove garlic, minced

¾ cup finely diced zucchini

½ cup peeled, seeded, and chopped tomato

2 tablespoons finely diced green chile or jalapeño peppers

1 teaspoon cornmeal

MASA MIXTURE:

¼ cup lard

3 cups blue corn *masa harina*

1¼ teaspoons salt

METHOD

The corn husks:

Submerge the husks in a pan of warm water for 2 to 3 hours.

The vegetable filling:

In a bowl, combine the eggplant and salt and let stand for 20 minutes.

In a medium skillet, heat the oil over moderate heat and sauté the onions and garlic until wilted.

Squeeze the moisture from the eggplant and add to the onion mixture. Sauté for 4 to 5 minutes.

Add the zucchini, tomatoes, and chile peppers and sauté for 3 minutes.

Stir in the corn meal and set aside to cool.

The masa mixture:

In a mixing bowl, beat the lard with a wooden spoon or electric mixer until soft and light.

Add the *masa harina* and salt and mix thoroughly.

Add enough water to make the mixture spreadable but firm. The amount of water will depend on the coarseness of the masa.

Assemble the tamales:

Drain the corn husks.

Using 3 or 4 of the split husks, pull off ¼-inch strips going with the grain of the husks to tie the tamales. Reserve.

With scissors, cut off 1 inch of the pointed smaller end of the husk and discard.

Place the husks on a flat working surface; there will be about 1½ dozen.

Place a rounded teaspoon of the masa mixture in the center of the husk and spread it out about ⅛-inch thick.

Spoon 1 teaspoon of the vegetable mixture into the center of the masa mixture.

Carefully wrap the husks around the masa and filling, pulling the sides around first and folding the top and bottom of the husks toward the center of the tamale to make a neat package.

Tie each tamale closed with a corn husk strip.

In a steamer, bring 2 cups of water to a boil.

Cover the base of the steamer container with a layer of the remaining corn husks, and set the tamales over the husks.

Cover and steam for 45 minutes, or until the masa mixture pulls away from the husks of the tamale.

To check for doneness, open one of the tamales. If not completely cooked, retie and continue steaming for another 5 minutes.

Makes 1½ dozen

GRILLED CHICKEN SALAD

INGREDIENTS

3 large whole chicken breasts, split

MARINADE:

¼ cup olive oil

½ cup fresh lime juice

1 medium onion, thinly sliced

6 cloves garlic, minced

Salt and freshly milled black pepper

DRESSING:

⅓ cup fresh lime juice

¼ cup olive oil

¼ cup vegetable oil

1 teaspoon chopped fresh mint

Salt and freshly milled black pepper

SALAD:

1 medium head iceberg lettuce—outer leaves discarded, cored, and thinly sliced

3 large ripe tomatoes—peeled, seeded, chopped, and chilled

6 green chile or jalapeño peppers—roasted, seeded, deveined, and chopped (see Basics, page 349)

½ cup piñon nuts, toasted (see Basics, page 349)

3 ripe avocados

TOOLS

Charcoal grill, with charcoal, piñon, or fruit wood

METHOD

Place the chicken breasts in a shallow nonaluminum
pan.

In a nonaluminum bowl, combine all of the ingredients
for the marinade.

Pour the marinade over the chicken breasts.

Cover and refrigerate for 6 hours, turning the breasts
at least once.

Prepare the fire.

When the charcoal or wood glows a dusty red, place
the breasts, skin side down, on the grill.

Grill on one side for about 10 minutes.

Turn breasts over and grill for about 15 minutes, or
until cooked through.

Do not overcook.

Remove from the heat and set aside to cool for 30
minutes (but do not refrigerate).

Mix the dressing, cover and reserve.

Meanwhile, compose the salad:

Remove the chicken from the bone with a sharp slicing
knife. Cut into long, thin slices including the skin.

Place the shredded lettuce in a large bowl.

Arrange the tomatoes, chiles, nuts, and chicken
attractively over the lettuce.

Peel the avocados and slice into long, thin strips.

Add the dressing and toss the salad at the table, or
each ingredient may be placed individually on
chilled plates, with the dressing served on the side.

Serves 6

CANTALOUPE WITH
TEQUILA LIME SYRUP

INGREDIENTS

4 limes
1 cup sugar
¼ cup tequila
2 ripe cantaloupes, chilled
Fresh mint

METHOD

Using a vegetable peeler, remove the zest from the
limes in long strips.

Cut the zest into fine, needle-thin julienne. Reserve.

Section the limes and remove the pith and membrane.
Reserve.

In a medium saucepan, combine the sugar with
1 cup of water and bring to a boil over high heat.

Continue boiling for 5 minutes and remove from
the heat.

Fold in the lime zest julienne and let steep for
2 minutes.

Remove the zest with a slotted spoon to a sheet of
waxed paper.

Add the tequila to the syrup.

Halve and seed the melons.

Cut into long 1-inch-wide strips.

Remove the melon rind with a sharp paring knife.

Arrange the melon slices attractively on a platter or
serving dish.

Sprinkle the lime sections and the lime julienne over
the melon.

Pour the syrup over the fruits and serve with the mint.

Serves 6

Posole

POSOLE STEW *

VEGETABLE CORN BREAD *

GREEN MANGO WITH
SALT AND LIME *

FETZER VINEYARDS
ZINFANDEL

Every region produces a dish that is reminiscent of another, similar dish somewhere else. Posole is the Southwestern version of hominy, not unlike large kernels of samp. Simply boiled up, it sustained the Pueblo community. "Posole" is generic for both the dry, treated kernel and for this stew. Over the years, each incoming settlement added an ingredient to the recipe for posole: a bone, morsels of meat, culminating with the addition of sausage and saffron. Not every region depended on sugar. Honey was easily available, but in these arid regions they developed a habit of salting sweet fruits.

POSOLE STEW

INGREDIENTS

3 thick slices slab bacon
¾ pound pork shoulder or neck, cut into 1-inch cubes
¾ pound lamb shoulder or neck, cut into 1-inch cubes
Salt and freshly milled pepper
2 medium onions, chopped
4 cloves garlic, minced
3 to 4 quarts Chicken Stock, as needed (see Basics, page 343)
2 pounds dried posole
10 fresh green chile peppers—seeded, deveined, and chopped
2 teaspoons chopped fresh oregano
2 pinches saffron threads
¾ pound linguiça sausage
¾ pound chorizo or Italian sweet sausage
1 tablespoon chopped fresh cilantro or parsley

METHOD

In a heavy skillet, render the bacon. Drain on paper towels when crisp.

Season the pork and lamb with salt and pepper.

Brown the meat in the bacon fat over moderately high heat. Cover and refrigerate.

Add the onions and garlic to the bacon fat and sauté until translucent. Set aside.

Add ½ cup of the chicken stock to the skillet and deglaze the pan, scraping up the brown bits that cling to the bottom.

Pour the liquid into a large kettle.

Add about 3 quarts of the chicken stock, the posole, green chiles, oregano, saffron, and 1 teaspoon salt.

Bring to a boil, reduce the heat, and simmer for 2 hours, stirring from time to time and adding more chicken stock or water as needed.

Add the pork and lamb, and continue to cook for 1 to 1½ hours, until the posole is tender.

Twenty minutes before the posole is ready to serve, prepare the sausages: Poach the linguiça in a pot of simmering water for 15 minutes.

In a medium skillet filled with ¼-inch of water, cook the
chorizo over moderately high heat until the water
evaporates and the sausages brown.

Place the posole in a heated crock or bowl.

Arrange the sausages in the posole.

Dust with the chopped cilantro or parsley and serve.

Serves 8 to 10

VEGETABLE CORN BREAD

INGREDIENTS

2 tablespoons butter, for the
    baking pan
1⅓ cups yellow cornmeal
1 teaspoon baking powder
2 teaspoons salt
¾ cup buttermilk
2 eggs, lightly beaten
¼ cup vegetable oil or rendered bacon fat
1 cup grated zucchini
½ cup peeled, seeded, and chopped tomatoes
¼ cup seeded, deveined, and chopped sweet red
    bell pepper
2 tablespoons chopped green chile or jalapeño
    peppers
1 ear fresh sweet corn, kernels removed

TOOLS

9-inch square baking pan

METHOD

Preheat the oven to 350°.

Butter the baking pan.

In a mixing bowl, combine the dry ingredients.

Add the liquid ingredients and mix well.

Fold in the vegetables.

Pour the batter into the pan and bake for 35 minutes,
    or until the edges turn golden and pull away from
    the sides of the pan.

Note: Any combination of leftover vegetables may be
    used. Timing here is set for low altitude cooking. In a
    high altitude, bake at 400° for 45 minutes.

Serves 8 to 10

GREEN MANGO WITH SALT AND LIME

INGREDIENTS

4 medium-size tart mangoes
4 to 8 limes, halved
Kosher salt

METHOD

Cut the mangoes flush against the pit on each side.
    (Reserve any leftover mango for chutney or another
    recipe.)

With a small sharp paring knife, score the fruit in a
    grid pattern; do not pierce the skin.

When eating the fruit, push the skin up in the center.
    Squeeze the lime juice over and sprinkle with salt.

Eat with your hands.

Serves 8

Mole Supper

SQUASH BLOSSOM SOUP*

TURKEY MOLE*
BLUE CORN PANCAKES*
HOT MANGO CHUTNEY*

FLAN WITH COCONUT CREAM*

DE LOACH VINEYARDS
CHARDONNAY

Squash blossom soup is a luxury to make if you have to buy blossoms at market; if you grow this prolific vegetable in your own garden, be sure to pluck only the male flowers (armed with pistils). This is a very delicate soup, a creamy prelude to the mole. Chocolate in its unsweetened state is used to enrich the flavor of many dishes. Our tendency to recoil when chocolate is used in a savory dish is based purely on our assumption that all chocolate is sweet. From Mexico to the Southwest, turkey and mole were synonymous. Shredded and served on buttered blue corn pancakes and with a fresh mango chutney hot with chiles, the turkey becomes anything but ordinary.

SQUASH BLOSSOM SOUP

INGREDIENTS

1 pound squash blossoms, reserve 8 of the choicest
   blossoms for decoration (about 60 blossoms)
2 tablespoons unsalted butter
1 bunch scallions, including some of the green, cut
   lengthwise and thinly sliced
1½ quarts Chicken Stock (see Basics, page 343),
   reduced by half
1½ to 2 pounds baby zucchini and yellow squash,
   chopped
2 cups heavy cream
Salt and freshly milled white pepper

TOOLS

Food processor or blender

METHOD

Remove the blossoms from the squash.
In a medium kettle or saucepan, melt the butter.
Sauté the scallions until wilted.
Add the reduced stock and bring to a simmer.
Add the blossoms and squash to the stock. Simmer for
   10 minutes.
Meanwhile, in a separate pan, reduce the cream
   by half.
Strain the broth into a clean saucepan.
Purée the solids in a food processor.
Fold the purée into the broth and add the cream.
Season to taste and chill for 1 hour.
When ready to serve, decorate each plate with a
   reserved squash blossom.

Serves 8

TURKEY MOLE

INGREDIENTS

18 dried New Mexican chile pepper pods
¾ cup lard
1 boneless turkey breast
   (about 4 pounds)
3 tablespoons raisins
2 tablespoons unroasted small skinless peanuts
5 cloves garlic
⅛ teaspoon coriander seed
¼ teaspoon cinnamon
¼ teaspoon aniseed
1 large green tomato, halved and seeded
1 ounce Mexican or unsweetened chocolate, chopped
1 quart Chicken or Turkey Stock
   (see Basics, page 343).

TOOLS

Food processor

METHOD

Remove the stems and seeds from the dried chiles.
   Reserve 2 tablespoons of the seeds.
In a large skillet, melt ¼ cup of the lard and briefly
   sauté the chiles until they turn dark red.
Remove immediately to a bowl, cover with water, and
   set aside to soak overnight.
Add ¼ cup lard to the skillet and brown the turkey
   breast, skin side down, for 10 minutes.
Turn and brown the other side for 10 minutes. Cover
   and refrigerate.
Purée the peppers in a food processor until they make
   a smooth paste. Add some of the soaking liquid, if
   necessary, to loosen the mixture.
In a large skillet, melt 2 tablespoons of lard over
   moderate heat. Add the purée and simmer for 5
   minutes.
Remove the purée to a large pot.
In the skillet, melt the remaining 2 tablespoons lard.
Add the raisins and simmer until they plump.

Remove with a slotted spoon to the food processor.

Lightly toast the peanuts, garlic, spices, and the reserved chile seeds in the skillet.

Remove to the food processor.

Add the green tomato to the food processor and purée the mixture until smooth.

Add the purée to the large pot.

Cook the purée mixture over moderate heat, stirring constantly, for 10 minutes.

Add the chocolate and stir until melted.

Add the broth and simmer for 10 minutes.

Remove the skin from the chilled turkey.

Cut the turkey breast into long ½-inch strips.

Prepare the pancake batter.

Add the turkey to the mole sauce and bring to a simmer until heated through.

To serve ladle turkey and some of the sauce over each stack of three blue corn pancakes.

Serves 8

BLUE CORN PANCAKES

INGREDIENTS

1½ cups blue cornmeal
½ cup all-purpose flour
1 teaspoon salt
1 tablespoon plus 1 teaspoon baking powder
2 eggs, lightly beaten
1½ cups milk
4 tablespoons melted butter
Unsalted butter, for the griddle

METHOD

Sift the dry ingredients into a mixing bowl.

Add the eggs, milk, and butter and mix thoroughly.

Cook the pancakes on a hot, buttered grill or skillet, using 2 tablespoons of batter for each pancake.

Keep the pancakes warm in a low oven until ready to serve.

Note: Blue corn meal is milled dry blue corn. Blue corn *masa harina* has been roasted before milling.

Makes about 25 small pancakes

HOT MANGO CHUTNEY

INGREDIENTS

1 dried New Mexican chile pepper pod, soaked in warm water for 20 minutes
2 large ripe mangoes, peeled and cut into ½-inch slices
1 tablespoon tequila
1 teaspoon sugar
2 tablespoons piñon nuts, toasted (see Basics, page 349)

METHOD

Remove the stem, seeds, and veins from the chile and cut into needle-thin julienne.

In a saucepan, combine the mangoes, tequila, and sugar over moderate heat.

Stir with a wooden spoon until the sugar dissolves and the mangoes begin to give off their juice.

Add the chile julienne and cook for another 2 to 3 minutes. Set aside to cool.

When the mixture has cooled, fold in the piñon nuts.

Serve at room temperature with the turkey mole.

Makes about 2 cups

FLAN WITH COCONUT CREAM

INGREDIENTS

¾ cup sugar
2 cups heavy cream
2 cups milk
4 egg yolks, lightly beaten
5 whole eggs, lightly beaten

TOOLS

9-inch flan mold

METHOD

Preheat the oven to 350°.
Place ½ cup of the sugar in a heavy skillet.
Melt the sugar over moderately high heat.
When the sugar begins to dissolve, stir constantly with a wooden spoon until all of the sugar melts and begins to turn a light golden color.
Remove from the heat and immediately pour into the flan mold. Lift the mold with a dry kitchen towel or hot pads and turn it until the bottom surface and sides are well coated with the sugar. Set aside.
In a heavy saucepan, scald the cream and the milk over moderately high heat.
Add the remaining ¼ cup sugar.
When the sugar dissolves, remove from the heat and whisk in the egg yolks and eggs.
Pour the flan into the prepared mold, and place the mold in a large pan. Add hot water to come halfway up the sides of the mold.
Bake for 45 minutes to 1 hour, or until a knife comes out clean when inserted in the center of the flan.
Remove from the oven and allow to set for at least 2 hours before unmolding.
To unmold, lift the flan and twist slightly. If loose, unmold. If not, return to a warm water bath to loosen the caramel. Invert the pan on a platter and serve with the Coconut Cream.

Serves 8

COCONUT CREAM

INGREDIENTS

1 fresh coconut
½ cup heavy cream
¼ cup sugar
3 egg yolks, lightly beaten

METHOD

Prepare the coconut:
Preheat the oven to 350°.
With a large nail or screwdriver, poke the 3 eyes of the coconut. Drain the milk and reserve.
Place the coconut in the oven and bake for 10 minutes.
Remove the coconut and reduce the oven temperature to 275°. Hit the coconut firmly with a hammer.
Peel the meat out of the shell.
With a vegetable peeler, peel off the outer brown skin.
Grate the flesh.
On a baking sheet, spread out ½ cup of the grated coconut and bake, tossing, until golden; reserve the remaining coconut for other use.
Prepare the sauce:
Strain the coconut milk into a saucepan and add the heavy cream and sugar.
Bring to a simmer, stirring until the sugar dissolves.
Remove from the heat and whisk half of the liquid into the eggs.
Return the milk and egg mixture to the saucepan, and cook, stirring constantly, until it thickens slightly.
Fold in the fresh toasted coconut, and serve at room temperature with the flan.

Makes 1 cup

Piñon-Grilled Dinner

MARINATED GRILLED BEEF HEARTS*
WITH SALSA RENA*

HOT NEW MEXICAN SALAD*

TORTILLAS

SQUASH PURÉE*

COCADA WITH FRESH CORN*

TEQUILA WITH SALSA

HAYWOOD WINERY
ZINFANDEL

Beef hearts are a chuckwagon legacy. The dish has a very aromatic blend of spices and herbs and is a simple preparation. The vegetable salad and squash purée are almost bland accompaniments, offset by the New Mexican habit of washing down fiery puréed dried pepper salsa with tequila. The cooling corn and coconut dessert helps to extinguish the fire.

MARINATED GRILLED BEEF HEARTS

INGREDIENTS

1 beef heart (3 to 4 pounds), fat and nerves removed, and cut into 1-inch cubes
12 cloves garlic, chopped
1 red onion, thinly sliced
¼ cup chopped fresh oregano
2 teaspoons ground cumin
Freshly milled black pepper
1 bottle (25.4 ounces) dry red wine
Salt, for grilling

TOOLS

Grill with piñon, mesquite, or charcoal
Stainless-steel skewers

METHOD

Place the cubed beef heart in a mixing bowl.
Add all the ingredients except the wine and mix.
Add the wine and mix.
Cover and refrigerate for 24 hours.
Prepare a fire of piñon, mesquite, or charcoal.
Drain the beef hearts, reserving the marinade.
Thread the cubes onto skewers and season with salt.
When the coals reach a dusty red glow, grill the hearts, turning often and basting with the remaining marinade.
Beef hearts are best served rare with salsa.

Serves 8 to 10

SALSA RENA

INGREDIENTS

12 dried New Mexican chile pepper pods
1 tablespoon chopped fresh oregano
Salt
2 to 3 tablespoons olive oil

TOOLS

Food processor

METHOD

Remove the stems and seeds from the chiles and soak in a bowl of warm water for 20 minutes.
Drain the chiles.
Process the chiles in a food processor, turning the machine on and off until they begin to purée.
Add the oregano and a generous amount of salt.
Turn the processor on and gradually add the oil.
For a very hot sauce, add chile seeds to suit your taste.
Serve with grilled beef hearts or with tequila as a chaser.

Makes ½ to ¾ cup

HOT NEW MEXICAN SALAD

INGREDIENTS

3 medium tomatoes—peeled, seeded, and finely chopped
3 ears sweet corn, blanched and the kernels cut off the cobs
2 green bell peppers—seeded, deveined, and finely chopped
1 sweet red bell pepper—seeded, deveined, and finely chopped
2 medium zucchini, finely chopped
3 ounces smoked slab bacon, finely diced
2 teaspoons chile powder
⅓ cup cider vinegar
¼ cup chopped fresh parsley
2 tablespoons chopped cilantro

METHOD

In a large bowl, toss all of the vegetables together and
set aside at room temperature. Do not refrigerate.
When ready to serve, in a large skillet, render the
bacon until crisp. Add the chile powder and stir.
Add the vinegar and bring to a simmer.
Add the herbs.
Pour the dressing over the vegetables and toss.

Serves 8 to 10

SQUASH PURÉE

INGREDIENTS

2 large butternut squashes
Salt and freshly milled black pepper
2 tablespoons butter, at room temperature
Freshly grated nutmeg

TOOLS

Food processor

METHOD

Place the squash in one or two large kettles filled with
cold water.
Bring to a boil and add 1 tablespoon salt per squash.
Reduce the heat and simmer until tender, about
30 minutes.
Drain.
Cut each squash in half and remove the seeds.
Remove the pulp from the rind.
Lightly purée the pulp in the food processor.
Add the butter, salt and pepper, and nutmeg to taste.
Serve hot.

Serves 8 to 10

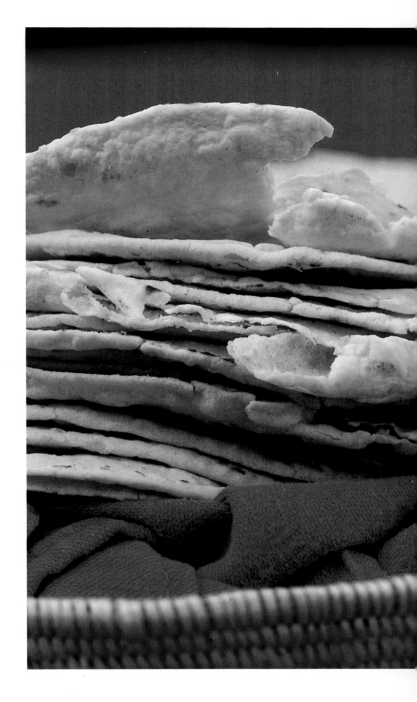

COCADA WITH FRESH CORN

INGREDIENTS

1½ cups sugar

1 vanilla bean, split

½ cup fresh coconut milk (see recipe for Coconut
    Cream, page 255)

2½ cups shredded fresh coconut

2½ cups milk

1 cup fresh corn kernels, cooked (about 2 ears)

2 eggs, separated

¼ cup toasted coconut

METHOD

In a heavy saucepan, combine the sugar, vanilla bean,
    and coconut milk.

Simmer over moderate heat until the sugar dissolves.

Add the shredded coconut and cook for 7 to 8 minutes
    to extract the flavors.

Pour in the milk, bring to a boil, reduce the heat, and
    simmer, stirring often, for about 20 minutes, until
    the mixture thickens.

Remove from the heat and add the corn kernels.

Whisk in the egg yolks. Turn the cocada into a bowl and
    refrigerate for 2 hours.

Before serving, beat the egg whites until stiff and
    glossy. Fold the whites into the custard mixture.

Turn into a serving dish and sprinkle with the toasted
    coconut.

Serves 8 to 10

Tequila

*Tequila, like any liquor, can be of the best or worst
quality. Made from cactus, it has influenced drinking habits from Mexico to the Southwest, and most
Spanish-speaking enclaves in our big cities. The
Mexicans take it with lime and salt to combat the
tequila's fire. The rugged ranchero laps up salsa
from a little tumbler, and shoots it down with a
jigger of tequila. Here, the tequila puts out the fire
of the chile.*

Green Chile Lunch

GREEN CHILE STEW*

MICHELLE NARANJO'S INDIAN BREAD*

GREEN SALAD WITH WATERMELON

ONION AND DILL VINAIGRETTE*

PIÑON BRITTLE*

CHARLES F. SHAW
VINEYARD NAPA GAMAY

The typical Southwesterner has a lusty passion for chiles. For the uninitiated, chiles are an education. In this case, a little meat and a pile of sweet hot chiles spiked with lemon zest make a refreshingly unexplosive stew. Fruit with salad greens was a Spanish combination, common here long before the Californians took it up. Be certain to serve this dense Indian bread hot from the oven. Piñon nuts make a brittle that's sweet and crunchy as one made from peanuts.

GREEN CHILE STEW

INGREDIENTS

2 tablespoons lard

Salt and freshly milled black pepper

1½ pounds lamb shoulder, trimmed and cut into 1-inch cubes

1½ pounds pork shoulder, trimmed and cut into 1-inch cubes

18 long, medium-hot, green chile peppers—stemmed, seeded, and deveined

1½ to 2 cups Chicken Stock (see Basics, page 343)

Zest of 1 lemon, cut into julienne and finely diced

METHOD

In a large heavy skillet, melt the lard over moderately high heat.

Lightly salt and pepper the lamb.

Brown the lamb on all sides and reserve.

Lightly salt and pepper the pork.

Brown the pork on all sides and reserve.

Cut the chiles into long, ½- or ¼-inch strips, depending on their size.

Lightly sauté the chiles in the lard until they begin to wilt.

Remove the chiles and reserve.

Add the stock to the skillet. Bring to a boil and reduce the heat.

Add the meats and simmer until tender.

Add the chiles and cook until heated through.

Fold in the zest and serve.

Note: For a salad accompaniment, combine ruby red lettuce leaves with ripe watermelon.

Serves 6

MICHELLE NARANJO'S INDIAN BREAD

INGREDIENTS

7 cups all-purpose flour
½ teaspoon salt
⅓ cup lard
1 teaspoon active dry yeast
1½ cups lukewarm water
½ teaspoon sugar

METHOD

In a large bowl, combine the flour and salt and cut in the lard until the mixture is crumbly.

In a small bowl, combine the yeast, lukewarm water, and sugar.

Set aside until the yeast and sugar dissolve and the mixture is foamy.

Mix the dissolved yeast mixture with the flour and lard.

Knead the dough until it becomes elastic and pliable, about 7 minutes.

Place the dough in a greased bowl. Cover the bowl and place it in a warm, draft-free place to rise until doubled, about 4 hours.

Punch down the dough and divide in half.

Shape the dough into 2 free form loaves and place them on an ungreased baking sheet, or place each loaf in a medium-size bread pan.

Cover the loaves and let rise again in a warm, draft-free place for another 2 hours.

Preheat the oven to 375°.

Bake the loaves for 45 to 60 minutes, or until the bottom of each loaf sounds hollow when tapped.

Makes 2 loaves

ONION AND DILL VINAIGRETTE

INGREDIENTS

Basic Vinaigrette (see Basics, page 345)
2 tablespoons finely chopped red onion
1 tablespoon chopped dill
1 clove garlic, minced

METHOD

Prepare the Basic Vinaigrette and whisk in the onion, dill, and garlic.

Cover and refrigerate for 30 minutes.

Whisk the vinaigrette before tossing with the salad greens.

Makes about 1¼ cups

PIÑON BRITTLE

INGREDIENTS

Vegetable oil, for the jelly roll pan
2 cups sugar
1 cup light corn syrup
2 tablespoons unsalted butter
2½ cups roasted piñon nuts
1 teaspoon baking soda

TOOLS

Candy thermometer
Jelly roll pan

METHOD

Generously coat a jelly roll pan with vegetable oil.
In a heavy saucepan, combine the sugar and corn
    syrup with ¼ cup water.
Bring to a boil and cook until the mixture reaches the
    soft crack stage (250°).
Add the butter and nuts.
Return to the heat and cook to the hard crack stage
    (295°).
Remove from the heat.
Stir in the baking soda.
Pour the brittle quickly over the oiled pan and spread
    as thin as possible with a spatula.
When the candy begins to harden, flip the brittle until
    completely cooled.
Break into irregular pieces.
Store in airtight containers.

Puye Picnic

GAZPACHO*

AVOCADO SANDWICHES*

JALAPEÑO PIE*

PEANUT SHORTBREAD*

POACHED PEACHES IN RED WINE*

ICED RED WINE
(FROM THE PEACHES)

KENWOOD VINEYARDS TABLE RED

This picnic is set on a mesa in the Puye ruins of New Mexico. Gazpacho traveled with the conquistadors from Spain to the Southwest. Too-often watery, this soup is meant to be thick with vegetables. When tomatoes are bursting-ripe, it is, above all, the proper time to make your gazpacho from scratch—forget store-bought tomato juice. The sandwiches are a sophisticated B.L.T., to be eaten with the soup. Jalapeño pie is a flavorful hot baked custard, and the peaches in wine provide both beverage and dessert. Shortbread sneaked into the territory with the Scots, and I've sneaked peanuts into the shortbread.

GAZPACHO

INGREDIENTS

2 quarts homemade tomato juice

4 to 5 cloves garlic, minced

1½ bunches scallions, including some of the green, split lengthwise and finely chopped

1 large sweet red bell pepper—seeded, deveined, and finely diced

2 green bell peppers—seeded, deveined, and finely diced

3 medium zucchini, grated (about 4 cups)

1 celery heart, finely diced

2 medium cucumbers—peeled, seeded, and chopped

¼ cup fresh lime juice

¼ cup tequila (optional)

2 teaspoons ground cumin

Salt and freshly milled black pepper

METHOD

In a large bowl, mix together all of the ingredients and chill for 4 hours.

Serve with the Avocado Sandwiches.

Serves 10

AVOCADO SANDWICHES

INGREDIENTS

¼ pound unsalted butter, at room temperature

1 teaspoon finely chopped cilantro

1 large ripe tomato—peeled, seeded, and chopped

6 slices crisp cooked bacon, chopped

2 medium-size ripe avocados

20 thin slices sprouted wheat bread

METHOD

In a small bowl, cream the butter with the cilantro.

Lightly butter each slice of bread.

Spread a little of the tomato on 10 slices of the bread and dust with the bacon.

Thinly slice the avocados and arrange over the bacon.

Top each sandwich with a slice of buttered bread.

Trim the crusts and cut in half diagonally.

Pack in an airtight container, covered with damp paper towels. Close tight until ready to serve.

Makes 20 half-sandwiches

JALAPEÑO PIE

INGREDIENTS

CORNMEAL CRUST:

1⅓ cups yellow or white cornmeal

⅔ cup all-purpose flour

½ teaspoon salt

½ cup lard

¼ cup cold water

FILLING:

1½ cups heavy cream

1½ cups milk

4 whole eggs, lightly beaten

3 egg yolks, lightly beaten

Salt, freshly milled pepper, and freshly grated nutmeg

1 cup grated Chihuahua or Monterey Jack cheese

7 fresh jalapeño peppers—seeded, deveined, and cut into ¼-inch strips

TOOLS

10-inch tart pan

Aluminum baking weights (optional)

METHOD

The cornmeal crust:

Preheat the oven to 350°

In a mixing bowl, mix the cornmeal, flour, and salt together.

Cut in the lard.

Add the cold water and mix.

Wrap the dough in waxed paper and refrigerate for at least 30 minutes.

Roll out the dough on a lightly floured surface.

Place the dough in a tart pan, fitting it evenly over the bottom of the pan and pressing it against the inside edges. Trim off excess dough by rolling a rolling pin over the top of the tart pan.

Cover the pastry with aluminum foil and weigh down with beans or aluminum baking weights.

Bake for 15 to 20 minutes, until the sides are set.

Remove the weights and foil and continue baking for 15 to 20 minutes, until light golden. Reserve; leave the oven on.

The filling:

In a large bowl, combine the heavy cream, milk, whole eggs, and egg yolks.

Blend thoroughly.

Season to taste with salt, pepper, and nutmeg.

Sprinkle the cheese over the bottom of the tart shell.

Arrange the strips of jalapeño over the cheese.

Pour the filling mixture into the shell.

Bake for about 40 minutes, or until the custard sets.

Allow to cool for 1 hour before cutting.

Serves 10

PEANUT SHORTBREAD

INGREDIENTS

½ pound unsalted butter at room temperature
½ cup sugar
2 cups all-purpose flour
¾ cup skinless roasted small peanuts

METHOD

In a mixing bowl, cream together the butter and sugar.

Blend in the flour.

Stir in the peanuts.

On a lighty dusted board, roll out the dough about ½-inch thick.

Cut the dough into 1½-by-2-inch rectangles.

Transfer the cookies to baking sheets.

Score the tops of the cookies in grid fashion with the edge of a paring knife.

Place the baking sheets in the refrigerator for 45 minutes.

Meanwhile, preheat the oven to 375°.

Place the baking sheets in the oven and reduce the temperature to 325°.

Bake for about 25 minutes, or until the bottoms are golden.

Cool.

Serves 8 to 10

POACHED PEACHES IN RED WINE

INGREDIENTS

10 ripe peaches
2½ cups sugar
Juice of 1 lemon
1 small cinnamon stick
2 bottles (each 25.4 ounces) dry red wine, chilled

METHOD

Place the peaches in a large pot with 1½ cups of the sugar, the lemon juice, and cinnamon stick. Add cold water to cover.

Cover the peaches with a round of waxed paper cut to fit the interior of the pot.

Set the pot over moderately high heat and bring the liquid to a simmer. Simmer until the peaches can be pierced easily with a sharp paring knife, about 10 to 15 minutes after the water begins to simmer.

Cool the peaches in the liquid.

Remove the skins with a paring knife. Strain the juice and reserve 3 cups for the syrup. Pour the remaining juice over the peaches.

Prepare the syrup:

In a heavy saucepan, heat the reserved 3 cups poaching liquid with the remaining 1 cup sugar.

Bring to a boil, reduce the heat, and simmer until reduced by one-third. Allow to cool.

Remove the peaches from their juice and place them in a large bowl. Discard the juices.

Add the wine and reduced syrup.

Serve the peaches as dessert and serve the wine as an accompaniment to the meal.

Serves 10

Frito Pie

Never underestimate the imagination of a fast-food vendor, and never doubt that when hunger strikes, we want it now. It's just a little bag of corn chips, cut along the side, and into this pouch they dump chili and cheese and onions and hand you a plastic fork, and you go to town.

Margarita

If ever a regional drink complemented the region's food, it is the Margarita, the champagne of the Southwest. Inevitably, drinks arrive with an assortment of velvety guacamole, hot salsa, and chicos fried up like popped corn.

MARGARITA

INGREDIENTS

1 lime slice
Kosher salt
Ice cubes
3 ounces tequila
1 ounce Triple Sec
2 ounces fresh lime juice

TOOLS

6- to 8-ounce Old Fashioned glass, chilled
Cocktail shaker
Cocktail strainer

METHOD

Rub the rim of the glass with the lime.
Pour a little salt in a flat dish and dip the glass in the salt to form a light coating around the rim.
Fill the cocktail shaker with 6 to 8 ice cubes.
Add the tequila, Triple Sec, and lime juice and shake briskly until the container begins to frost.
Strain into the salt-rimmed glass and serve.

Serves 1

STREET FOOD

CHIMAÝO COCKTAIL

INGREDIENTS

Ice cubes
1¼ ounces tequila
2 ounces apple cider
1½ teaspoons fresh lemon juice
1½ teaspoons crème de cassis

TOOLS

6- to 8-ounce tall glass
Cocktail shaker
Cocktail strainer

METHOD

Fill a cocktail shaker with 6 to 8 ice cubes.
Add all of the ingredients and shake briskly 6 or
   7 times.
Strain into the glass and serve.

Note: This drink was invented at the Rancho de
   Chimaýo. It provides a happy way of using the cider
   from their apple orchards.

Serves 1

GUACAMOLE WITH TOSTADOS

INGREDIENTS

4 ripe avocados
2 small ripe tomatoes—peeled, seeded, and chopped
¼ cup chopped cilantro
2 to 3 fresh green chiles or jalapeño peppers—
   deveined, seeded, and chopped
2 tablespoons fresh lime juice
2 cloves garlic, minced
1 small onion, minced (about ¼ cup)
Salt
Tostados, for serving

METHOD

Mash the avocados in a bowl.
Add the remaining ingredients, and mix together
   thoroughly.
Serve with tostados.

Makes about 3 cups

RED SALSA

INGREDIENTS

12 dried New Mexican chile pepper pods
½ cup vegetable oil
3 cloves garlic
1 teaspoon chopped fresh oregano
6 large ripe tomatoes, peeled and seeded
Salt
Tostados, for serving

TOOLS

Food processor

METHOD

Cut the chiles in half and devein and seed them.
In a heavy skillet, heat the oil and fry the chiles quickly
   until they begin to turn a brighter shade of red.
Remove with a slotted spoon and place in a bowl
   of water.
Let the chiles soak for 30 minutes.
In the skillet with the hot oil, toast the garlic cloves
   until golden.
Place the garlic in a food processor and chop. Add the
   drained chiles and chop coarsely.
Add the oregano and tomatoes and chop coarsely.
Remove the salsa to a bowl and set aside at room
   temperature for 2 hours.
Before serving, season to taste with salt.
Serve with tostados.

Makes 2 to 2½ cups

West Coast

"The beginning of vine planting is like the beginning of mining for the precious metals: the wine grower also 'prospects'. One corner of land after is tried with one kind of grape after another. This is a failure; that is better; a third best. So, bit by bit, they grope about for their Cloz Vougeot and Lafite.

"Those lodes and pockets of earth, more precious than the precious ores, that yield inimitable fragrance and soft fire; those virtuous Bonanzas, where the soil has sublimated under sun and stars to something finer, and the wine is bottled poetry: these still lie undiscovered; chaparral conceals, thicket empowers them; the miner chips the rock and wanders further, and the grizzly muses undisturbed. But there they bide their hours, awaiting their Columbus; and nature nurses and prepares them, the smack of Californian earth shall linger on the palate of your grandson."
—from SCOTLAND TO SILVERADO *by Robert Louis Stevenson, The Belknap Press of Harvard University Press, Cambridge, MA, 1966*

Los Angeles in 1820 was just a small town, numbering a few thousand. It was populated for the most part by the Spanish, Mexicans, and Indians whose lives revolved around the Franciscan missions that devoted its efforts to prayer and evangelizing the natives and to tilling the land. The friars brought their European olive, grape, and fig cuttings to these fertile valleys where the climate, so like the Mediterranean, was ideal. The sun-drenched soil produced wine grapes, table grapes, and raisins; dates, figs, and pistachios from Persia thrived. In the arid south, citrus and semitropical fruits included limes, oranges, grapefruits, mangoes, papayas, apricots, and plums; English walnuts, artichokes, garlic, and berries flourished in the moist earth of the north. At the time the Franciscans began building their missions in 1769, the nomadic tribes that inhabited the desert land of California and Nevada depended on the acorn as their staple; acorns, hulled and ground, were made into bread or gruel, just as hominy had been used elsewhere. The cooking method preferred by these tribes was a full day's project. Baskets

sunk in shallow pits were filled with water and hot stones. The food was added to the basket where it absorbed the stones' heat, and the cool stones were replaced with newly heated ones until the food was cooked. Unlike so many other ingenious cooking techniques devised by natives across the country, this was one the settler never really accepted.

By the 1850s, much of what is now Orange County was settled by Southerners—first, by the gold diggers, their pockets heavy with the dust of the Sierra Nevada lode, and later, by refugees of the war-ravaged states. In their "transplanted" southern gardens, magnolia and jasmine bloomed next to exotic pomegranates, avocados, quince, and cherimoya (the creamy, vanilla-fragrant fruit native to this arid soil). In the canyons, artichokes grew wild alongside cactus, whose leaves were used to pepper stews and were also thrown together with garden chard and beet greens to be boiled up with pork scraps for pot liquor. Southerners continued to feast on familiar fried hominy, pancakes studded with corn kernels, and fried apple rings, and the pig continued to play a major role. (From New England to California, that pork barrel followed the settler right across the country.) Los Angeles could boast a population of 100,000 by the turn of the century. During the summer months, fashionable families would have their trunks packed onto the small, independently run steam engine that chugged to Santa Monica, and they would "summer" there by the seashore. Little cups of steaming samp and sausages could be purchased from carts by midsummer strollers, and figs and guavas were plucked fresh from the trees lining the driveways.

The discovery of gold nearly emptied some of the Western states in 1851. Americans from every corner of the Union were joined by English, French, and Germans who sailed to Panama and then up the Pacific coast. Fortune seekers of every description—farmers, engineers, lawyers, doctors, merchants, the footloose, and the young—clambered aboard whaling boats, skiffs, and sailing vessels of all sizes, some holding as few as 10 passengers, some scarcely seaworthy. Many went north to seek excitement in San Francisco, and others packed off to the Sierras to join the frantic hunt. "Hangtown," the commonly used name given to

Placerville, was the gold miners' unofficial headquarters where saloons, boarding houses, dance halls, gambling houses, and bordellos were eager to accommodate the flood of business. From Hangtown's early unsavory years (though perhaps later years were no more savory) comes the story of its baptism. Three fugitive murderers were judged by a civil court of vigilantes and strung up from a great oak at one end of this muddy, one-street town. Hangtown's reckless reputation was established. Streets were littered with empty bottles, sardine boxes, and old bones. Dry goods stores and outfitters offered speculators their essential supplies at inflated prices. Boarding houses shoveled up greasy steaks, salt pork, pickles, and bad coffee to the 40 customers who fit at the oilcloth-covered tables, but the price of a square meal in a local eatery far exceeded its style. A plate of fried oysters, eggs, and bacon was bought with raw gold, and the infamy of this town is remembered not for its hot-headed vigilantes, but for this commonplace oyster fry, the "Hangtown Fry."

San Francisco, by contrast to dusty Los Angeles, was a makeshift town of plank and mud streets. Housing, such as it was, could be found in canvas tents, corrugated iron shacks, and prefabricated cottages complete with flimsy shutters. Immigrant-filled boats passing through the Golden Gate in the 1880s, a last wave from starving Europe, were greeted by what was described by the adventuring Scotsman J.D. Borthwick as "a ready-made population of active and capable men of every trade and profession." California had actually been colonized by her own "native" sons. Of the many nationalities to be found in San Francisco, each left its mark. The Chinese who came to work the railroads entrenched themselves in their own quarter. Their shops were filled with dried fish, glazed dried ducks, weird-looking vegetables, and foreign smelling teas; their "100-year-old eggs" and rumors of rat pies didn't stir a sense of culinary adventure in the general public. By mid-century, sections of San Francisco were completely French, others completely Italian, in appearance. There were several French-speaking theatres, Italian operas, concerts, and masquerades. San Francisco was becoming rather elegant—for an outpost! Restaurants provided excellent fare but found competition in the feasts offered at many bars and saloons—a groaning board set with sumptuous meats, fishes, and soups, available at no charge, the expectation being that the diner would make his contribution in buying some kind of "punch," "sling," or "cocktail." In San Francisco, one could indulge in the basic unelaborate American fare of corn bread, buckwheat cakes, pickles, grease, molasses, and pies. And although many ethnic cooks entered the service of the wealthy, the Chinese cook was preeminent. Some employers didn't necessarily like to "eat Chinese," but this approach, using finely cut, briefly cooked vegetables and meats would bring about an awareness of their cuisine and establish San Francisco as one of the capitals of Chinese cookery.

The city market was one enormous larder of deer, rabbit, and little quail hailed as the most delectable in the country (fetching an impressive $4 the dozen during the Gold Rush). Cabbages, turnips, potatoes, and onions were as fine as any grown, and broccoli, zucchini, artichokes, and garlic, with the profusion of wild and cultivated herbs, comforted the European. California farming was big thinking right from the start, producing remarkably large, succulent vegetables and fruits. A beetroot weighing in at 100 pounds was not thought too freakish (but it does defy the thought of attacking it for the pot), and what would those first farmers think of today's sudden affection for minature this and miniature that?

The Sacramento River ran with excellent salmon and sturgeon during the spawning months of the spring and fall. The Pacific coast was fished mainly by Italians, and there was an easy awareness of Italian cookery at the time, what with popular Italian restaurants as well as the fish shacks along the wharf that heated up cauldrons of an invention called "cioppino," a stew of Dungeness crabs, mussels, clams, and cod simmered in stock, tomatoes, oil, and herbs. Perhaps sweetest of all treats was batter-fried abalone. (Abalone is now making something of a comeback after the ravages of pollution and the greedy sea otter.)

On the drive through the San Joaquin, or "Central" Valley in spring, lunar landscape hills are already burnished with hip-high grasses shimmering in shades of copper brown to gold. This valley is a technological masterwork, an overwhelming feat of farming. Imagine it as a series of huge cultivated tracts, for example, of 20-mile stretches of bell pepper fields between farms. Miles of pipeline and wheels dizzily spout thousands of gallons of water, coaxing rich soil from desert. The agribusinessman (or "desktop farmer" as he is sometimes called) has left the pickup truck in favor of air-conditioned, stereo-equipped cabs that sit on huge tractors. These farmers go to any length to "up" production, even bringing in bees to pollinate stone fruits, pistachios, almonds, and walnuts. (Walnuts, for instance, illustrate America's methodical approach to crop raising. In France, the typical walnut grower hopes for three weeks of clear weather to dry his three-acre crop. In northern California, monstrous farms dry theirs artificially in a couple of days. It's hard to imagine that production on such a huge scale gives us an equally delicious walnut, when a single California grower outstrips the whole of France's annual harvest by 160 million pounds.)

On vegetable farms, migrant workers are in the fields before sunup, and the moment the sun peeks over the distant hills the day's picking begins. The workers are paid by the pound, and frantically pick as fast as they possibly can to make their buck. Canvas bags are filled rapidly and transported by conveyor belt to wheeled gondolas. Produce is hand-sorted and packaged in nearby packing sheds. "How're your peppers doin'?" is a refrain sung out as farmer passes farmer, the lyrics changing from peppers, to melons, to nectarines, to tomatoes, to beans, as the endless growing season stretches on toward autumn. By midday the light is white and the heat typically reaches a mean of 100 degrees. During the hell of summer, picking continues on through the night with tractors floodlighting the fields as pickers work through a heavy rain of insects. Onions are harvested and sacked right in the fields, likewise garlic, and then are left there until they dry. Lack of moisture is no enemy here. In vineyards, plastic hoses run down the rows, dripping precisely controlled amounts of water to produce the perfect looking table grape. Large-scale farming would hardly be possible without today's scientific manipulation. When 80 percent of a grape stem has bloomed, a spray is applied to thin out the buds, and eventually elongate the grape. Later, second and third sprayings stretch the maturing grape to achieve a larger size. These sprays increase the visual attractiveness of each bunch, as well as the total yield per acre. These sprays are water-soluble and though the chemicals don't enter the fruit, they do produce a tougher skin. We habitually wash fruits purchased from the market in cold water, but the pickers choose to dip theirs first in hot, then in cold water before eating the fruit.

Though the table grape grower can manipulate his fruit with chemicals, he must carefully harvest, or "pack" the fruit by hand. However, the wine grape grower demonstrates the trend of modern agriculture with a mechanical grape harvester that straddles the vine and shakes off the grapes, sucking up leaves and stems with a fan and setting the clusters in gondolas. A couple of workers sit on the harvester's "wings", pulling out unwanted branches and debris. Yet like most of the hand-picked produce of the valley, hand-picked wine grapes fetch a higher price, as they carry more weight, and less undesirable material.

Eighty percent of this region's produce is shipped east, and most of the remaining tonnage is sent to the canning factories and markets of California. The yield is simply astonishing, a legacy of Luther Burbank, who left New England for the west in the 1920s and will be remembered as one of America's great horticulturists. During the rushed picking season, the strain of round-the-clock work is felt night and day at the little Mexican fondas that keep the workers going, dishing out burritos and frijoles refritos with store-bought tacos, or at the cozy diners where they still serve stacks of pancakes, fresh farm eggs, sausages, grits, and good coffee with fresh cream.

The United States government brought a number of Basque sheep farmers from Spain and France for few Americans felt inclined to herd. The Basques settled primarily from Idaho to the San Joaquin Valley, and Bakersfield is virtually all Basques, Mexicans, farmers, and cowboys. It has a midwestern feel, with oil derricks pumping away right in the middle of the farmland. Local farmers permit Basque herds to come down from the hills in winter and forage for whatever they can find in the harvested fields, and in exchange, the shepherd gives up one of his lambs.

Bakersfield may be a city in some respects, but more than anything else it is a farmtown, with farm ethics and the good fun of race car heats and rodeos. On Sunday nights, the local Basque restaurant is crowded with farmers, families in tow, all speaking French. First they have a drink of fizzy picon punch, and then the doors open onto a room with long, cloth-covered tables. A battery of dishes appears, one following the other: tureens of vegetable soups, cold veal's tongue with vinaigrette and onions, beef stews with noodles, grilled chicken with fried potatoes, leafy salads, brie and bread, crème caramel to polish it off, and big bottles of plonk red to wash it all down. These farmers defy the dictates of California cookery today, that to eat cool is to stay cool, and the whole occasion is a 19th–century throwback.

America's native grape, *Vitis labrusca*, didn't flourish west of the Rockies. Circa 1770, Franciscan friars planted their first vines in California. The Mission grape, grafted from Spanish and Mexican vines, is said to have been brought by Padre Junípero Serra in 1769 from Baja to San Diego. At this time the heart of the wine region was in the Los Angeles basin (it would move three times in two centuries to make room for urban sprawl and still accommodate the thirst for this greatest of elixirs). Missionaries produced as many as 50,000 gallons a year—the grapes trampled by local Indians and the wine stored in barrels and cowhide bags to ferment. In the 1830s, when the Mexican government stripped California's 21 missions of their religious authority, the Mission grape became a secular concern. The classic European varieties of *V. vinifera,* which failed so miserably in every attempt to grow them in the East, would thrive in California as though native to the soil. Still, though the grapes may have been good, winemaking techniques were not, and so, for many long years, neither was the wine.

New England colonists explored some 40 grape varieties, calling the common grape a "fox" grape for its muskiness; they used it primarily for juice and jelly for it made awful wine. Thomas Jefferson certainly didn't fail at viticulture for lack of trying, but couldn't manage to coax his European *V. vinifera* cuttings to grow successfully on vineyard scale, and by the turn of the 19th century his extensive vineyards had been given up as hopeless. William Prince of Long Island, whose family established nurseries and vineyards in Flushing, was an ardent early–19th–century horticulturist who wrote enthusiastically on winemaking and took great pains to classify and grow literally hundreds of varieties. In fact it was Prince (as scholars Janice and Daniel Longone have pointed out) who introduced the Zinfandel grape to America, long before Agoston Haraszthy took it to California. Haraszthy brought many European varieties to California in addition to Zinfandel, arranging for the import of 100,000 healthy vines. He labored over sparkling wines too, but his developments were later eclipsed by the Czech Korbel brothers. It is Bordeaux-born Jean-Louis Vignes who is often considered the father of California wine. By 1840, he was cultivating 100 acres (mostly Mission vines with some French varieties as well), which lie today beneath Union Station in Los Angeles. Vignes aged his wine eight to 10 years, unheard-of devotion at that time, and induced a considerable number of Frenchmen to emigrate to California and enter the wine industry.

The French in California were soon joined by Germans and Italians who established vineyards of their own. Meanwhile, the wine industry stirred to life in the Midwest, notably in Ohio and Missouri. Missouri was actually one of our leading wine producers, and the huge Catawba vineyards of Cincinnati in the 1850s produced popular and sparkling wines until suddenly the vines fell to a devastating disease which cut the Cincinnati industry dead.

Large scale California wine-making began in the early 1940s when master vintner Paul Masson's vineyards were bought up by a large concern. Sonoma, Mendocino, and Napa counties were then our source of inexpensive table wines. Competition among vineyards and a growing public awareness of good wine have encouraged the older, larger wineries of these valleys to turn from jug wine to more reputable labels. Today the small wineries produce varietal wines that are elegant competition for any European contender. The

drive to compete with European wine, to create wines on a par with those of the French in particular, prompted California vintners to purchase wooden aging barrels made of oak from the forests of Limousin and Nevers, France. Wine makers over the years have experimented with native California oak or redwood, but many prefer the French wood. Today enormous stainless steel vats store wine until it is ready to age in the barrels before bottling.

These valleys have become a mecca for wine lovers. In just a decade, these quiet villages practically have become chic resorts. Property values have skyrocketed, and the result is a movement north to the Alexander Valley, where the newest vineyards are sprouting. The valley towns still project a 19th–century tranquility, looking perhaps just the way wine country towns ought to look. But because this industry is so tightly bound with the American "discovery" of food, it happily has brought in numbers of young people who have not only opened some great restaurants, but are devoted to producing wonderful cheeses from goats and sheep, drying and packaging herbs, developing virgin olive oil, raising game on farms, and bottling local preserves, honeys, and mustards.

The character and quality of a region will eventually tell in all its wines. As one wine maker says, "California wine from any given valley is the same—it's just a question of how much love you want to put into it."

Pioneer spirit brought the wine makers to California, and it is this spirit that is so evident today, keeping California a vanguard of perpetual pleasures. And though the food sometimes smacks of trendiness, think twice! California cooking is a very clear derivative of American cooking, done with the raw materials California has made her own. In no other part of the country do we have such a strong feeling that the foods and drink wholly complement each other. This is a new experience for Americans, to visit an area and dine on its local warm goat cheese in a salad, roast quail, and homegrown vegetables, persimmon sherbet and nut tortes, accompanied by a true *vin du region*. Not one of these valleys was developed by a single nationality but by blends of Finns, Czechs, Germans, Hungarians, Spanish, French, and Italians.

LAMB FRIES

INGREDIENTS

24 lamb fries
All-purpose flour, to dust the fries
Salt and freshly milled black pepper
½ to ⅔ cup Clarified Butter (see Basics, page 344)
3 cloves garlic, minced
½ cup chopped fresh parsley
34 thin rounds of French or sourdough bread

METHOD

Preheat the oven to 275°.

Lightly dust the lamb fries with flour and season with salt and pepper.

In a large heavy skillet, heat half of the butter over moderate heat.

Add the garlic and sauté until it begins to wilt.

Add the lamb fries and cook for 8 to 10 minutes, until golden, adding more butter as the fries absorb it.

Fold in the parsley and keep the fries warm on a serving platter in the oven.

Add the remaining butter, increase the heat slightly, and toast the bread until golden.

Serve the fries immediately, surrounded by the toast.

Serves 4 to 6

Lamb Fry Lunch

LAMB FRIES° GARLIC TOAST
ICED FRESH FRUITS
FRESH ALMONDS

RIO BRAVO RANCH FRENCH
COLOMBARD RESERVE or
QUPÉ VINEYARD SYRAH

Every spring the shepherds send down buckets of lamb fries, nipped from would-be rams. This delicacy rarely goes beyond the rancher's kitchen. Sun-ripened fruits are refreshed in bowls of ice. Branches of green almonds, picked almost before they are ready to be harvested, are heavy with silken nutmeats. You can break the velvety outer skin with your teeth to reach the inner shell, full of soft, pungent, almondy fruit. Green almonds were as much a surprise to these growers as they were to me, when bowls of them were set out after dinner in the orchards of Corsica.

Roast Lamb on a Spit

ROAST LAMB LIMA BEAN PURÉE

POTATO TART *

SOURDOUGH BREAD
(see page 292)

PLUM TART *

LAUREL GLEN VINEYARDS
CABERNET SAUVIGNON

Though I prefer my gigot with juices running pink, a whole roasted lamb should be cooked until the flesh can be picked from the bone. Young lamb does not require marinating but does require constant basting when roasted on a spit. A "broom" made of wild rosemary and thyme branches, with cut bulbs of garlic on their stalks will do. Dipped in a bowl of local olive oil, the broom brushes the meat as it roasts. A smaller lamb could be oven roasted. This spit is makeshift, the lamb securely fastened with wire; a second cook should turn the spit and keep the small beast in place.

POTATO TART

INGREDIENTS

6 large Idaho potatoes, peeled
1 cup Clarified Butter (see Basics, page 344)
Salt and freshly milled black pepper

TOOLS

10-inch pie pan, 2 inches deep (preferably glass)

METHOD

Preheat the oven to 500°.

Thinly slice the potatoes about ⅛-inch thick and wash them thoroughly in cold running water.

Drain and place them in a bowl of lightly salted ice water for up to 1 hour.

Drain and thoroughly dry the slices with paper towels.

Coat the pie pan with 3 tablespoons of the butter.

Arrange the potatoes in an overlapping spiral on the bottom of the pan.

Season the first layer with salt and pepper and coat with butter.

Continue making layers, alternating potatoes, seasonings, and butter and ending with a layer of potatoes, until the pan is filled.

Place a clean kitchen towel over the pan and weigh down with a second pan or baking sheet and a heavy weight for 10 minutes.

Remove the weights, pan, and towel and coat the tart with the remaining butter.

Bake for 45 minutes, or until the bottom crust is golden.

Let the tart rest for 5 minutes.

Place a serving platter over the tart and invert.

If the potatoes do not immediately release, run a metal spatula around the rim of the pan.

Slice into pie wedges and serve hot.

Note: The tart can be prepared and weighed down and refrigerated about 1 hour before baking.

Use a glass pan to check the degree of doneness on the bottom of the tart.

Serves 6 to 8

PLUM TART

INGREDIENTS

1 recipe Pie Dough, made with butter (see Basics, page 346)
12 to 16 ripe red plums
Grated zest of 1 lemon
3 tablespoons sugar
⅓ cup apricot jam

METHOD

On a lightly floured surface, roll out the pastry dough to form a 28-by-10-inch rectangle, about ¼-inch thick.

Place the dough on a baking sheet.

Cover with waxed paper and refrigerate while you prepare the plums.

Preheat the oven to 400°.

Cut the plums in half, remove the pits, and cut each half into quarters.

Toss the plums with the lemon zest.

Starting at the center and working out to within 1 inch of the sides, arrange the plums on the pie dough, slightly overlapping the pieces.

Roll in the edges of the dough to meet the plums.

Dust with the sugar and bake for 30 to 40 minutes, or until the outer crust is crisp and golden.

In a small saucepan, melt the jam over moderate heat and brush the top of the tart with the jam.

Slice the tart into strips and serve warm.

Serves 10 to 12

Samp Dinner

SAMP WITH FRESH LIMA BEANS
AND SMOKED EEL*

POUSSIN WITH OLIVE PURÉE
AND SWEET PEPPERS*

PARKER HOUSE ROLLS
(see Basics, page 343)

POPPY SEED CAKE WITH
CARAMEL FROSTING*

FOPPIANO VINEYARDS
PETITE SIRAH
WILLIAM WHEELER WINERY
SAUVIGNON BLANC

Samp found its way from the coastal towns of New England, Long Island, and the South. It was the Southerners who brought it to Los Angeles, and cooked it up with bits of meat and shanks. It became the custom at the southern tip of Long Island to add a little smoked eel to the cooked kernels. Poussin is a little chicken—not to be confused with a game hen or a Cornish hen—that weighs about a pound or less, and is best when simply roasted. Local ripe olives puréed with garlic and oil, similar to the southern French tapenade, are stuffed between the skin and the flesh to infuse the chicken with pungent olive flavor. The cake is loaded with poppy seeds, which was the custom at the time when a cake was really a cake.

SAMP WITH FRESH LIMA BEANS AND SMOKED EEL

INGREDIENTS

1½ cups samp (coarse hominy)
About 1 quart Chicken Stock (see Basics, page 343)
2 cups heavy cream
1 cup shelled fresh lima beans
1 smoked eel, peeled and flaked from the bone
(about 1½ cups)
1 tablespoon unsalted butter
2 to 3 gratings of nutmeg
Salt and freshly milled pepper

METHOD

In a large bowl or pot, cover the samp with 3 quarts of water and soak for 12 hours or overnight.

Drain and place the samp into a stockpot with the chicken stock.

Add water to cover and simmer until tender, adding more water or stock as needed.

When tender, drain and return the samp to the pot.

Add the heavy cream and place over low heat.

In a pot of lightly salted water, cook the lima beans until tender.

Drain and fold into the samp mixture.

Fold in the flaked eel.

Add the butter and seasonings to taste.

Serve hot.

Note: The samp will take 2 to 3 hours of watchful cooking; add additional liquid as necessary, stirring often.

Serves 4 to 6

POUSSIN WITH OLIVE PURÉE AND SWEET PEPPERS

INGREDIENTS

OLIVE PURÉE:

1 cup small salted black olives, pitted
1 clove garlic, chopped
About 1½ tablespoons olive oil

POUSSIN:

4 poussins or very young chickens (each about
    1¼ pounds)
Salt and freshly milled black pepper
Olive oil, for the birds
2 sweet red bell peppers—cored, seeded, deveined,
    and cut into 1-inch strips
2 yellow bell peppers—cored, seeded, deveined,
    and cut into 1-inch strips
3 tablespoons olive oil
½ cup dry white wine
1 cup Chicken Stock (see Basics, page 343)

TOOLS

Food processor

METHOD

The olive purée:
Blend the olives, garlic, and oil in a food processor
    until smooth.
If too dry, add an additional ½ tablespoon of oil.
    Reserve.

The poussin:
Preheat the oven to 400°.
Remove the fat from the cavities of the chickens.
Salt and pepper the cavities.
Using your index finger, carefully loosen the skin from
    the breasts.
Spread a little of the olive purée into the pockets.
Truss the birds and brush with olive oil.
Set the birds on a rack in a roasting pan and roast,

basting frequently, for 30 to 40 minutes,
    or until the juices run clear when the
    legs are pierced.
Meanwhile, in a large skillet, sauté the red and yellow
    bell peppers in the olive oil over low heat, until they
    wilt and are tender. Season with salt and pepper.
Transfer the birds to a warm platter.
Spoon off any excess fat from the roasting pan.
Add the wine and stock and deglaze the pan over
    moderate heat, scraping up any brown bits that
    cling to the bottom of the pan.
Season the sauce with salt and pepper and cook until
    reduced by one-third. Strain and reserve.
Serve the birds with the sautéed peppers and
    the sauce.

Serves 4

POPPY SEED CAKE WITH CARAMEL FROSTING

INGREDIENTS

CAKE:

Butter and flour, for the cake pans
1 cup poppy seeds
1 cup sour cream
¼ pound butter
⅔ cup granulated sugar
2 cups all-purpose flour
2 teaspoons baking powder
¼ teaspoon ground cardamom
1 teaspoon grated lemon zest
4 egg whites

FROSTING:

2 cups brown sugar
1 cup granulated sugar
1½ cups heavy cream
3 tablespoons butter

TOOLS

Two 9-inch round cake pans
Electric mixer
Candy thermometer

METHOD

The cakes:
Preheat the oven to 350°.
Butter and flour the cake pans; set aside.
In the top of a double boiler, combine the poppy
    seeds and sour cream.
Cook over simmering water until warmed through.
Remove the pot from the heat and set aside for 1 hour.
In a mixing bowl, cream together the butter
    and the sugar.
Combine all the dry ingredients, including the
    cardamom and lemon zest.
Alternately add the dry ingredients and the poppy seed
    mixture to the creamed butter until the ingredients
    are blended.
In the bowl of the electric mixer, beat the egg whites
    until stiff and glossy.
Fold one-third of the whites into the batter. Fold in the
    remaining whites.
Divide the batter between the cake pans and bake for
    40 minutes, or until the cake pulls away from the
    sides of the pan.
Immediately remove the cakes from the pans and set
    on a rack to cool.
The frosting:
In a heavy saucepan, bring the sugars and cream to a
    boil, stirring constantly.
When the sugars dissolve, stop stirring, place a candy
    thermometer in the syrup, and cook until the mix-
    ture almost reaches the soft ball stage (232°).
Remove the syrup from the heat and add the butter,
    stirring until incorporated. Set aside to cool.
When the syrup is lukewarm, beat with a wire whisk or
    electric mixer until thick and creamy.
Hold the frosting in a warm water bath while
    icing the cake.
To assemble:
With a serrated knife, trim the top and bottom crusts of
    both cake layers.
Using a spatula, spread the caramel frosting on the
    bottom layer, placing the second layer on top
    of the first.
Spread the frosting evenly over the top and sides
    of the cake.

Serves 8 to 10

Sashimi Supper

SASHIMI NAPOLEON*

FRESH FRUIT WITH
TRIPLE SEC CREAM*

HACIENDA WINE CELLARS
CHENIN BLANC

Possibly the freshest fish to be found in Los Angeles comes from the markets of Little Tokyo—likewise, the best sushi bars. If the French borrowed the Japanese aesthetic in creating nouvelle cuisine, the Japanese in turn have embraced the principles of French sauces. The stark look of these Los Angeles eateries—the straight-forward lighting, the marble, the neon—is the American touch, but the dishes are an amalgam of East and West.

SASHIMI NAPOLEON

INGREDIENTS

VEGETABLES:
¼ of a whole daikon (Japanese white radish), peeled—cut into needle-thin julienne, and soaked in ice water
1 bunch radish sprouts, roots trimmed
4 *shiso* leaves (grape-type leaf, sometimes called "beefsteak")
8 long fresh chives

DRESSING:
3 tablespoons sherry vinegar
⅛ teaspoon wasabi horseradish, or to taste
1 tablespoon soy sauce
⅓ cup mild olive oil

FISH:
½ pound fresh tuna
½ pound smoked salmon
½ pound halibut fillets, with skin intact

WONTONS:
8 wonton skins, about 5 inches square
½ cup Clarified Butter (see Basics, page 344)

METHOD

The dressing:
In a small bowl, whisk together the vinegar, wasabi, and soy sauce until dissolved.
Gradually whisk in the olive oil. Reserve.

The fish:
With a very sharp thin-bladed knife, very thinly slice the fish against the grain.
When cutting the halibut, slice against the skin as you would smoked salmon. Reserve.

The wontons:
Cut the wonton skins crosswise in half, making 16 pieces.
In a skillet, heat ¼ cup of the clarified butter over moderate heat.

Fry the wonton skins until golden on each side, adding more butter as needed.

Remove and drain on paper towels.

To assemble:

Place a wonton skin on each of four plates.

Layer the fish to fit the wonton skin, separating the fish with the wonton leaves and ending with a layer of fish layers (4 layers per plate, creating a Napoleon effect).

Tuck a *shiso* leaf under the corner of each Napoleon.

Drain and dry the radish julienne and scatter with the daikon, sprouts, and chives over the top. Sprinkle with the dressing and serve.

Serves 4

FRESH FRUIT WITH TRIPLE SEC CREAM

INGREDIENTS

FRUIT:

Choose any combination of strawberries, raspberries, and figs; orange, grapefruit, or lime sections; sliced starfruit; peeled and quartered kiwi fruit

TRIPLE SEC CREAM:

4 egg yolks, at room temperature

½ cup sugar

¼ cup Triple Sec

2 cups heavy cream, scalded

TOOLS

4 ovenproof shallow plates

METHOD

Wash and dry the fruit. Set aside.

In the top of a double boiler, beat the egg yolks until smooth and lemon colored.

Fold in the sugar.

Place the yolk mixture over simmering water and gradually whisk in the Triple Sec.

As the mixture begins to thicken, gradually add the hot cream.

When the mixture thickens enough to coat the whisk, remove from the heat and reserve.

Arrange the fruits on the plates and divide the sauce among them.

Place each plate on a pan under the broiler for 15 seconds, or long enough to glaze the cream.

Serves 4

STREET FOOD

Hamburger

I had my first drive-in meal in Los Angeles, when I was 17. From the car window all I could see was net stockings on a pair of legs. A tray was slapped on the side of the door, and I had my lunch, and I just thought I'd been to the end of the plastic rainbow.

Breakfast

Sourdough bread is popular from Bakersfield to Sonoma, and is synonymous with San Francisco. The recipe given here, with the gracious permission of James Beard, is the best one I know. Because of the difficulty involved in making good sourdough, I saw no point in developing another one, and would rather rely on the techniques of the master. I also agree with Mr. Beard that attempting to make good French bread without a fired stone oven isn't always worth the effort. Nothing is more pleasing than running home with a loaf of bread warm from the oven of a local baker. Fresh local figs, sweet butter, and jam make an uncomplicated, satisfying breakfast.

JAMES BEARD'S SOURDOUGH RYE BREAD

INGREDIENTS

THREE DAYS IN ADVANCE:

1 package active dry yeast
2 cups lukewarm water
2 cups all-purpose flour

ONE DAY IN ADVANCE:

2 cups rye flour
1 cup lukewarm water

BREAD:

1 package active dry yeast
2¼ cups lukewarm water
2 teaspoons salt
1 tablespoon caraway seed
1½ teaspoons poppy seed
2 tablespoons melted butter
3 tablespoons granulated sugar
4 cups all-purpose flour
Butter and cornmeal, for the baking sheets
1 egg lightly beaten with 1 tablespoon water, for egg wash

METHOD

Three days in advance:
In a bowl, combine the yeast with the lukewarm water.
Add the 2 cups flour and blend.
Pour the starter into a container and seal tightly.
Allow starter to sit at room temperature for 2 days.
    Then place in the refrigerator for 1 day.
One day in advance:
Place 1 cup of the "starter" in a bowl. Measure in the
    rye flour and lukewarm water.
Mix together and cover with plastic wrap.
Let stand overnight at room temperature.
The bread:
Dissolve the yeast with ¼ cup of the lukewarm water.
Stir down the dough that has been standing overnight.
Add the dissolved yeast, salt, caraway seeds, poppy
    seeds, melted butter, and sugar.
One cup at a time, add 4 cups of the flour, stirring to
    make a stiff dough.
Turn the dough out onto a clean surface and knead for
    10 to 12 minutes.
Shape the dough into a ball and place in a
    buttered bowl.
Turn the dough over to coat it with butter.
Cover and place in a warm draft-free place to rise until
    doubled in bulk, about 2 hours.
Meanwhile, butter 2 baking sheets and generously
    sprinkle with cornmeal.
Punch down the dough and divide it in half.
Shape each piece of dough into a free-form loaf and
    place it on the prepared baking sheets.
Cover and let rise for 1 hour.
Preheat the oven to 375°
Brush the loaves with the egg wash and bake for 30
    minutes, or until the bread is golden and sounds
    hollow when the bottom is tapped.
Cover the sourdough loaves with kitchen towels to
    prevent the crust from hardening.

Makes 2 loaves

Fish Stew Dinner

GRILLED SHIITAKE MUSHROOMS*

SAUTÉED FISH STEW*

NASTURTIUM AND
WATERCRESS SALAD*

A VARIETY OF CALIFORNIA
GOAT CHEESES

ARMENIAN SESAME SEED
CRACKERBREAD

BLACKBERRIES AND RASPBERRIES
WITH CREAM

RIDGE WHITE ZINFANDEL

Shiitake mushrooms are an Oriental mushroom cultivated from California to Vermont. Sometimes called "golden oak" or "black forest" mushrooms, they are as common in the Orient as our American commercially grown mushrooms are here but have a woodsier flavor. They can be pan-sautéed, but the charred flavor from grilling is very nice. The fish stew is like a quick sauté, the ingredients added one at a time to preserve their individual character and tenderness. Goat cheeses, aromatic with herbs and pepper, and ranging from soft to hard, are locally produced in French fashion. The edible nasturtiums are not store-bought but rather picked from the profusion of blossoms that grow in the pots and gardens of so many California homes.

GRILLED SHIITAKE MUSHROOMS

INGREDIENTS

⅓ pound shiitake mushrooms (per serving)
Olive oil, for basting
Kosher salt and freshly milled black pepper
Fresh thyme leaves

TOOLS

Charcoal grill or broiler

METHOD

Prepare a charcoal grill.
When the coals turn dusty red, set an oiled rack 4 to 5
    inches above the coals.

Brush the mushrooms with oil and sprinkle with a little salt and pepper.

Place the mushrooms on the rack and grill until they blister and become slightly limp.

Serve with a sprinkling of thyme leaves.

Note: You may cook the mushrooms on a low flame of a broiler or on a rack over a gas flame, but charcoal enhances the flavor more effectively.

Serves 1

SAUTÉED FISH STEW

INGREDIENTS

½ cup olive oil
1 large yellow bell pepper—cored, seeded, deveined, and cut into long julienne
1 large sweet red bell pepper—cored, seeded, deveined, and cut into long julienne
2 large white onions, very thinly sliced
2 cloves garlic, minced
6 large ripe tomatoes—peeled, seeded, and chopped with juices reserved
1 tablespoon fresh tarragon leaves
1 teaspoon fresh thyme leaves
1 quart Fish Stock (see Basics, page 344)
1 pound lingcod or bass
1 pound Pacific snapper
1 pound prawns or large shrimp
1 pound sea scallops
1 pound squid, cleaned and cut into ½-inch rings
1½ to 2 dozen Pacific Coast littleneck clams
½ cup wild fennel leaves, torn into bits

METHOD

In a large skillet or sauté pan, heat the oil over moderately low heat.

Sauté the yellow peppers just until they wilt.

Remove and reserve.

Sauté the red pepper strips in the same manner and reserve.

Sauté the onions and garlic until the onions wilt.

Add the tomatoes and simmer for 5 minutes.

Add the herbs and fish stock and bring the mixture to a slow simmer.

Add the fish and shellfish in the order listed. As each fish takes on color, add the next one.

Add the clams last. (Unlike East Coast clams, they require little cooking to open.)

Quickly fold in the peppers.

Transfer the stew to a heated tureen and stir in the fennel leaves.

Serve with slices of sourdough bread brushed lightly with olive oil and baked briefly in a 400° oven just until the edges begin to turn golden and the bread is still soft.

Serves 6 to 8

NASTURTIUM AND WATERCRESS SALAD

INGREDIENTS

2 bunches watercress, stems trimmed

¼ cup olive oil

Juice of 1 lemon

Salt and freshly milled black pepper

2 dozen nasturtium flowers, pistil and base removed

METHOD

In a salad bowl, toss the watercress with the olive oil and lemon juice, and seasonings.

Place the flowers over the watercress and serve.

Serves 6 to 8

hominy, liked by San Francisco Italians who doctor up the bland grit. The little quail are set on the polenta, soaking it with their juices while they are picked apart and eaten with the fingers. Berries with angel food cake are a must. The addition of this tart lemon sauce makes this sweet, cottony cake more palatable.

FENNEL-GRILLED SHRIMP

INGREDIENTS

2 pounds medium shrimp in their shells
   (6 to 7 per person)
¾ cup olive oil
½ cup chopped fresh fennel sprigs

TOOLS

Grill with charcoals or fruit wood
Dried fennel stalks

METHOD

Prepare a charcoal or wood fire.
Off the heat, cover the rack with foil and make slits in the foil with a paring knife.
Place the shrimp in a bowl.
Add the olive oil and fennel and toss.
When the coals are dusty red, set the grill in place to heat up.
When ready to cook the shrimp, add the dried fennel stalks to the coals; they will ignite almost immediately.
Quickly arrange the shrimp on the grill to infuse with the fennel stalk flavor.
Grill the shrimp on each side for 1 to 2 minutes, until they turn pink.

Serves 4

Fennel-Grilled Lunch

FENNEL-GRILLED SHRIMP*

QUAIL* ON POLENTA*

CARAMELIZED ONIONS*

MELTED BERRIES*

ANGEL FOOD CAKE*
WITH STRAWBERRIES,
RASPBERRIES, AND LEMON CREAM*

ACACIA WINERY PINOT NOIR *or*
NEYERS WINERY CHARDONNAY

Throughout the Bay area, wild fennel is like the dandelion—growing in fields, abandoned lots, and along roads—it's there for the taking. Bundles are tied and set to dry, and the fennel is used as cooking fuel to infuse fish with a marvelous flavor. If fennel isn't handy, you can always splash the fish with Pernod. Polenta is an Italian version of

QUAIL

INGREDIENTS

8 quail, washed and patted dry
Salt and freshly milled pepper
16 juniper berries, crushed
⅓ cup olive oil

TOOLS

Grill and charcoals

METHOD

Prepare the charcoal fire.
Salt and pepper the cavities of the birds.
Place 2 juniper berries in each cavity.
Truss the birds, brush with olive and set aside.
Preheat the oven to 400°.
When the coals reach a dusty red glow, lightly oil
    the grill.
Brown the birds on the grill, turning often.
Place on a heatproof pan and baste with a
    little more oil.
Bake in the oven for 5 to 10 minutes, until rare
    and juicy.
Serve the quail on the fried polenta cakes so that the
    polenta will absorb the juices.

Serves 4

POLENTA

INGREDIENTS

2 cups milk
1 teaspoon salt
½ cup yellow cornmeal
2 egg yolks, beaten
¼ cup plus 1 tablespoon olive oil

METHOD

Lightly oil a baking sheet.
In a heavy saucepan, bring the milk to a low boil over
    moderate heat and add the salt.
Slowly pour in the cornmeal, stirring constantly with a
    wooden spoon.
Continue to cook, stirring constantly, for 30 minutes,
    or until the polenta pulls away from the sides
    of the pan.
Off the heat, briskly fold in the eggs, beating until
    incorporated.
Pour the polenta onto the prepared baking sheet and
    spread out a little less than ½-inch thick.
Allow to cool thoroughly and cut the polenta into
    rectangular or diamond shapes large enough to
    hold the birds.
In a cast-iron skillet, heat the olive oil over
    moderate heat.

When the oil is hot, fry the polenta on each side until golden.

Place the polenta on a heated serving dish and set a hot roasted bird on each slice of polenta. Serve immediately.

Note: The consistency of cornmeal varies and the addition of more liquid may be necessary. Have ready a small pan of boiling water and, if the mixture becomes too tough, add boiling water, a little at a time, stirring vigorously to avoid any lumps.

Serves 4 to 8

CARAMELIZED ONIONS

INGREDIENTS

2 pints pearl onions
4 tablespoons unsalted butter
2 tablespoons sugar

METHOD

Make an "X" in the root end of each onion.

In a pot of lightly salted boiling water, blanch the onions for about 1 minute.

Cool and peel.

Return the onions to boiling water, reduce the heat, and simmer until tender. Drain.

In a skillet, melt the butter over moderate heat.

Add the onions, shaking the pan to coat the onions with butter.

Sprinkle with the sugar and cook until the sugar begins to caramelize.

When the onions take on a caramel color, serve.

Serves 8

MELTED BERRIES

INGREDIENTS

1 pint blueberries, huckleberries, or Concord grapes
2 tablespoons sugar
3 thin lemon slices
1 tablespoon fresh lemon juice

METHOD

In a small nonaluminum saucepan, combine the berries or grapes with the sugar, lemon slices, and lemon juice.

Warm the berries over moderate heat, gently tossing to coat with the sugar.

Cover tightly and cook until the sugar has melted and the berries begin to give off their juice. Remove from the heat and serve immediately with the birds.

Serves 4 to 8

ANGEL FOOD CAKE

INGREDIENTS

1⅓ cups sugar
1 cup all-purpose flour
11 egg whites, at room temperature
1½ teaspoons cream of tartar
1 teaspoon salt
1 teaspoon vanilla extract

TOOLS

10-inch tube pan, ungreased
Electric mixer

METHOD

Preheat the oven to 350°.
Sift the sugar 3 times into a mixing bowl.
In a separate mixing bowl, sift the flour 5 times.
Mix ⅓ cup of the sugar with the flour.
With an electric mixer, beat the egg whites until foamy.
Add the cream of tartar and salt and continue beating.
As the whites begin to stiffen, gradually add the remaining sugar and continue whipping until the whites form stiff glossy peaks.
Add the vanilla and beat for 1 to 2 seconds.
With a rubber spatula, gently fold in the flour, ¼ cup at a time.

Pour the cake batter into the pan and bake for 40 minutes.
Invert the pan on a rack to cool, leaving at least 1 inch air space between the rack and the table. (You might want to "hang" the pan over the neck of a tall bottle to accomplish this.)
When *completely* cooled, pull the sides away from the pan with a fork and unmold the cake.
Serve with Lemon Cream and strawberries.
Note: Angel food cake is not everyone's favorite treat. The tart lemon sauce and strawberries cut the sweetness and complement this all-American dessert.

Serves 8 to 10

LEMON CREAM

INGREDIENTS

¾ teaspoon arrowroot
½ cup fresh lemon juice
3 egg yolks
½ cup sugar

METHOD

In the top of a double boiler set over simmering water, whisk the arrowroot into the lemon juice until thick and shiny. Cook until warmed through.
In a small bowl, whisk the egg yolks with the sugar until smooth and lemon colored.
Add the lemon juice mixture to the sugar and yolks and stir.
Return the mixture to the double boiler and whisk over simmering water for 10 minutes, or until thick.
Set aside and keep warm.
Serve the Lemon Cream with Angel Food Cake, accompanied with strawberries and raspberries.

Makes about 1 cup

Cioppino Dinner

SPAGHETTI CIOPPINO*

DAY-OLD CAKE WITH FRESH
STEWED FRUITS AND ZABAGLIONE*

GLEN ELLEN WINERY
SAUVIGNON BLANC or

MONTEREY PENINSULA
CALIFORNIA ZINFANDEL

*I've always found that fresh pasta is best treated
with delicate sauces. The availability of this fresh
noodle in countless forms has caused us to forget
plain old spaghetti. The wonderful confusion of
ingredients in this recipe calls for a sturdy pasta.
The confusion continues in a fantasy dessert that
offers one way to rid yourself of day-old cake (but
it's really quite delicious).*

SPAGHETTI CIOPPINO

INGREDIENTS

Juice of ½ lemon

8 tablespoons olive oil

12 baby artichokes

1 clove garlic, crushed

1 medium yellow bell pepper—cored, seeded,
    deveined, and cut into julienne

1 medium sweet red bell pepper—cored, seeded,
    deveined, and cut into julienne

2 large ripe tomatoes—peeled, seeded, and chopped
    with juice reserved

1 dozen small clams

1 dozen mussels, scrubbed and debearded

½ pound spaghetti

½ pint bay scallops

½ pound small bay shrimp, cooked

4 tablespoons golden caviar, for serving

METHOD

Stir the lemon juice and 1 tablespoon of the olive oil into a large pot of salted boiling water.

Add the artichokes and boil for 3 to 5 minutes.

Cool under cold running water and reserve.

Fill a large kettle with lightly salted water and bring to a boil.

Meanwhile, prepare the sauce:

In a large skillet, slowly heat the remaining 7 tablespoons olive oil with the garlic.

Add the peppers and sauté until they wilt.

Remove the garlic clove when it turns golden.

Add the tomatoes and their juice and bring to a simmer.

Add the clams, mussels, and artichokes; cover.

Add the spaghetti to the boiling water.

When the clams and mussels begin to open, add the scallops and cook uncovered for 2 to 3 minutes.

Add the shrimp and cook just to warm through.

When the spaghetti is cooked but still firm to the bite, drain in a colander and return to the pot.

Toss with a cup or two of the sauce so the spaghetti does not stick.

Turn the spaghetti out onto heated plates and divide the sauce.

Mount 1 tablespoon or more of the golden caviar in the center of each plate of spaghetti.

Note: Because of the quantity of the ingredients in Cioppino, ½ pound of spaghetti is sufficient for 4. However, there is enough Cioppino for ¾ pound of spaghetti.

Serves 4

DAY-OLD CAKE WITH FRESH STEWED FRUITS AND ZABAGLIONE

INGREDIENTS

1 cup raspberries
1 cup blueberries
1 cup strawberries
6 tablespoons sugar

ZABAGLIONE CREAM:

6 egg yolks
⅔ cup sugar
⅔ cup Marsala wine
2 cups heavy cream, whipped

Unsweetened cocoa powder
3 to 4 slices day-old yellow cake or sponge-type cake, cut into 1-inch cubes
Ground cinnamon

METHOD

The fruit:

In separate saucepans, lightly stew the berries with 2 tablespoons of sugar each, just until they begin to give off their juices.

Cool and reserve.

The zabaglione cream:

Bring water to a simmer in the bottom of a double boiler.

Off the heat, in a heatproof bowl, whisk the egg yolks until they are smooth and lemon colored.

Set the bowl over the simmering water and, whisking constantly, slowly add the sugar.

As the eggs begin to thicken, gradually add the Marsala and continue to whisk for about 20 minutes, until the zabaglione coats the back of a spoon.

If the mixture begins to curdle, remove the bowl from the heat and whisk in a little cold heavy cream. Beat vigorously.

Cool the mixture over ice water. Cover with a sheet of plastic placed directly on the surface of the cream.

Refrigerate.

To assemble:

Fold the whipped cream into the zabaglione mixture; do not overblend.

Place the cubed cake onto a deep platter and smother with the berries.

Spoon the zabaglione cream over the berries.

Allow to rest for 15 to 20 minutes before serving.

Liberally sprinkle with cinnamon and cocoa and serve.

Serves 6

Swan's Oyster Depot

Swan's Oyster Depot supplies San Francisco with some of the best and freshest fish. They make their own chowders and will poach a salmon to order. Their counter is open at eight o'clock in the morning and I never fail to breakfast there (before catching a morning flight back home) on little oysters, Pacific Coast clams, Dungeness crabmeat with homemade Louis dressing, good sourdough bread, coffee, and beer. It's a bit self-indulgent, but then I don't eat lunch on the plane!

LOUIS DRESSING

INGREDIENTS

1 cup homemade Mayonnaise (see Basics, page 345)
¼ cup ketchup
1 teaspoon fresh lemon juice
3 scallions, including some of
   the green, finely chopped
¼ cup finely chopped sweet or dill pickle
2 tablespoons finely chopped fresh parsley
1 teaspoon Worcestershire sauce
3 to 4 drops Tabasco sauce

METHOD

Combine all the ingredients and refrigerate until
   ready to serve.

Note: Serve with cold crab, lobster, or shrimp

Makes 1½ cups

Dim Sum

The Golden Dragon rooms of Chinatown still offer platters of dim sum and tea. For the past couple of years, little "holes in the wall" have been steaming up these savory pleasures as snack food. Baby gets her snack.

Irish Coffee

Rumor has it that Irish coffee was first served in the bars on San Francisco's wharves. Whether this is true or not, the practice of a little nip in the coffee has become a warming habit, no matter what the time of day. Unlike the flood of liqueurs with their johnny-come-lately coffee tricks, Irish coffee is the most straightforward of all coffee concoctions and is a perfect way to end a meal.

INGREDIENTS

1 teaspoon superfine sugar
1½ ounces Irish whiskey
5 ounces hot espresso coffee
1 heaping tablespoon unsweetened whipped cream

TOOLS

8-ounce goblet or mug

METHOD

Warm the glass with boiling water and shake dry.
Place the sugar and whiskey in the glass.
Add the espresso and stir to dissolve the sugar.
Float the whipped cream on top.

Serves 1

In addition to the great wineries that spread across the valleys of California, there are numerous cottage industries producing all manner of cheeses, olive oils, breads, preserved olives, and as recently as this year, sun-dried tomatoes. This little feast is a tribute to those who toil for an eager and appreciative public. The menu, built around the wines served, is decidedly Mediterranean.

Wine Tasting Picnic

FRESH GOAT CHEESE WITH
OLIVE OIL AND HERBS

FRESH CRANBERRY FAVA BEANS
WITH HERBS AND OLIVE OIL

SUN-DRIED TOMATOES*

CALIFORNIA OLIVES

SOURDOUGH BREAD

FOCACCIA* WITH
AGED GOAT CHEESE,
OIL-CURED OLIVES AND ROSEMARY

SWISS CHARD AND ARUGULA SALAD

SHREDDED AGED GOAT CHEESE
AND SALTED BUTTERED ALMONDS

DRIED FRUIT, NUTS, AND GRAPES

ALMONDS/WALNUTS/DRIED FIGS

DRIED PRUNES/GRAPES

RUTHERFORD HILL MERLOT

RUTHERFORD HILL
SAUVIGNON BLANC

SUN-DRIED TOMATOES

INGREDIENTS

Salt
Plum tomatoes
Garlic cloves
Rosemary sprigs
Olive oil

METHOD

Salt the tomatoes and set on a wire rack raised 12- to 18-inches off the ground, directly in hot sunlight. Sun-dry for 8 to 10 days.

Remove the tomatoes from the rack and pack in sterilized canning jars with 1 clove of garlic and 1 sprig of rosemary per jar.

Fill each jar with olive oil.

Note: The tomatoes must be dried in a very dry climate. It is not necessary to bring them indoors at night.

FOCACCIA

INGREDIENTS

2 packages active dry yeast
1 cup lukewarm water
3 teaspoons salt
3½ cups all-purpose flour
⅓ cup mashed potatoes
7 tablespoons olive oil
¼ pound oil-cured black and green olives, pitted
¼ pound medium-soft goat cheese, crumbled
1 tablespoon lightly chopped rosemary

METHOD

In a large bowl, dissolve the yeast in the
    lukewarm water.
Add the salt and set aside until it begins to foam
    and bubble.
Gradually add the flour and mashed potatoes, mixing
    until the dough forms a sticky ball.
Add 1½ tablespoons of the olive oil.
Coat a bowl with 2 tablespoons of the olive oil.
Place the dough in the bowl and turn to coat with
    olive oil.
Cover with a damp cloth and let rise in a draft-free
    place for 25 minutes.
Punch down the dough and place on a baking sheet
    coated with ½ tablespoon olive oil.
Shape it into a ½-inch-thick round or oval.
Randomly press the olives into the dough.

Sprinkle with the remaining 3 tablespoons olive oil,
    the goat cheese, and rosemary.
Allow to rest for 20 minutes.
Preheat the oven to 400°.
Bake the focaccia for 30 minutes, or until golden.
Serve warm.

Serves 6

SWISS CHARD AND ARUGULA SALAD

INGREDIENTS

2 tablespoons butter
¼ pound slivered almonds
Salt
2 bunches (about ½ pound) young Swiss chard leaves
    with stems, washed and thoroughly dried
1 to 2 bunches arugula, washed and thoroughly dried
½ to ¾ cup Vinaigrette (see Basics, page 345)
Hard goat cheese, for grating

METHOD

In a small skillet, melt the butter and sauté the
    almonds until they begin to turn golden.
Remove from the pan with a slotted spoon and
    salt lightly.
Toss the greens with the vinaigrette and divide
    among six plates.
Sprinkle with the warm almonds and grate a little goat
    cheese over each salad. Serve.

Serves 6

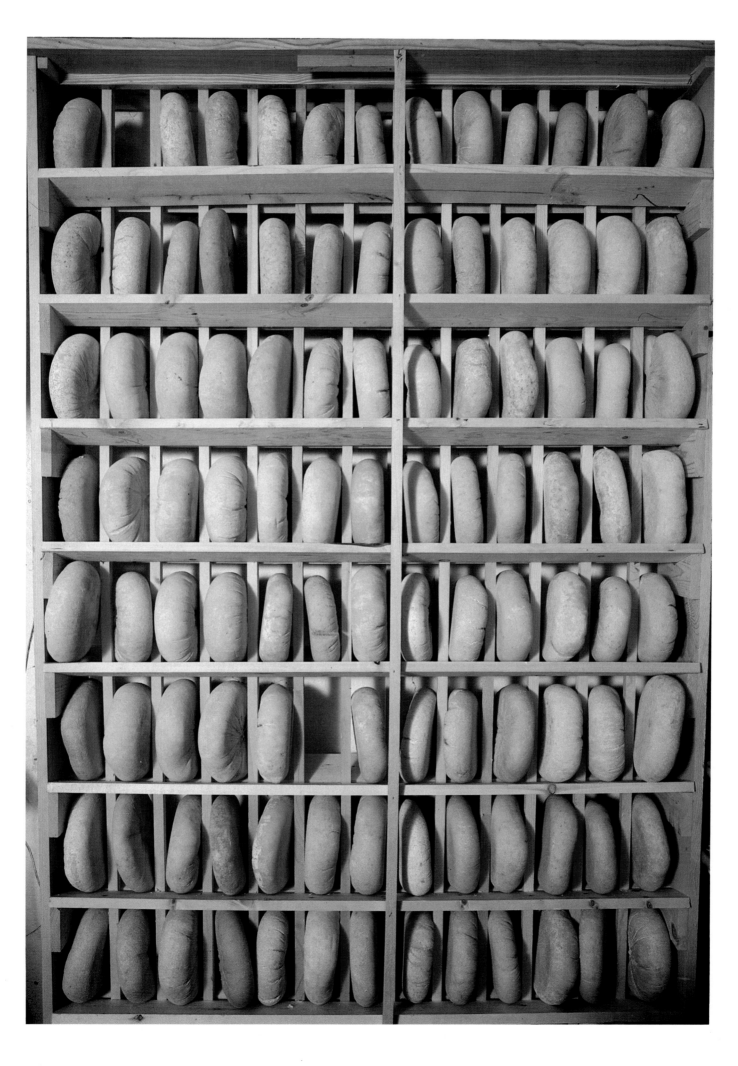

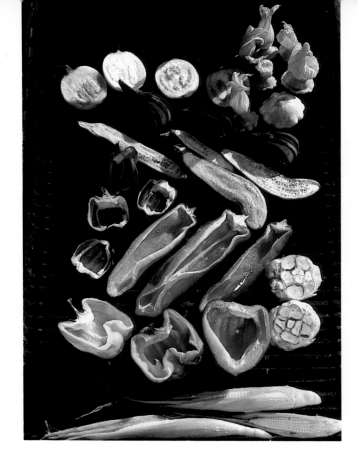

GRILLED MINIATURE VEGETABLES

INGREDIENTS

6 long Japanese and white baby eggplant
3 each of red, yellow, and chocolate bell peppers
3 heads of garlic
6 ears of baby sweet corn
12 zucchini and yellow squashes with blossoms
6 small pattypan squashes with blossoms
1 cup olive oil
Salt and freshly milled black pepper

TOOLS

Grill with charcoal and a small bundle of grapevine
   clippings

METHOD

Prepare the grill.
When the coals have reached a dusty red glow, grill the
   vegetables in the following manner:
Thinly slice the larger eggplants up to the stem and fan
   out the slices.
The smallest eggplants can be grilled whole.
Halve the peppers and remove the stems, seeds,
   and veins.
Cut a small slice off the stem and root ends of the
   garlic. Cut the bulb horizontally in half.
Remove the silk but leave the baby corn in their husks.
Brush all of the vegetables with olive oil and lightly
   sprinkle with salt and pepper.
Place the vegetables on the grill, browning on each
   side until tender.
Serve with sliced grilled lamb.

Serves 6

Grilled on Grapevines

GRILLED MINIATURE VEGETABLES*

GRILLED BUTTERFLIED
LEG OF LAMB*

WALNUT AND PRUNE TART*

CAYMUS VINEYARDS
CABERNET SAUVIGNON

The abundance of grape prunings in the wine country makes for good kindling to start the grill. It's a common practice throughout Bordeaux and Burgundy, not because the cuttings impart a very strong flavor to the cooking meats, but rather to utilize what is available. Unlike tiny bonsai trees, which are miniature but mature, these miniature vegetables are picked before reaching maturity, more to amuse our aesthetic sense than to satisfy our stomachs. It is an uneconomical trend, a flirtation that will not reach most consumers, but is suitable for expensive restaurants and the home gardener who has a vegetable patch which he can capriciously invade for his own amusement. The grilled meat and generously nut-filled tart bring us back to our senses and fill us happily with substantial good food.

GRILLED BUTTERFLIED
LEG OF LAMB

INGREDIENTS

1 leg of lamb (5 to 6 pounds), butterflied
1¼ cups olive oil
2 teaspoons chopped fresh rosemary
1 teaspoon lemon thyme leaves
1 tablespoon red pepper flakes
Salt and freshly milled pepper
3 cloves garlic, minced
Zest of ½ navel orange, finely diced
12 large basil leaves, cut into fine ribbons

TOOLS

Grill with charcoal and a small bundle of dry grapevine
    clippings that have been soaked in water for 2
    hours.

METHOD

Place the leg of lamb in a shallow baking pan.
In a bowl, combine the olive oil, rosemary, lemon
    thyme, and red pepper flakes.
Pour the oil mixture over the lamb, turning the meat
    from side to side until well coated.
Cover and marinate for 2 hours, 1 hour in the
    refrigerator and 1 hour at room temperature.
Prepare the charcoal grill.
Preheat the oven to 250°.
When the coals reach a dusty red glow, add a small
    bundle of grapevine clippings.
Brush the grill with olive oil.
Season the meat with salt.
Place the meat on the grill and cook for 5 minutes
    on each side.
Transfer the meat to a baking pan and place in the oven
    for 10 minutes.
Allow the lamb to rest for 10 minutes before slicing.

While the meat is roasting in the oven, grill the
vegetables lightly on each side.

Serve rare.

To assemble:

Very thinly slice the meat allowing about 3 slices
per person.

Sprinkle with a little of the minced garlic, orange zest,
and basil.

Serves 5 to 6

Continue to boil until the thermometer registers 215°.

Fold in the walnuts and prunes and mix thoroughly.

Pour the mixture into the prebaked pie shell.

Bake for 25 minutes, or until the mixture is bubbly and
the nuts are glazed and golden brown.

Cool on a rack for 30 minutes before serving.

Serve in small wedges with unsweeetened
whipped cream.

Serves 10

WALNUT AND PRUNE TART

INGREDIENTS

2 cups heavy cream

1 cup honey

½ cup sugar

6 tablespoons unsalted butter

5 cups shelled walnuts

18 prunes, pitted and quartered

1 recipe Cookie Crust Pie Dough (see Basics, page
347), prebaked in an 11-inch loose-bottomed pie pan

Whipped heavy cream, for serving

TOOLS

Candy thermometer

METHOD

Preheat the oven to 350°.

In a heavy saucepan, combine the cream, honey, sugar,
and butter over high heat.

Place the thermometer in the mixture and
bring to a boil.

White Wine

Since the 1970s, white wine has been
the cocktail. A good bottle of white wine,
lightly chilled, is tailored to refresh
and please, no matter what the
hour of the day.

Northwest

"The beet is the most intense of vegetables. The radish, admittedly, is more feverish, but the fire of the radish is a cold fire, the fire of discontent not of passion. Tomatoes are lusty enough, yet there runs through tomatoes an undercurrent of frivolity. Beets are deadly serious....

"Slavic peoples get their physical characteristics from potatoes, their smouldering inquietude from radishes, their seriousness from beets.

"The beet is the melancholy vegetable, the one most willing to suffer. You can't squeeze blood out of a turnip...

"The beet is the murderer returned to the scene of the crime. The beet is what happens when the cherry finishes with the carrot. The beet is the ancient ancestor of the autumn moon, bearded, buried, all but fossilized; the dark green sail of the grounded moon-boat stitched with veins of primordial plasma; the kite string that once connected the moon to the EARTH, now a muddy whisker drilling desperately for rubies."
—JITTERBUG PERFUME *by Tom Robbins; 1984.*

The Pacific Northwest is still young, and still wild. It is a revelation of hope to sail its crystal waters through the archipelagos of islands, to walk its rain forests of cascading ferns and silken moss, to climb its alpine heights carpeted with close-cropped bells and tiny daisies, and to watch deer dance over the sponge of leaves and needles. This land is green in spite of us. George Vancouver was 34 years old in 1792 when he set anchor in the sound with his Lieutenant, Peter Puget. The Indians they met showed little interest in their arrival, leaving the navigators to explore and claim on their own. By 1818, Britain and the United States shared the Northwest, and the Hudson's Bay Company soon followed, opening the wilds to fur traders. By 1843, American settlers began to trickle in by land and water route—scores of them pioneers from New England who came with their chowders and their curries, bringing the settlement of America full circle. History repeated itself. The natives showed the new-comers where to fish the great king salmon and where to harvest

clams, mussels, and crabs. The Indians themselves dined on clams and berries to such a hearty extent that visitors were appalled at the very consumption. Clams, smoked and dried, were oftentimes strung and worn around the neck, to be nibbled whenever hunger struck. The Indians roasted chunks of salmon or whole fish on spears, leaving gills and bladders standing like flags to mark that the fishing had been good. With nets, spears, and traps, they harvested salmon like a crop, just as land farmers pulled their harvest from moist earth. Settlers were shown how to make a flour from the inner stalks of cattails, and the Indians shared their meadows, growing with wild chickweed, dandelion, burdock, nettles, and lamb's quarters, along with the secrets of edible fungi. Spring morels, summer cèpes, and autumn's boletus, chanterelles, alpine white chanterelles, "cauliflower", and coral mushrooms were available and some were dried for storage. The first settlers did not fish, but farmed instead, and their plantings couldn't fail in these valleys of fertile volcanic soil protected from the cold salt air of the Pacific by the Cascade range.

The apple seed was a long way short of reaching the Pacific Northwest, but by the mid-19th century, Conestoga wagons filled with earth and seedlings trundled over the plains. Today, of course, the reputation of these apples is unsurpassed, and Oregon apples and pears are flown to the food halls of Europe and the Orient. The Northwest supplies the United States with nearly all of her lentils, not to mention most of her hops (for the beer industry) and soft wheat. Idaho potatoes are fried up on the boulevards of Paris and in the streets of Tokyo. Near Seattle, Dutch farmers cultivate acres of tulips, and Scottish descendants tend their flocks of clover fattened sheep and cattle. Down in Kent, the Carnation milk factory continues to put up tins of condensed milk, that have nourished countless American babies and become a family staple.

The Northwest of 1893 was like the rest of the country: in a state of financial panic. The Klondike gold strike was kept nearly secret for a year, until word leaked out in the July 17, 1897 *Seattle Post-Intelligencer* that the steamship Portland had arrived with more than a ton of gold on board. Desperate fortune-seekers—farmers,

bank clerks, doctors, teachers, lawyers, policemen, prostitutes, missionaries, firemen—abruptly packed their belongings and headed for Alaska, many with only the vaguest notion as to where that territory actually was. Not every prospector had luck, and few were prepared for the hardships of survival, but this flood was a boon to Seattle. Canada was decidedly hesitant, however, and the Mounted Police refused entry to anyone not carrying a year's food supply. Merchants got rich selling gold diggers the usual list of staples: bacon, 100 to 200 pounds; flour, 400 pounds; dried fruits, 75 pounds; cornmeal, 50 pounds; coffee, 25 pounds; sugar, 25 to 100 pounds; beans, 100 pounds; cases of condensed milk and tins of dried meat and fish—all in all, weighing down a dogsled with enough clothing and equipment to daunt the most loyal team of huskies plunging through the drifts.

The French from Brittany, followed closely by Scandinavians, were the first to show real interest in fishing. They homesteaded prime locations, at the mouth of estuaries and rivers on Indian land holdings. They too often built too close to the banks, their cabins and barns swept away time and again by rivers swollen with glacial run-off, so determined were they to claim this land for themselves. These early disputes, the first hint of the settler's offense, challenged the native American for his fishing rights. As far as the Indians were concerned, the right to fish these waters was God-given; they could scarcely fathom the notion of owning or selling land, sea, or air, cherished collective holdings had always passed from generation to generation.

The Great Council of Walla Walla, signed in 1855, relieved five major Indian tribes of all rights to fishing territories from the Columbia River through its tributaries to the Strait of San Juan de Fuca—a total of some 60,000 square miles in eastern Oregon and east-central Washington—prime land compensated at the equivalent of three cents an acre. The settlers lusted not so much after the fish that ran these waters as for the virgin timber that lined them, and by 1888, the Northern Pacific railroad had reached the terminus of Tacoma and logging went full tilt. Forests closest to the rivers fell first, the river itself providing the timber's

transport to the railways. In this manner logging gravely disrupted spawning and fish runs; this early manifestation of pollution seriously hindered species of fish that were accustomed to the clearest waters in the hemisphere. Power boats appeared in the 1920s and worsened the downhill slide, as did the seal, salmon's natural predator. Between Russian traders and the Hudson's Bay Company, the seal was at first over-hunted, but, when it was later realized that a seal can effortlessly consume 200 to 300 pounds of salmon daily, it was clear that new laws were needed to protect the fish and the seals from man. Fishing rights have now returned to the native Indians, and fishermen settlers, their fleets of fishing boats anchored in Seattle, Port Townsend, and Port Angeles, wait for the word from the Fish and Game Department that will allot them a day's fishing. Indian fishermen maintain a commercial foothold in an industry that was once their birthright, while the children of the settler fishermen abandoned the local waters for another way of life.

Coho is the term for silver salmon, a small variety, and Humpi are the smallest of all, pink and perfect for poaching and smoking. King salmon are commonly fished at 70 pounds (at the turn of the century, 100 pounds at the end of a hook was not amazing). This is the salmon the Indians love to roast or bake. When the flesh is to be grilled on open fires, wood spears as sharp as arrows are carved from an ocean spray bush called "ironwood," as tough as steel and flame resistant. The preferred fuel for roasting is alderwood, and for kippered and smoked salmon, a combination of alderwood and cherry. When pulled from the bay, the kings are fat and pink; caught upstream, they have paled from their exhausting journey (but are preferred for smoking, as they last better throughout the winter; the fattier kings mold more quickly).

Along the coast all the way up to Alaskan waters, the Northwest is extraordinarily rich in shellfish—Dungeness, Alaskan King and snow crabs, abalone, shrimps, and oysters and clams of many varieties. The Pacific razor clam, which at maturity resembles a pen knife, is perhaps the most prized of the clams. Digging this clam requires a keen eye and vigorous work with a shovel, but that hasn't kept the razor clam population safe from over-hunting; a limit has been set on the number of clams that can be harvested per person, but the creature is perilously close to disappearing altogether.

The Northwest is a region of easy bounty, burgeoning with riches for the taking. The trees of valley orchards are heavy with fruit, the waters wait to be reaped of their harvest, and the air is full of life-giving moisture. It will take all of our discipline to keep the Northwest a frontier.

LAMB SAUSAGE PATTIES

INGREDIENTS

1 pound lean lamb, ground twice
⅓ pound pork fat, ground twice
1 clove garlic, minced
2 teaspoons rubbed sage, crumbled
½ teaspoon coarsely milled black pepper
2 tablespoons chopped fresh parsley
½ teaspoon chopped fresh rosemary
¾ teaspoon salt
2 tablespoons unsalted butter

METHOD

In a mixing bowl, combine the lamb and pork fat.
Add the seasonings and mix well.
Using about ¼ cup for each, shape small round patties.
   Set aside.
Melt the butter in a skillet over moderately high heat.
Add the sausage patties and reduce the heat
   to moderate.
Brown the patties evenly on both sides, turning once.
Serve with freshly opened oysters.

Makes 12 patties

Breakfast

QUILCENE OYSTERS
LAMB SAUSAGE PATTIES*
OOMA'S DILL BREAD*
AQUAVIT

HOGUE CELLARS
CHENIN BLANC

The Pacific Northwest oyster is the only oyster native to this region, and its little spoonful of flesh is a distillation of all the flavors of the best bivalves found in this country. There are some people who absolutely love oysters, and there are some people utterly horrified by the mucilaginous quality of them, and still others will eat them the size of baseball gloves. (At the turn of the century, a pond on Montauk at the end of Long Island was harvesting oysters a foot long and bigger, grilling them up like steaks.) What may seem an odd coupling, sausages and oysters, was a popular turn-of-the-century combination. Yeasty warm dill bread is a definite Scandinavian influence, and Aquavit is an eye-opener for this fisherman's breakfast.

OOMA'S DILL BREAD

INGREDIENTS

1 package active dry yeast
¼ cup lukewarm water
1 cup small curd cottage cheese, at room temperature
2 tablespoons sugar
½ small onion, minced
1 teaspoon salt
1 teaspoon baking soda
1 tablespoon unsalted butter, melted
4 teaspoons dill seed
3 fresh dill flower sprigs, chopped
1 egg
2½ cups all-purpose flour, sifted
Vegetable oil, for the bowl
Kosher salt

TOOLS

1½-quart ovenproof mold or loaf pan

METHOD

In a small bowl, dissolve the yeast in the lukewarm water and set aside until foamy.

In a bowl, combine the cottage cheese with the sugar, onion, salt, baking soda, butter, dill seed, dill flowers, and egg.

Add the yeast and mix.

Stir in the flour and knead to make a stiff dough.

Place the dough in a lightly oiled bowl, cover with a damp cloth, and set in a warm draft-free place until doubled, about 50 minutes.

Punch down the dough and place in a well-oiled baking pan.

Cover and let rise until doubled in volume, about 30 minutes.

Meanwhile, preheat the oven to 350°.

Brush the top of the bread with water and sprinkle liberally with kosher salt.

Bake for 50 minutes, or until the bread is golden brown.

Makes 1 loaf

Veal and Parsley Pie Dinner

CRUSTACEANS, HERRINGS,
AND SMELTS

VEAL AND PARSLEY PIE*

PLUM KETCHUP*

BLACK PEPPER CAKE*
WITH STEWED QUINCE*

SOKOL BLOSSER VINEYARDS
CHARDONNAY *or*
EYRIE VINEYARDS PINOT NOIR

Meals are made from the abundance of salted, cured, and pickled herring, smelts, and the versatile Dungeness and Alaskan King crab. The fishes are put up in true Scandinavian fashion. It is arguable whether the bigger-than-life crabs are comparable to the blue crab of the East—they are a different kettle of fish. Sweet and firm, they can be served hot, cold, unadorned, or enveloped in sauces. They take to embellishment as gracefully as lobsters.

For this meal any selection of herrings, smelts, or crustaceans, served simply, make for a nice opening. Cold crab or shrimp with Louis dressing, local oysters on the half shell with a squeeze of lemon and a grinding of pepper, mussels in a mustardy mayonnaise, or any variety of pickled herring or smelt would be ideal. Parsley pies, like shepherd's pie, were served from leftovers; the dish included ground or chunked meats and parsley was incorporated as a filler. These Victorian meal extenders were covered with pastry or mashed potatoes, but this Veal and Parsley Pie is begun fresh from scratch, elevated by pieces of white veal, chanterelles, and a piping of mashed potatoes. The Oriental quince replaces the spoonful of applesauce that so frequently accompanied spice cakes.

VEAL AND PARSLEY PIE

INGREDIENTS

FILLING:

½ cup vegetable oil
Salt and freshly milled black pepper
2½ pounds lean veal, trimmed and cut
    into 1½-inch cubes
All-purpose flour
½ cup dry white wine
1 cup Veal or Beef Stock (see Basics, page 343)
1 cup heavy cream
6 tablespoons unsalted butter
1 pound fresh chanterelles

MASHED POTATO:

4 medium potatoes, peeled
½ cup milk, scalded
4 tablespoons unsalted butter
Salt and freshly milled black pepper

1 cup minced fresh parsley

TOOLS

2-quart ovenproof casserole
Pastry bag fitted with star tube

METHOD

Heat ¼ cup of the oil in a large skillet.
Salt and pepper the veal and lightly dredge with flour.
Working in batches, brown the meat, adding more oil
    as necessary. (If the pan becomes overly browned,
    deglaze with some of the stock, scraping with a
    wooden spoon; reserve. Add more oil and
    continue to brown the veal.)
When all the veal has been browned, drain off any
    excess oil from the pan.
Add the wine and deglaze the pan, scraping up the
    brown bits that cling to the bottom of the pan.
    Cook until reduced to a thick glaze.
Add the stock and simmer for 5 minutes.
Strain the liquid and return it to the pan.
Add the cream and bring it to a slow boil. Reduce the
    heat and simmer for 15 minutes. Reserve.
Melt the butter in a skillet and lightly sauté the
chanterelles over moderate heat just until they give
    off their juices.
Drain and reserve the mushrooms; add the juices to
    the cream.
Boil the potatoes in a pot of lightly salted water.
Mash the potatoes using ⅓ to ½ cup of the
    scalded milk.
Stir in the butter and season to taste with salt
    and pepper.
To assemble:
Preheat the oven to 350°.
Toss the veal with the chanterelles and place in
    the casserole.
Add the parsley to the cream sauce and pour over the
    meat mixture.
Fill a pastry bag with the potatoes and decoratively
    pipe the mixture over the meat.
Bake for 50 to 60 minutes, until tender and just
    cooked through.

Serves 6

PLUM KETCHUP

INGREDIENTS

1 quart small, black Italian-type plums, pitted and cut
    into eighths (about 4 cups)
¼ cup raspberry or blueberry vinegar
1 small cinnamon stick
¼ teaspoon black peppercorns, crushed
2 strips lemon zest, diced

METHOD

In a large pot, combine all of the ingredients.
Place over moderately low heat and simmer for 30
    minutes, or until most of the juice evaporates.

Makes about 4 cups

BLACK PEPPER CAKE

INGREDIENTS

Butter and flour, for the mold
¼ pound plus 4 tablespoons unsalted butter
¾ cup packed dark brown sugar
1 cup granulated sugar
3 eggs
1 teaspoon vanilla extract
2¼ cups all-purpose flour
1 teaspoon baking powder
½ teaspoon salt
½ teaspoon ground cloves
¼ teaspoon ground ginger
¾ teaspoon cinnamon
2 teaspoons freshly milled black pepper
1 cup buttermilk

TOOLS

1-quart kugelhopf mold
Electric mixer

METHOD

Preheat the oven to 350°.
Butter and flour the kuglehopf mold; set aside.
In a mixing bowl, cream together the butter and sugars.
One at a time, add the eggs and mix well. Beat in the vanilla.
Sift together the dry ingredients and spices.
Alternately add the dry ingredients and the buttermilk to the butter and egg mixture.
Pour the butter into the mold and bake for 1 hour, or until the cake pulls away from the sides of the pan.
Cool in the pan for 10 minutes. Invert the cake onto a serving plate and unmold.

Serves 8 to 10

STEWED QUINCE

INGREDIENTS

4 large quince
Juice of 1 lemon
¾ cup sugar
1 small cinnamon stick

METHOD

Peel, core, and roughly chop the quince.
Place the fruit in a small nonaluminum saucepan and toss with the lemon juice, sugar, and ¼ cup water.
Add the cinnamon, place over low heat and cover.
Simmer, stirring from time to time, until the fruit begins to give off juice and soften.
Serve warm with the pepper cake.

Makes about 3 cups

Fish Soup in a Cup

I know of no market in the entire country that glitters and sparkles with the region's produce as the Pike Place Market does. The joy of this market is that you can find there everything you need for a meal, including meat and fish. It has been touted as a tourist trap; still, it wasn't born yesterday and serves Seattle residents as honestly today as 80 years ago. Tucked away in an alley behind this market is a restaurant-in-miniature, where one can sample local Quilcene oysters, chowders, smoked salmon and trout, and a spicy fish soup, all ready-to-go on paper plates and in styrofoam cups.

Seattle Fish Stew

*ADAPTED FROM
EMMETT WATSON'S OYSTER BAR*

INGREDIENTS

1 quart Fish Stock (see Basics, page 344)
¼ cup olive oil
1 medium onion, finely chopped
2 cloves garlic, minced
3 cups tomatoes—peeled, seeded, and chopped
    with juices reserved
½ teaspoon chopped fresh rosemary leaves
¼ teaspoon fresh thyme
¼ teaspoon fresh oregano
1 cup dry white wine
2 dozen Pacific Coast littleneck clams, washed
2 dozen mussels, scrubbed and debearded
1 pound bay scallops
1 pound baby shrimp, shelled and cooked
1 teaspoon sweet paprika
4 to 5 drops Tabasco sauce
Salt

METHOD

In a nonaluminum soup kettle, heat the stock over moderately low heat.

In a large skillet, heat the olive oil over moderate heat. Add the onions and garlic and sauté until translucent.

Add the chopped tomatoes and their juices.

Add the rosemary, thyme, and oregano.

Add the white wine and bring to a simmer. Simmer for 10 minutes.

Add the vegetable mixture to the heated fish stock and bring to a simmer.

Add the clams and mussels, cover tightly, and simmer until the clams and mussels open, about 5 minutes. Discard any that do not open.

Add the scallops and simmer for 3 minutes.

Add the shrimp, paprika, Tabasco, and salt to taste. Simmer for 2 minutes more.

Serve hot.

Serves 5 to 6

Gravlax Lunch

GRAVLAX*

MUSTARD DILL SAUCE*
(see Basics, page 346)

BLACK BREAD

BEER or
LOUIS FACELLI RIESLING

Indians stood on catwalks that stretched across the river, to spear salmon as the fish leapt to clear the barrier dams. Many salmon that escaped their spears tumbled into nets erected behind these dams. The first settlers were quick to apply the Indian skill for catching salmon, and it became an early basis of their commerce. The endless supply was brought to the fishing stations, salt-cured, pickled, and barreled in 42-gallon casks. Curing preserved the fish for at least three years, and this salmon was considered emergency food throughout the interior. The industry was transformed by 20th-century fish canneries which dot the territory where sport fishermen can leave their catch to be custom canned. The age-old Northwest Indian method of smoking or kippering salmon has led to a separate industry. The Scandinavians were equally at home with this fish, using a quick salt and dill method of curing that is as popular here as in their homeland. Served with thinly sliced buttered black bread, gravlax is a perfect hors d'oeuvre or a nice little lunch.

GRAVLAX

INGREDIENTS

2 fresh salmon fillets with skin intact (about 3 pounds)
¼ cup kosher salt
⅓ cup sugar
2 tablespoons black peppercorns, crushed
2 large bunches dill

METHOD

Wash and pat the salmon dry with paper towels.
In a bowl, combine the salt, sugar, and pepper.
Arrange a few sprigs of dill in the center of a sheet of foil large enough to envelop the fish.
Place 1 fillet, skin side down, on top of the dill.
Sprinkle with half the seasonings and some of the dill.
Place the remaining fillet, the skin side up, on top of the seasonings.
Sprinkle with the remaining seasonings and dill.
Tightly wrap the foil around the fish, set the fish on a baking dish, and weigh down with a heavy board.
Refrigerate for at least 2 days, turning once every 12 hours and basting with its natural juices.
When the gravlax is ready, wipe off the dill and seasoning with a paper towel.
Thinly slice on the diagonal, removing the rosy flesh from the skin as you would smoked salmon.
Serve with Mustard Dill Sauce, freshly milled pepper, and black bread.

Serves at least 12

Baked Potato Supper

BAKED POTATO WITH
INDIAN-CURED SALMON*

CHANTERELLE AND
CORAL MUSHROOMS*

PEAR AND BLACK HEART
CHERRY STRUDEL*

AQUAVIT or
OAK KNOLL PINOT NOIR

The woodlands of the Pacific Northwest are a mycologist's dream come true, and in fact mushrooms grow practically everywhere out here. Platoons of hunters forage from spring to fall, and the markets are filled with heaps of morels, hedgehogs, boletus, the Japanese matsutake (which fetch an astounding $100 a pound), and the most prolific of all, the yellow chanterelle. They are delectable and versatile fungi: morels are dried and used with game; the boletus, which is our porcini, or cépe enliven pasta and risotto as well as soups. But the chanterelle remains the most available and popular of all. Though easily put up in brine, they are best served fresh as soon after picking as possible; some say the flavor is lost in 24 hours. I tend to agree. Like many regional foods, they are cheap here, and the price doesn't soar until they wing their way East and West. This Pacific mushroom gives off an enormous quantity of liquid and should be drained before the sautéeing process is complete. A rare coral mushroom was a present to me from a local purveyor, who had set it out to adorn his basket of chanterelles.

BAKED POTATO WITH INDIAN-CURED SALMON

INGREDIENTS

4 baking potatoes
3 tablespoons butter
3 tablespoons all-purpose flour
1 teaspoon dry mustard
¼ teaspoon cayenne pepper
1 cup milk, scalded
1 cup heavy cream, scalded
1¼ pounds Indian-cured salmon or other smoked
    flaky fish, skinned and flaked
¼ cup chopped fresh dill

METHOD

Preheat the oven to 400°.

Wash and dry the potatoes.
Bake the potatoes until easily pierced with a
    sharp paring knife.
Melt the butter in a saucepan over moderate heat.
When the foam subsides, remove the pan from the heat
    and whisk in the flour.
Whisk in the mustard and cayenne.
Return to the heat and add the milk and cream.
Bring to a boil, whisking constantly.
Add the flaked salmon and dill, reduce the heat,
    and simmer for 4 minutes, or until the salmon
    is heated through.
Keep warm on the warm side of the stove.
Slit the top of the potatoes and scoop out a little
    of the pulp.
Place on serving plates and ladle the salmon mixture
    into each potato.
Serve immediately.

Serves 4

CHANTERELLE AND CORAL MUSHROOMS

INGREDIENTS

½ pound fresh coral or boletus mushrooms
½ pound fresh chanterelles
8 tablespoons unsalted butter

METHOD

In a pot of salted boiling water, blanch the coral mushrooms for 2 minutes.

Drain and set aside.

In a large skillet, melt 4 tablespoons of the butter over moderate heat. Sauté the chanterelles until tender, about 8 minutes.

In a medium skillet, melt the remaining 4 tablespoons butter. Sauté the coral mushrooms for 5 minutes, until tender.

Combine and serve.

Serves 4

PEAR AND BLACK HEART CHERRY STRUDEL

INGREDIENTS

6 pears, such as Bosc, Comice, or Seckels—peeled, cored, seeded, and chopped (about 6 cups)
1½ cups black heart or bing cherries, split and pitted
½ teaspoon ground ginger
⅓ cup sugar
Grated zest and juice of ½ lemon
4 leaves strudel dough
¼ pound unsalted butter, melted
½ cup ground blanched almonds

TOOLS

Large baking sheet lined with parchment paper

METHOD

Preheat the oven to 450°.

In a bowl, combine the pears, cherries, ginger, sugar, lemon juice, and lemon zest.

Spread 1 leaf of strudel dough on a flat surface, one of the long sides at the bottom. Brush with butter and sprinkle with 2 tablespoons of the almonds.

Repeat this layering process, stacking the remaining 3 leaves.

Spoon the pear filling in a 3-inch strip along the edge nearest you, leaving 3 inches at each end.

Fold the ends over the filling and roll the dough around the filling, jelly roll fashion.

Brush the strudel with melted butter and place in the center of the baking sheet.

Bake for 10 minutes, reduce the heat to 400°, and bake for 20 minutes more.

Cool for 1 hour before serving; serve warm with whipped cream.

Note: This strudel can be reheated.

Serves 6 to 8

Alderwood Grilled King Salmon

PACIFIC COAST
LITTLENECK CLAMS
—THE INDIAN WAY
—THE WHITE MAN'S WAY
GRILLED SALMON
LENTIL SALAD WITH
YELLOW AND RED PEPPERS*

PRESTON WINE
CELLARS FUMÉ BLANC (WA)

For all its abundance, salmon is revered by the Indian. The tribal custom continues. From the moment the fish were caught, I felt as though we were witness to something ritual, sacrificial, almost mythic. Each family member performs a single task, handed down from generation to generation. They work together like a primitive, living machine: one man catches the salmon, one man guts the fish and then builds the fire, a woman braids the salmon on ironwood stakes that have been carved by yet another person. The stakes are set about the alderwood fire that perfumes the fish, and if a breeze comes up, logs fence the fire like totems to stay the wind. "Our people used to cook clams and mussels gathered from the beach and rocks over hot coals, and cover them with kelp and seaweed to steam them. We still do this. And sometimes we use curry too." If I lived by the sea, I would choose to give up the embellishments of curry and cream in favor of clams steamed open in a broth of seawater.

CLAM CHOWDER

THE INDIAN WAY: Skagit Clams and Broth: ½ bushel Pacific Coast Clams, seawater to cover. The clams are brought to a boil over an open fire, and are served immediately after they open. They are then picked from the pot and eaten with bread, which is dipped into the broth.

CURRIED CLAM CHOWDER

THE WHITE MAN'S WAY:

INGREDIENTS

3 tablespoons unsalted butter
3 tablespoons all-purpose flour
1 tablespoon curry powder
1½ cups Fish Stock (see Basics, page 344)
3 cups heavy cream
4 dozen Pacific or East Coast littleneck clams, scrubbed
Freshly milled black pepper

METHOD

In a heavy saucepan, melt the butter over moderate heat.
When the foam subsides, remove the pan from the heat.
Whisk in the flour until smooth.
Return to heat and whisk in the curry powder.
Add the stock and cook until the mixture thickens.
Add the cream, reduce the heat, and simmer, stirring from time to time, for 15 minutes.
Add the clams and cover until the clams open. Discard any that do not open.
Season with pepper and serve in heated bowls.

Serves 6

LENTIL SALAD WITH YELLOW AND RED PEPPERS

INGREDIENTS

2 cups lentils
1 onion, studded with 3 whole cloves
3 cloves garlic
2 teaspoons salt
2 sweet yellow bell peppers—cored, seeded, deveined, and diced
2 sweet red bell peppers—cored, seeded, deveined, and diced
1 cup Vinaigrette (see Basics, page 345)
Salt and freshly milled black pepper

METHOD

Wash the lentils thoroughly and drain.
In a large pot, bring 2 quarts of water to a boil.
Add the lentils, onion, garlic, and salt.
Simmer for 30 minutes, or until the lentils are tender.
Drain, discarding the onion and garlic. Set aside.
Just before serving, toss the lentils with the peppers and vinaigrette; check for seasonings.
Serve at room temperature.

Serves 8 to 10

EPILOGUE

The pond broke last night, as it must have done numberless times over the centuries. When the brackish waters creep too high, the ponds on the south fork of Long Island overrun their banks and rush in a flood to the ocean a few hundred feet away. Carving out a channel, the waters snake their way to the ocean—the seasonal infusion of salty water with the fresh water run-off rests in shallow pools. These shallows are the breeding ground for the blue crabs, eels, silver minnows, and oysters that fed the Indians from Shinnecock to Montauk. These Indians have all but disappeared but they left their legacy to the Bonacers, descendants of the British who settled here in the 17th century, many of whom still support themselves with local fishing.

Before the pond breaks, long before dawn, the light of an occasional battery lamp can be seen shining on its surface. The shallow pond dances with light when everyone comes out to net the season's last crabs and eels as the waters rush out. Crabs not already burrowed or safe in the grasses will wash into the sea. Nature flushes these ponds annually, and if she should forget, the local townships will bulldoze a path to the sea, to prevent the ponds from flooding the nearby fields and farms that stretch to the dunes, the same fields tilled by native Americans so long ago.

The fishing season has ended. The men who haul seine have stored their dories in the barn. A lonely trawler can be seen a few miles out at sea. Hunters tread back and forth stealthily. With the occasional shot, a duck falls from the sky, and a flurry of ducks and honking geese speed away, flying out beyond the breakers and sand-bars, stretching their number out in one long, dark thread on the horizon where they bob on the ocean like decoys, waiting for the shooting to stop. The potato fields are carpeted with new green rye, a winter's rest before spring's planting.

It would seem nothing ever changes here, but for the distant din of pylons being driven into the ground, making way for the next vacation house that has taken away another acre.

DECEMBER 26, 1984
SAGAPONACK, NEW YORK

Basics

PIQUANT RELISH

INGREDIENTS

2 bunches fresh parsley, chopped
4 sprigs fresh sage, chopped
1 cup flaked smoked eel
1 Cortland apple—peeled, cored, and grated
Salt and freshly milled pepper
¼ cup olive oil
2 tablespoons sherry vinegar

METHOD

In a nonaluminum bowl, combine all of the ingredients.
Taste for seasonings and cover with plastic wrap.
Refrigerate for up to a few hours and remove 30
    minutes before serving.

Makes about 2 cups

CHICKEN, BEEF, OR VEAL STOCK

INGREDIENTS

5 pounds chicken, beef, or veal bones
2 medium onions, peeled and coarsely chopped
3 celery ribs with leaves, coarsely chopped
3 carrots, tops removed and coarsely chopped
2 leeks, green part only
2 teaspoons dried thyme
1 teaspoon dried rosemary
2 bay leaves
15 peppercorns
6 parsley sprigs
1 large clove garlic

TOOLS

Large stockpot
Fine wire mesh strainer

METHOD

Rinse the bones under cold running water.
Place the vegetables and remaining ingredients in the
    stockpot. Add the bones and pour in water to cover.
Bring the stock to a boil, reduce the heat to low and
    simmer, skimming the foam from the surface, for
    2½ hours.
Line a fine strainer with a double thickness of
    dampened cheesecloth and set the strainer over
    a clean pot.
Ladle the stock into the strainer, pressing lightly on
    the bones and vegetables to release their liquid.
Allow the stock to cool completely.
Cover and refrigerate. When the stock has chilled,
    skim off the fat that rises to the surface and
    hardens.
The stock will keep under refrigeration if brought to a
    boil daily; indefinitely, if frozen.

Makes about 4 quarts

COURT BOUILLON

INGREDIENTS

1 large carrot
3 shallots, peeled
1 leek, green part only
½ cup celery leaves
1 bottle (25.4 ounces) dry white wine
6 peppercorns, crushed
¼ teaspoon dried thyme
1 bay leaf
1 teaspoon salt, optional
3 cloves garlic, crushed

TOOLS

Large stockpot
Fine wire mesh strainer

METHOD

Chop the vegetables coarsely.
Combine all the ingredients in the stockpot.
Add 2 quarts of water and bring the bouillon to a boil.
Reduce the heat to low and simmer for 30 minutes.
Strain the court bouillon into a large clean saucepan.
Refrigerate until ready to use or freeze in
    1-quart containers.

Makes about 2½ quarts

FISH STOCK

INGREDIENTS

5 pounds white fish bones, tails and heads,
2 medium onions, coarsely chopped
3 celery ribs, coarsely chopped
3 carrots, tops removed and coarsely chopped
2 teaspoons dried thyme
2 bay leaves
20 black peppercorns
6 parsley sprigs
2 cups white wine

TOOLS

Large stockpot
Fine wire mesh strainer

METHOD

Rinse the fish bones under cold running water, making
    sure the gills and blood pockets have been removed.
Place the vegetables and remaining ingredients
    in a stockpot.
Add the fish bones and cold water to cover.
Bring the stock to a boil and reduce the heat
    to low.
Simmer, skimming the foam that forms on the surface,
    for 30 minutes.
Line a strainer with a double thickness of dampened
    cheesecloth and place the strainer over a clean pot.
Ladle the stock into the strainer.
Let the stock cool completely.
Cover and refrigerate for up to 2 days or freeze
    indefinitely.
Makes about 3 quarts

BROWN SAUCE

INGREDIENTS

5 pounds veal bones, or 4 pounds veal bones
    and 1 pound chicken bones
2 cups coarsely chopped onion
2 cups coarsely chopped carrot
2 cups coarsely chopped celery
1 tablespoon peppercorns, crushed
2 bay leaves
2 cloves garlic, crushed
1 teaspoon dried thyme
2 teaspoons dried rosemary
1 cup parsley leaves and stems
2 very ripe tomatoes, cubed
2 cups dry red wine

TOOLS

Roasting pan
Large stockpot
Fine wire mesh strainer

METHOD

Preheat the oven to 400°.
Wash the bones under cold running water and drain.
In a roasting pan large enough to hold them, brown the
    bones in the oven, turning them every 30 minutes,
    for a total of 2½ hours. Scatter the vegetables over
    the bones for the last 20 minutes of roasting. The
    bones should be deep brown in color.
Transfer the bones and vegetables from the roasting
    pan to a stockpot.
Pour 1 quart of water into the roasting pan and deglaze,
    scraping the brown bits that stick to the bottom of
    the pan.
Pour the liquid into the stockpot. Add the remaining
    ingredients and water to cover.
Bring the stock to a boil and reduce the heat to low.
    Simmer, skimming the foam from the surface, for 12
    hours.
Line a strainer with a double thickness of dampened
    cheesecloth or a clean cotton towel.
Place the strainer into a clean pot and ladle the stock
    into the strainer.
Let the stock cool completely.
Cover and refrigerate for up to 3 days, or freeze
    indefinitely in 1-quart containers.
Makes about 2 quarts

CLARIFIED BUTTER

INGREDIENTS

1 pound unsalted butter

METHOD

In a saucepan, melt the butter over moderate heat.
Remove the pan from the heat and set aside for
    30 minutes.

Skim off the foam from the top of the melted butter.

Slowly pour the clear liquid into a clean container, carefully stopping before the milky white sediment pours out.

Discard the milky solids.

Note: Clarified butter will keep indefinitely since the milk solids (the part that can spoil) have been removed.

Makes about 1¾ cups clarified butter

GIN-LIME BUTTER

INGREDIENTS

¼ cup dry gin

3 tablespoons fresh lime juice

¼ pound plus 4 tablespoons cold unsalted butter, cut into bits

METHOD

In a small nonaluminum saucepan set over moderate heat, combine the gin and lime juice and cook until reduced to a thick glaze, almost to the point of evaporation.

Off the heat, whisk in 1 to 2 tablespoons of the butter.

Return the saucepan to moderately low heat and add the remaining butter bit by bit, whisking constantly. The sauce will take on the texture and thickness of hollandaise.

Set aside on the warm side of the stove until ready to serve with the fish.

Makes ¾ cup

VINAIGRETTE

INGREDIENTS

⅓ cup red wine vinegar

1 teaspoon Dijon-style mustard

⅓ cup safflower oil

⅓ cup olive oil

Salt and freshly milled black pepper to taste

METHOD

In a small bowl, whisk together the vinegar and mustard.

Gradually whisk in the oils.

Season with the salt and pepper.

Makes 1 cup

MAYONNAISE

INGREDIENTS

4 egg yolks, at room temperature

1 teaspoon Dijon-style mustard

Salt and freshly milled white pepper

Dash of cayenne pepper

1½ cups olive oil, or ¾ cup olive oil and ¾ cup vegetable oil

2 tablespoons fresh lemon juice

1 tablespoon boiling water

TOOLS

Electric mixer or food processor

METHOD

Place the egg yolks, mustard, salt, pepper, and cayenne in the bowl of a mixer or food processor and beat at high speed for 2 minutes, or until the mixture is creamy.

In a slow, thin stream, gradually add all of the oil.

Add the lemon juice and taste for seasoning.

Add the boiling water and mix for 2 to 3 seconds, just until incorporated.

Refrigerate the mayonnaise in a covered container.

Makes about 2 cups

TARTAR SAUCE

INGREDIENTS

1 cup good quality store-bought mayonnaise

⅛ teaspoon cayenne pepper

½ teaspoon dry mustard

1 medium-sweet pickle, thinly sliced and finely diced

4 scallions, including some of the green, finely chopped

1 teaspoon fresh lemon juice

Grated zest of ½ lemon

METHOD

In a small bowl, combine the mayonnaise with the remaining ingredients.

Mix well, cover, and chill.

Makes about 1 cup

MUSTARD DILL SAUCE

INGREDIENTS

¼ cup Dijon-style mustard
½ teaspoon dry mustard
2 tablespoons sugar
2 tablespoons white wine vinegar
2 tablespoons dry white wine
¼ cup olive oil
¼ cup chopped fresh dill

METHOD

In a mixing bowl, combine the prepared and dry
    mustards.
Whisk in the sugar, vinegar, and wine.
Slowly whisk in the oil to make a sauce that is the
    consistency of mayonnaise.
Fold in the dill and chill.
Serve with the gravlax.

Makes ¾ cup

KETCHUP

INGREDIENTS

6 pounds very ripe tomatoes, peeled and seeded
    with juices reserved
1 onion
6 whole cloves
4 whole allspice berries
6 peppercorns
1 sprig fresh rosemary
1 celery heart, with leaves
2 tablespoons brown sugar
¼ cup cider or raspberry vinegar
Salt

TOOLS

Large nonaluminum kettle
Food mill

METHOD

Coarsely chop the tomatoes and place them in the
    kettle with the reserved juice.

Stud the onion with the cloves and tie it in a double
    layer of dampened cheesecloth along with the all-
    spice, peppercorns, and rosemary.
Add the cheesecloth bag, celery heart, brown sugar,
    vinegar, and a little salt to the tomatoes and bring to
    a boil, stirring from time to time, over high heat.
Reduce the heat to low and simmer, stirring frequently,
    for 1½ to 2 hours, or until reduced by half.
Purée the ketchup in a food mill and taste for
    seasoning.
Return the ketchup to the kettle and bring to a boil.
    Reduce the heat and simmer for 15 minutes.
Immediately pour the ketchup into sterilized jars and
    seal according to the manufacturer's directions.

Note: Tomatoes can be very watery. If not reduced
    enough, a layer of water will form in the bottom of
    the jars. If this should develop, unseal the jars
    and gently plunge a bulb baster to the bottom of
    the jar to extract the water. This ketchup will keep,
    refrigerated, for 2 weeks.

Makes about 2½ pints

PIE DOUGH

INGREDIENTS

2 cups all-purpose flour
⅛ teaspoon salt
12 tablespoons (¾ cup) unsalted butter or lard,
    chilled and cut into bits
4 to 5 tablespoons ice water

TOOLS

Electric mixer (optional)

METHOD

Combine the flour, salt, and butter or lard in a
    mixing bowl.
Using an electric mixer at low speed, or your fingers,
    cut the butter into the flour until the mixture
    resembles fine cornmeal.
One tablespoon at a time, gradually mix in the ice
    water until the pastry can be shaped into a ball.
    If using a mixer, the dough will pull away from

the sides of the bowl and adhere to the beater.

Wrap the dough in waxed paper or plastic and refrigerate for at least 20 minutes before using.

To prebake the pie crust:

Preheat the oven to 350°.

On a lightly floured surface, roll out the dough ¼-inch thick.

Place the dough in a pie pan, fitting it evenly over the bottom of the pan and pressing gently against the inside edges.

Crimp the edges or trim away excess pie dough with a sharp paring knife.

Cover the dough with a sheet of foil and weigh down with aluminum baking weights, dried beans, or rice.

Bake for 10 minutes.

Remove the weights and foil and bake for 15 minutes, or until golden brown.

Remove to a rack to cool.

Note: To make tartlets, roll out the dough ⅛-inch thick and fit rounds of the dough into the molds. Bake thoroughly to ensure that the shell will hold its shape.

Makes one 9-inch two-crust pie or 48 2-inch tartlets

COOKIE CRUST PIE DOUGH

INGREDIENTS

¼ pound unsalted butter, at room temperature
¼ cup sugar
2 eggs
2½ cups all-purpose flour, sifted
2 to 3 tablespoons ice water

TOOLS

Electric mixer
Aluminum baking weights (optional)

METHOD

In a medium bowl, cream together the butter and sugar.

Add the eggs and blend thoroughly.

Add the flour and blend, gradually adding the water, until the dough forms walnut-size balls.

Shape the dough into a ball, wrap in waxed paper or

plastic, and refrigerate for at least 20 minutes before using.

To prebake the pie crust:

Preheat the oven to 350°.

On a lightly floured surface, roll out the dough ¼-inch thick.

Place the dough in a pie pan, fitting it evenly over the bottom of the pan and pressing gently against the inside edges.

Crimp the edges or trim away excess pie dough with a sharp paring knife.

Cover the dough with a sheet of foil and weigh down with aluminum baking weights, dried beans, or rice.

Bake for 10 minutes.

Remove the weights and foil and continue to bake for 15 minutes, or until golden.

Remove to a rack to cool.

Makes one 9- to 11-inch pie crust

PARKER HOUSE ROLLS

INGREDIENTS

1 package active dry yeast
1 teaspoon sugar
1¼ cups milk, warmed
2¾ cups all-purpose flour
3 tablespoons butter, melted
1 teaspoon salt
Vegetable oil, for the bowl and the baking sheet
1 egg, lightly beaten with 1 tablespoon cold water, for the egg wash

TOOLS

3-inch round cutter

METHOD

In a bowl, dissolve the yeast and sugar in the warm milk.

Set aside until the mixture becomes frothy.

Add the flour, melted butter, and salt.

Stir until the mixture becomes a firm dough.

On a lightly floured surface, knead the dough until elastic and smooth.

Form into a ball and place in an oiled bowl. Turn the dough to coat it with oil.

Cover and set aside in a warm, draft-free place to rise until doubled, about 2 hours.

Lightly oil a baking sheet.

Turn out the dough on a lightly floured surface and roll out ¾-inch thick.

Using a 3-inch round cutter dipped in flour, cut out rounds of dough, using all of the dough.

Crease the center of each round with the back of a floured table knife.

Fold the dough along the crease and press down on the fold; the edges will fan out.

Arrange the rolls 2 inches apart on the baking sheet and set aside in a warm, draft-free place to rise for 30 minutes.

Meanwhile, preheat the oven to 400°.

Brush the tops of the rolls with the egg wash.

Bake the rolls for 20 minutes, or until the bottoms sound hollow when tapped.

Serve hot with sweet butter.

Makes about 15 rolls

SIMPLE SYRUP

INGREDIENTS

2 cups sugar

METHOD

Place the sugar and 4 cups of cold water in a saucepan and bring to a boil over high heat, stirring with a wooden spoon until the sugar has dissolved.

Continue to boil for 5 minutes and remove from the heat.

When the syrup is cool, refrigerate in a covered container.

The syrup will keep for two weeks under refrigeration and can be frozen indefinitely.

Makes 1 quart

RUM HARD SAUCE

INGREDIENTS

½ pound unsalted butter at room temperature
¾ cup confectioners' sugar
2 tablespoons rum or brandy

TOOLS

Electric mixer

METHOD

With an electric mixer, cream the butter until fluffy.

Gradually add the sugar and cream together with the butter.

Gradually add the rum or brandy.

Scrape the butter onto a sheet of plastic wrap.

Roll the plastic wrap around the butter into a log that is about 1½ inches in diameter.

Chill until hardened.

Remove the butter about 20 minutes before serving.

Cut into ¼-inch medallions and serve it on top of the hot mincemeat.

Makes about 1 cup

ENGLISH CREAM

INGREDIENTS

1 quart millk
2 vanilla beans, split lengthwise
12 egg yolks
1 cup sugar

TOOLS

Double boiler

METHOD

In a heavy saucepan, scald the milk with the vanilla beans.

Set aside.

In the top of a double boiler, whisk the egg yolks with the sugar until frothy and lemon colored.

Place over simmering water and cook gently, stirring constantly, until the yolks are warmed through.

Slowly pour in the scalded milk and cook, stirring, until the cream coats the back of a metal spoon, about 20 minutes.

Strain the English Cream into a clean bowl and set in a larger bowl of ice and water. Stir until completely cooled.

Cover and refrigerate for up to 2 days.

Makes about 1½ quarts

TOASTED NUTS

METHOD

Preheat the oven to 400°.

Spread the nuts evenly over a dry baking sheet.

Place the cookie sheet in the oven and toast for 4 minutes, tossing the nuts to ensure even browning.

Watch the nuts closely and when they turn golden brown, remove from the oven.

Allow the nuts to cool slightly before removing from the baking sheet.

ROASTED PEPPERS

INGREDIENTS

For all types of peppers—bell peppers, jalepeños, or green chiles

METHOD

Char the peppers directly on the open flame of a gas range or in the broiler of an electric oven, turning until the peppers are thoroughly blackened on all sides.

Remove, place the peppers in a paper bag, and close tightly.

Allow them to steam in the bag for 3 to 5 minutes. Remove the peppers and peel off the outside skins. Discard the stem end and seeds.

Proceed with the appropriate recipe.

OLD STAND-BYS
CREAMY MACARONI AND CHEESE

INGREDIENTS

½ pound elbow macaroni

8 tablespoons butter

¼ cup all-purpose flour

1 teaspoon dry mustard

3 cups milk

½ teaspoon salt

⅛ teaspoon cayenne pepper

¾ pound sharp cheddar cheese, shredded

½ cup fresh bread crumbs

TOOLS

Ovenproof baking dish

METHOD

In a pot of lightly salted boiling water, cook the macaroni until almost tender. Do not overcook.

Drain under cold running water and reserve.

Butter an ovenproof baking dish.

In a heavy saucepan, melt 4 tablespoons of the butter over moderately high heat.

Off the heat, whisk in the flour.

Return the saucepan to moderate heat and whisk for 3 to 4 minutes, until the flour is cooked.

Blend in the dry mustard and add the milk, whisking constantly.

When the mixture bubbles and begins to thicken, remove from the heat and add the salt and cayenne.

Fold in the cheese and blend.

Fold in the macaroni and pour the mixture into an 8-inch square baking dish and reserve.

Preheat the oven to 350°.

In a small saucepan, heat the remaining 4 tablespoons butter over moderate heat.

Add the bread crumbs and toss for 1 or 2 minutes, until lightly toasted.

Sprinkle the crumb mixture over the macaroni.

Bake for 25 minutes and serve hot.

Serves 6

HAM CROQUETTES

INGREDIENTS

WHITE SAUCE:

3 tablespoons unsalted butter

3 tablespoons all-purpose flour

1 cup milk, scalded

½ bay leaf

1 small onion, halved, each half studded with 2 whole cloves

1 leaf fresh sage

HAM:

1¼ cups chunked cooked country ham

1 teaspoon fresh lemon juice
2 tablespoons minced onions
Dash of Tabasco sauce
Freshly grated nutmeg
1 leaf fresh sage, chopped
3 tablespoons finely chopped fresh parsley
2 eggs, lightly beaten with ¼ cup milk, for egg wash
2 cups dried bread crumbs
Vegetable oil

TOOLS

Food processor or meat grinder

METHOD

The white sauce:

In a heavy saucepan, melt the butter. Add the flour
and combine.

Off the heat, add the hot milk and whisk to combine.

Return the pan to moderate heat and cook the roux,
whisking constantly, for 1 minute, until the
flour is cooked through.

Add the bay leaf, onion, and sage and cook for
2 minutes.

Strain the sauce; discard the solids.

To make the croquettes:

Chop the ham through the fine blade of a meat grinder,
or chop medium-fine in a food processor, pulsing
to chop but making sure the ham does not
become too soft.

Combine the ham with the lemon juice, onions,
Tabasco, nutmeg, sage, parsley, and ½ cup of the
white sauce.

Refrigerate for at least 1 hour.

Shape the mixture into small cakes or croquettes and
dip in the egg wash, then in the bread crumbs. Coat
again in the egg wash and bread crumbs to make a
good crusty coating.

Fry the croquettes in about 1 inch of hot oil (365°) until
golden brown. Drain on paper towels and serve with
the Mustard Sauce.

Serves 4

MUSTARD SAUCE

INGREDIENTS

1½ teaspoons butter
1½ teaspoons all-purpose flour
1⅓ cups heavy cream, scalded
3 tablespoons Dijon-style mustard
Freshly grated nutmeg
Pinch of cayenne pepper
1 teaspoon minced onion
1 tablespoon capers—washed, drained,
    and lightly chopped

METHOD

In a saucepan, melt the butter. Off the heat, add the
flour and whisk to combine.

Off the heat, add the heavy cream and whisk.

Return to moderate heat and cook, whisking constantly, for at least 1 minute, until thick.

Add the remaining ingredients and cook until
warmed through.

Serve warm.

Makes about 1½ cups

HAM SALAD

INGREDIENTS

1 pound cured baked ham, trimmed of all fat, cut into
    2-inch julienne (about 3½ cups)
½ red bell pepper, cut into fine julienne
1½ celery ribs, peeled and cut into fine julienne
2 dill pickles, cut into fine julienne (about 1 cup)
½ cup Mayonnaise made without salt
3 tablespoons chopped fresh chives
Yolk of 1 hard-boiled egg

METHOD

In a bowl, combine the ham and vegetable julienne.

Toss with the mayonnaise and sprinkle with chives.

Push the egg yolk through a fine sieve and sprinkle
    over the top of the salad.

Chill briefly and serve.

Serves 3 to 4

CHICKEN SANDWICHES

INGREDIENTS

1 large poached chicken breast, split
Thinly sliced white bread or white toast
Homemade Mayonnaise (see Basics, page 345)
Salt and freshly milled pepper
Leafy lettuce such as Boston, oak leaf,
   or butter crunch

METHOD

Thinly slice the chicken breasts diagonally.
Lightly coat the bread with the mayonnaise.
Place one or two layers of chicken on half of the
   slices of bread.
Lightly season the chicken slices with salt and pepper.
Cover with one piece of lettuce and top with a slice
   of bread.
Trim the crusts and cut the sandwiches in half.

Note: The breast of a 3-pound poached chicken will
   yield 4 to 5 sandwiches. The combination of sweet
   chicken, sweet white bread, and sweet mayonnaise
   was a specialty available at most soda fountains and
   good hotels until the 1960s. It has since fallen on
   hard times.

Serves 4 to 5

MEATLOAF

INGREDIENTS

1 pound ground lean beef
½ pound ground lean veal
½ pound ground lean pork
1 medium onion, finely chopped
1 clove garlic, minced
1 teaspoon chopped fresh tarragon
¼ cup chopped fresh parsley
1 cup fresh whole wheat bread crumbs
   (from about 4 very thin slices)
1 egg
½ cup store-bought chili sauce
1 tablespoon heavy cream
Salt and freshly milled black pepper
4 thick slices slab bacon, cut ¼-inch thick
¾ cup sour cream, at room temperature

TOOLS

Loaf pan
Bulb baster

METHOD

Preheat the oven to 325°.
In a large mixing bowl, combine all of the ingredients
   except the bacon and sour cream. Mix well.
Shape the mixture and place it in a loaf pan. Cover the
   top with the bacon slices, tucking the bacon
   between the meatloaf and the sides of the pan.
Cover the meatloaf with foil and bake for 1 hour.
   Remove the foil and bake for an additional
   15 minutes.
Remove the bacon and suction off the cooking liquid
   with a bulb baster. Measure ¼ cup of the cooking
   liquid and stir it into the reserved sour cream.
   Blend thoroughly and serve with the meatloaf.
To serve cold, thinly slice the meatloaf and accompany
   with hot jalapeño relish or hot pepper relish.

Serves 6

ACKNOWLEDGMENTS

Every once in a while, a few people come into your life, become fired by your idea, and then help to give it shape and make it happen. The pleasure of realizing this book in its original hardcover form began with Lena Tabori and Jason Epstein, who gave me their time, guidance, enthusiasm, and heartfelt support; Lena, in her role as president and publisher of Stewart, Tabori & Chang, again gave this book life in 1994, this time as a paperback. I am grateful for the memory and friendship of James Beard, who was there to encourage and question my thoughts and ideas. To Rena Coyle, who held this book as dear a dream as I and devoted hours of her time preparing research, and to Gary and Catelyn, who let her go. For Rebecca Wolcott Atwater, who delighted in co-researching this project and gave her advice and sincerity in helping shape this book. For Mardee Haidin Regan, for quickly and brilliantly editing what at times seemed unending amounts of corrections. For the pleasure of working once again with Penni Wisner, who helped so much to make the valleys of California a joy. And to the people at Random House who so generously gave their time and support, especially Laura Schultz and Bob Scudellari. For Tom Eckerle, whose patience and hard work brought a vision and dimension to this book. And for Maryann Page, who was cheerful chauffeur, laundress, assistant cook, and merry-maker. And for Todd Weinstein, who jumped in to save the last of New England. For Lafcadio Cortese, Jimmy Eckerle, and Chechi Gallini, who bounded along with us.

For the people who opened their doors and their hearts:

NEW ENGLAND

Felicity Pratt Morgan
Ralph Gray
Nicholas Love
Mrs. Ruth P. James
Thomas, Susie and Seth Wilbur
Norman Miller
Randy Durkee
K. Eric Weiss
Vernon B. Miller
Diana Conklin
Clifford Klenk
Polly and Joseph Kraft
Peaches and Raymond Halsey and their family
Ceil and Stanley Knight
Arnold Leo—East Hampton Town Baymen's Association and the
    haulseiners: Bill Lester, Calvin Lester, Donald Eames, Ernie Green,
    Jr., Walter Burnett
William Serter
John Hassler—The Seafood Shop
Andrea Terry—The Lobster Roll
Bruce and Maryann Bozzi—The Palm restaurants
Peter Schub
Robert Bear
Eric Villency
Mark Sudack
Labinia and Joachim Esteve

THE MID-ATLANTIC

Judith Van Amringe
Jean de Castella Delley
Beati and Hart Perry
Everett Nak
Leo Steiner—Carnegie Deli
Big Apple Circus: Eileen Condon, Ruth Schuman, Jane Lahr
Bill Blass
Mrs. Kenyon Boocock
Frolic Weymouth
Joanne Dupont
Manuel Nunez
Jessica Myers
Lisa Babinski
Mrs. Barbara Munves—James II Gallery
Mrs. John M. Gates
Zoe Lewis
Felipe Rojas-Lombardi
Helen Fraser

SOUTH

Nancy and Neil Smith
Bart Murphy and The Ruby Ford
Billy Wood Bradshaw and The Maggie Lee
Ralph Ruark and The Wilma Lee
Corporal Nick Nazare, Jr., and Sgt. Joseph H. Jones—Maryland Natural
    Resources Police
Didi and Neil Rheiland
William R. "Bill" Jones—The Crab Claw
Caleb Cliff
Richard Jenerette
Bob Bray
Nell Dillow Thomas
Beth Spary
Owen Lee
Mr. and Mrs. Charles Atkins
Mrs. Perry Lewis
Mrs. Sidney Le Gendre
Sam Washington
Fleeta Fox—Charleston Foundation
The Stockpot—Charleston
Mrs. A.L. Jennings
Ken Jennings

DEEP SOUTH

Mr. and Mrs. Jimmy Boulet
Henri Boulet
Shella Duplessis
Douglas Hayward—Belle Helene Plantation
J. Lawrence Hill
Joe Mizelle
Michael Myers
Russell Albright
Mrs. Donald J. Nalty
Adam Steg
Soniat House—Rodney Smith
Shirley Ratterree
Flo Treadway, Scott Ratterree—Longuevue House and Gardens
Edith Morgan
Ella Brennan
Edmund McIlhenny—Avery Island
Acme Oyster House
Mr. and Mrs. Lloyd English, Jr.—Mandiche's
Lee Brian Schrager
Dr. and Mrs. Anthony Petro
Mr. and Mrs. John Peet, Jr.
Mr. and Mrs. Thomas E. Goodman
Mr. and Mrs. William Wallace
Carol Puckett Daily—The Everyday Gourmet
Ernie Knight

MIDWEST

Mary Reisinger
Deborah Buell
Nancy and George Buell
Marcia Goldberg
Gladys Delight Hilgert

NORTHERN REGIONS

Snake River Ranch: Nancy and Chuck Resor, Jane and Stan Resor, Story and Bill Resor, Susan Hauge
Ted Kimmel
Bernie Shrable—Wyoming Department of Fish and Game
The Hardeman Ranch: Earl Hardeman, Jerry Jacobson
Dick Best
Ad Lib
Ann Stewart

SOUTHWEST

Janie and Hank Coleman
The Bar K Ranch: Ann and Hamp Smead, John and Leah Darby, Jeff and Catherine Steinmeyer, Ab Crawford, David Smelley, Derwood Smelley, Mary and Sylvester Perry, Gaspar Herrera, Dale Savell, Grady Crawford, C.W. Bardwell, Cotton McLeroy
Rose and Kenneth Kirkpatrik
Billy Sue Turner Antiques
Coty Bliss
Sunny Bryant's
Joan Baker
Sarah Moody
Michelle Tsosie Naranjo—Santa Clara Pueblo
Mr. and Mrs. Keith Wofford
Mr. and Mrs. Arturo Jaramillo
Forrest Moses
Ramona Scholder
Anne Ferrier
Rosalea Murphy
Alan Smith—The Stockpot
Nedra Mateucci

WEST COAST

The Rio Bravo Ranch: Mr. and Mrs. George Nickel, Kathi and Miller Nickel, Andre Honesté
Steve Couture
John J. Kovacevich
Jacinto Sarabia
Sue Campoy
Mr. and Mrs. Arthur C. Withrow II
Suzannah Love
Tom and Patty Skouras
Ames Cushing
Gijsbert Paul Bozuwa
Maggie Waldron
Mrs. Richard K. Miller
David Miller
Jim Mays
Ira Kirlander
Mrs. Ivy Rosequit
Carmella Scaggs
Sal Sancimino and Sons—Swan's Oyster Depot
Wendra Liang
Haywood Winery: Peter Haywood and Dennis Bowker
Rutherford Hill Winery: Mr. and Mrs. William Jaeger, Robert Hardy
Belle Rhodes
Laurie Chenel—Laurie Chenel California Chevre
Ignazio A. Vella—Vella Cheese Company

NORTHWEST

Astrida R. Blukis Onat
Don Foster
Rosalynn G. Powell
Benjamin Woo—The Morel Society
Michael Erikson
Peter Hasson—Hasson Brothers Fruit and Produce
Mike Osborn—Pure Food Fish Market
Emmett Watson's Oyster Bar
Larry Hansen
Members of the Swinomish tribe: Maxine Williams, Gus "Stoney" Stone, Bernadette Stone, Ken Edwards

The New York Public Library
The New York Society Library
The New York Academy of Medicine Library
The American Cookbooks and Wine Books 1797-1950 exhibition from the collection of Janice Bluestein Longone and Daniel T. Longone, courtesy of The William L. Clements Library of American History and the Food Library, Ann Arbor, Michigan.

And all the friends and advisors who put up with me:

Rico Puhlmann
Geoffrey Drummond, Bruce Franchini and the crew from Exploration Television
James Steinmeyer
Barry and Linda Donahue
Geraldine Stutz
Gail Levenstein
Steve Weiss
Marjorie Benchley
Eugenie Voorhees
Cheryl Merser
Robert Reynolds
David Easton
Enid Futterman
Robert Dash
Peter Stephan
Gary Stephan
Richard Nimmo
Carolyn Stewart
Kenn Ferguson
Libba Esteve
Kim Esteve
Ann Johnson
Dena Schmidt

SELECTED BIBLIOGRAPHY

Adams, Ramon F. *Come An' Get It: The Story of the Old Cowboy Cook.* Norman, Okla.: University of Oklahoma Press, 1952.

Anderson, Ken. *Eagle Claw Fish Cookbook.* Cambridge, Mass.: Dorison House, 1977.

Baker, Charles H., Jr. *The Gentleman's Companion: An Exotic Drinking Book.* New York: Crown, 1946.

Bandera Library Association. *Cooking Recipes of the Pioneers.* Bandera, Tex.: Frontier Times, 1936.

Beard, James. *Beard on Bread.* New York: Knopf, 1977.

　　　James Beard's New Fish Cookery. Boston: Little, Brown, 1976.

　　　James Beard's American Cookery. Boston: Little, Brown, 1972.

Beecher, Catherine Esther. *Domestic Receipt Book.* New York: Harper and Brothers, 1846.

Beeton, Mrs. Isabella. *The Book of Household Management.* London: Warwick House, Salisbury Square, E.C.: Ward, Lock and Company, 1880.

Berglund, Berndt, and Clair E. Bolsby. *The Edible Wild.* Toronto: Pagurian Press, 1971.

Bivins, S. Thomas. *The Southern Cookbook.* Hampton, Va.: Press of the Hampton Institute, 1912.

Boorstin, Daniel J. *The Americans: The Democratic Experience.* New York: Random House, 1973.

Borthwick, J.D. *Three Years in California.* Edinburgh and London: Wm. Blackwood and Sons, 1857.

Bowles, Ella, and Dorothy Towle. *Secrets of New England Cooking.* New York: M. Barrows, 1947.

Brown, Dale. *American Cooking: The Northwest.* Alexandria, Va.: Time-Life Books, 1970.

Bujzek, Beatrice Ross. *The Cranberry Connection.* Brattleboro, Vt.: The Stephen Green Press, 1978.

Carson, Jane. *Colonial Virginia Cooking.* Williamsburg, Va.: University Press of Virginia in Charlottesville, 1968.

Challenger, Jean. *How to Cook Your Catch.* Sidney, B.C.: Sallaire Publishing Co., 1973.

Chase, Joan. *During the Reign of the Queen of Persia.* New York: Ballantine Books, 1983.

Christ Church. *Christ Church Cook Book.* Savannah, Ga.: Kennickell Printing Co., 1978.

Colquitt, Harriet Ross. *The Savannah Cookbook.* New York: Farrar and Rinehart, 1933.

Commercial Fisherman Wives, Port of Coos Bay. *Cookbook Presented by the Wives of Charleston, Oregon.* Charleston, Ore.: Wegford Publications, 1972.

Cone, Joan. *Easy Game Cooking.* Mclean, Va.: EPM Publications, 1974.

The Democratic Women of Maine. *The State of Maine Cookbook.* 1924.

Dillow, Louise B., and Deenie B. Carver. *Mrs. Blackwell's Heart of Texas Cookbook.* San Antonio: Corona Publishing Co., 1980.

Doar, David. *Rice and Rice Planting in the South Carolina Low Country.* Charleston: The Charleston Museum, 1936.

Field, S.S. *The American Drink Book.* New York: Farrar, Straus, Young, 1953.

Fisher, M.F.K. *As They Were.* New York: Knopf, 1982.

Fox, Minnie C. *The Blue Grass Cook Book.* New York: Fox, Dunnfield and Co., 1904.

Frederick, J. George. *The Pennsylvania Dutch and Their Cookery.* New York: The Business Bourse, 1935.

The Friday Club. *The Friday Club Menus: A Capecod Cookbook.* Yarmouthport, Ma.: The Register Press, 1912.

Glasse, Hannah. *The Art of Cookery, made Plain and Easy; Which far exceeds any Thing of the Kind yet published.* London: Wm. Strahan, 1770.

Gleig, George Robert. *A Narrative of the Campaigns of the British Army of Washington and New Orleans, under Generals Ross, Pakenham, and Lambert, in the years 1814 and 1815.* 2d ed. London: John Murray, Albemarle Street, 1826.

Hack, Virginia, and Ann Andersen, eds. *100 Years of Good Cooking.* St. Paul: Minnesota Statehood Centennial Commission, 1958.

Hawkins, Nancy and Arthur, and Mary Allen Havermeyer. *Nantucket and Other New England Cooking.* New York: Hastings House, 1976.

Hayes, W.T. *Kentucky Cookbook.* St. Louis: J.H. Tomkins Printing Co., 1912.

Hearn, Lafcadio. *La Cuisine Creole.* New Orleans: Pelican Publishing House, 1967.

Hess, John L., and Karen Hess. *The Taste of America.* New York: Grossman Publishers, 1977.

Hewitt, Jean. *The New York Times Southern Heritage Cookbook.* New York: G. P. Putnam's Sons, 1976.

Horne, Viola, comp. *Milton Cookbook.* Boston: Boston Press of George H. Ellis, 1918.

Hosmer, Susan Harris Coleman. *Nantucket Recipes.* Nantucket, Ma.: The Inquirer and Mirror Press, 1915.

Howard, Mrs. B. C. *Fifty Years in a Maryland Kitchen.* Baltimore: Norman Remington Co., 1913.

Jones, Cranston. *Homes of the American Presidents.* New York: Bonanza Publishers, 1962.

Jones, Evans. *American Food: The Gastronomic Story.* New York: E. P. Dutton, 1975.

Junior League of Baton Rouge. *River Road Recipes.* Baton Rouge, La.: 1972.

Junior League of Charleston. *Charleston Recipes.* Charleston: Walker, Evans, Cogswell Co., 1966.

Junior League of Shreveport. *A Cook's Tour of Shreveport.* 1964.

Junior League of Tampa. *The Gasparilla Cookbook.* 1961.

Kahn, E.J., Jr. "The Staffs of Life." *The New Yorker,* June 18, November 12, December 17, 1984.

Kimball, Marie. *Thomas Jefferson's Cook Book.* Charlottesville: University Press of Virginia, 1976.

King, Caroline B. *Victorian Cakes.* Idaho: Caxton Printers, 1941.

Kramer, Mark. *Three Farms.* Boston: Little, Brown, 1977.

Lang Varley. *Follow the Water.* Winston-Salem: John F. Blair, 1961.

Lewis, Meriwether, and William Clark. *The Journals of Lewis and Clark.* Edited by Bernard DeVoto. Boston: Houghton Mifflin Company, 1953.

Luchetti, Cathy. *Women of the West.* St. George, Utah: Antelope Island Press, 1982.

MacFadyen, J. Tevere. *Gaining Ground: The Renewal of America's Small Farms.* New York: Holt, Rinehart and Winston, 1984.

Marrow, Kay. *The New England Cookbook.* Reading, Pa.: Culinary Arts Press, 1936.

McCla e, A.K. *The Encyclopedia of Fish Cookery.* New York: Holt, Rinehart and Winston, 1977.

McCulloch-Williams, Martha. *Dishes and Beverages of the Old South.* New York: McBride, Nast and Co., 1913.

Michaux, François André. *Travels to the West of the Alleghany Mountains.* 2d ed. London: D.N. Shury for B. Crosby and Co., 1805.

Michener, James A. *Chesapeake.* New York: Random House, 1978.

Mitcham, Howard. *Creole Gumbo and All That Jazz: A New Orleans Seafood Cookbook.* Reading, Pa.: Addison-Wesley Publishing Co., 1978.

Morgan, Edmund S. *Virginians at Home.* Williamsburg: The Colonial Williamsburg Foundation, 1983.

Morgan, Murray. *Puget's Sound.* Seattle: University of Washington Press, 1980.

Morison, Samuel Eliot. *The Maritime History of Massachusetts, 1783–1860.* Boston: Houghton Mifflin Company, 1922.

Mosser, Marjorie. *Good Maine Food.* New York: Doubleday, 1947.

Ortiz, Elisabeth Lambert. *The Book of Latin American Cooking.* New York: Random House, 1979.

Ott, Eleanore. *Plantation Cooking of Old Louisiana.* New Orleans: Harmanson Publisher, 1938.

Parkman, Francis. *The Oregon Trail.* Boston: Little, Brown, 1902.

Perl, Lila. *Hunter's Stew and Hangtown Fry: What Pioneer America Ate and Why.* New York: a Clarion Book, Seabury Press, 1977.

　　　Slumps, Grunts, and Snickerdoodles: What Colonial America Ate and Why. New York: Houghton Mifflin, 1975.

Pixley, Aristene. *The Green Mountain Cook Book.* New York: Stephen Day Press, 1934.

Randolph, Mary. *Virginia Housewife.* Baltimore: J. Plaskett, 1836.

Reidpath, Stewart. *The Angler's Cookbook.* London: A.H. and A.W. Reed, 1973.

Rombauer, Irma S., and Marion Rombauer Becker. *Joy of Cooking.* Indianapolis and New York: Bobbs-Merrill Company, 1979.

Ronald, Mary. *Mary Ronald's Century Cook Book.* New York: Century Company, 1897.

Root, Waverly. *Food.* New York: Simon and Schuster, 1980.

Russel, Howard S. *A Long Deep Furrow: Three Centuries of Farming in New England.* Hanover, N.H.: University Press of New England, 1976.

The Silver Thimble Society. *How We Cook in Tennessee.* Jackson, Tenn.: The Silver Thimble Society of the First Baptist Church, 1906.

Scott, Natalie Vivian. *Two Hundred Years of New Orleans Cooking.* New York: J. Cape and H. Smith, 1931.

Stieff, Frederick Phillip. *Eat, Drink and Be Merry in Maryland.* New York: G.P. Putnam's Sons, 1932.

Stratton, Dorothy. *Pioneer Women.* New York: Simon and Schuster, 1981.

Talmadge, Betty. *How to Cook a Pig: And Other Back-to-the-Farm Recipes.* New York: Simon and Schuster, 1977.

Thoreau, Henry David. *The Annotated Walden, or Life in the Woods.* New York: Clarkson Potter, 1970.

　　　Cape Cod. Cambridge, Mass., Houghton Mifflin, Riverside Press, 1914.

　　　A Week on the Concord and Merrimack Rivers. Princeton: Princeton University Press, 1980.

Tocqueville, Alexis de. *Journey to America.* Translated by George Lawrence. New Haven: Yale University Press, 1960.

Turner, Harry Baker. *Nantucket Cookbook.* Nantucket, Mass.: Inquirer and Mirror Press, 1927.

Twain, Mark. *A Tramp Abroad.* New York: Harper and Brothers, 1907.

Tyree, Marion Cabell, ed. *Housekeeping in Old Virginia.* Louisville, Ky.: J.P. Morton and Co., 1890.

Voltz, Jeanne A. *The Flavor of the South.* New York: Doubleday, 1977.

Warner, William. *Beautiful Swimmers.* Boston: Atlantic, Little, Brown, 1976.

Weatherwax, Paul. *Indian Corn in Old America.* New York: Macmillan, 1954.

Weygandt, Cornelius. *A Passing America: Considerations of Things of Yesterday Fast Fading from Our World.* New York: Henry Holt and Co., 1932.

White, Mrs. Peter A. *Kentucky Cookery Book.* Chicago: Belford Clarke Co., 1891.

INDEX

CONVERSION TABLES

LIQUID MEASURES

Fluid Ounces	U.S. Measures	Imperial Measures	Milliliters
	1 tsp.	1 tsp.	5
1/4	2 tsp.	1 dessert spoon	7
1/2	1 tbs.	1 tbs.	15
1	2 tbs.	2 tbs.	28
2	1/4 cup	4 tbs	56
4	1/2 cup or 1/4 pint		110
5		1/4 pint or 1 gill	140
6	3/4 cup		170
8	1 cup or 1/2 pint		225
9			250, 1/4 liter
10	1 1/4 cups	1/2 pint	280
12	1 1/2 cups or 3/4 pint		240
15		3/4 pint	420
16	2 cups or 1 pint		450
18	2 1/4 cups		500, 1/2 liter
20	2 1/2 cups	1 pint	560
24	3 cups or 1 1/2 pints		675
25		1 1/4 pints	700
27	3 1/2 cups		750
30	3 3/4 cups	1 1/2 pints	840
32	4 cups or 2 pints or 1 quart		900
35		1 1/4 pints	980
36	4 1/2 cups		1000, 1 liter

SOLID MEASURES

U.S. and Imperial Measures Ounces	Pounds	Metric Measures Grams	Kilos
1		28	
2		56	
3 1/2		100	
4	1/4	112	
5		140	
6		168	
8	1/2	225	
9		250	1/4
12	3/4	340	
16	1	450	
18		500	1/2
20	1 1/4	560	
24	1 1/2	675	
27		750	3/4
28	1 3/4	780	
32	2	900	
36	2 1/4	1000	1
40	2 1/2	1100	
48	3	1350	
54		1500	1 1/2

OVEN TEMPERATURE EQUIVALENTS

Fahrenheit	Gas Mark	Celsius	Heat of Oven
225	1/4	107	very cool
250	1/2	121	very cool
275	1	135	cool
300	2	148	cool
325	3	163	moderate
350	4	177	moderate
375	5	190	fairly hot
400	6	204	fairly hot
425	7	218	hot
450	8	232	very hot
475	9	246	very hot

INGREDIENTS AND EQUIPMENT GLOSSARY

The following ingredients and equipment are basically the same on both sides of the Atlantic, but have different names.

AMERICAN	BRITISH
arugula	rocket
baking soda	bicarbonate of soda
bell pepper	sweet pepper (capsicum)
Bibb and Boston lettuce	soft-leaved, round lettuce
broiler/to broil	grill/to grill
celery stalk	celery stick
cheesecloth	muslin
confectioners' sugar	icing sugar
cookie sheet	baking sheet
eggplant	aubergine
fava bean	broad bean
ground beef/pork	minced beef/pork
heavy cream (37.6% fat)	whipping cream (35–40% fat)
hot red pepper flakes	dried crushed red chilli
parchment paper	nonstick baking paper
Romaine lettuce	cos lettuce
scallion	spring onion
semisweet chocolate	plain chocolate
shrimp	prawn (varying in size)
skillet	frying pan
squab	young pigeon
unsweetened chocolate	bitter *chocolat pâtissier*
whole milk	homogenized milk
zucchini	courgette

INGREDIENTS

BUTTER
In the United States, butter is generally sold in a one-pound package, which contains four equal "sticks." The wrapper on each stick is marked to show tablespoons, so the cook can cut the stick according to the quantity required. The equivalent weights are:
1 stick = 115 g or 4 oz.
1 tablespoon = 15 g or 1/2 oz.

FLOUR
To achieve a near equivalent to American all-purpose flour, use half British plain flour and half strong bread flour. American cake flour can be replaced by British plain flour alone.

SUGAR
American granulated sugar is finer than British granulated, closer to caster sugar, so British cooks should use caster sugar throughout.

YEAST
Quantities of dried yeast (called active dry yeast in the United States) are usually given in number of packages. Each package contains 7 g or 1/4 oz. of yeast, which is equivalent to a scant tablespoon.